BE YOUR OWN
CONTRACTOR
THE AFFORDABLE WAY TO
HOME OWNERSHIP

BE YOUR OWN
CONTRACTOR
THE AFFORDABLE WAY TO
HOME OWNERSHIP

BY MAX & CHARLOTTE ALTH

TAB **TAB BOOKS Inc.**
BLUE RIDGE SUMMIT, PA. 17214

TAB BOOKS Inc. offers software for sale. For information and a catalog, please contact TAB Software Department, Blue Ridge Summit, PA 17294-0850.

Questions regarding the content of this book should be addressed to:

Reader Inquiry Branch
TAB BOOKS Inc.
Blue Ridge Summit, PA 17294-0214

FIRST EDITION

FOURTH PRINTING

Printed in the United States of America

Library of Congress Cataloging in Publication Data

Alth, Max, 1917-
Be your own contractor.

Includes index.
1. House construction—Amateurs' manuals.   I. Alth,
Charlotte.   II. Title.
TH4815.A48   1984   690'.837   83-24375
ISBN 0-8306-0254-2
ISBN 0-8306-0154-6 (pbk.)

Contents

Dedicated to
Erin
Shannon
Kim
Simon
Mich
Mike
Darcy
and Mendle

BE YOUR OWN

CONTRACTOR

THE AFFORDABLE WAY TO
HOME OWNERSHIP

Introduction

MOST OF US WOULD LIKE TO OWN OUR OWN HOME. The drawback is money. There are two solutions to this problem. You can somehow secure the funds you need or you can reduce the purchase price of a home.

This book deals with reducing the cost of building a home. It has been done and is being done by thousands of people all over the country. The cost of a new home can be reduced by 30 percent or more by building it or contracting the building yourself.

As a general contractor, you might consider yourself completely incapable. You are an accountant, a beekeeper, a lifeguard, or a housewife. You can't really tell one end of a hammer from another. No matter. You can contribute management, and if your back is strong enough, labor—cleaning, painting, and the like. You can hire the skills. That is what all builders do. There is no reason why you cannot do the same. You might not know much about building or the building trades now, but by the time you finish this book you will be ready to be your own builder/contractor.

This is a how-to-build/contract-your-own-home book. It differs from other books on the same subject in one major respect. This is a practical book. It is not a dream book in the sense that it does not discuss construction that is impractical for the do-it-yourself builder. It does not discuss beautiful, wonderous dream homes. They make for exciting pictures in magazines, but very few people can afford them.

The goal of this book is to show you how to secure a good, comfortable home for a minimum expenditure of labor and money. The constant theme is the method or technique that will provide a well-built, comfortable home. We spend no time with "gimmick" homes that might be wonderful for certain people in certain areas, but which you will never be able to sell or for which a bank will not advance a mortgage.

We do not describe the construction of any particular home nor type of home. That would be limiting. Instead we present and develop the general principles and sequence of small-structure construction so that you can apply this information to any type or size of building you want to build.

All major building trades—with the exception of the licensed trades: plumbing, electrical, and, in some areas, heating—are discussed and illustrated. The coverage is by no means complete. It is not intended to be a series of courses on home construction. The subject is much too large to be covered in any one book. The building trades are reviewed so that you, the builder, can appreciate what is involved and determine if you have the time and the skill to do one or more of them. Reviewing the sections on the construction trades will prevent you from undertaking a task that is beyond your present skill or passing up a job that you can easily accomplish.

Reviewing the trades will also give you a better position from which to discuss contracts and work schedules with the craftsmen you employ. Knowing to some degree what you are speaking about will gain you some respect and probably a better deal.

In addition, tips are provided on scheduling to save money, on purchasing material, on selecting the most efficient house designs, and more.

Chapter 1

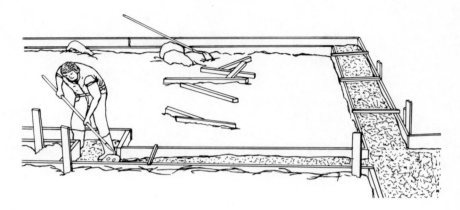

The Preliminaries

THE BOOK COMBINES TWO TECHNIQUES USED BY IN-dividuals with limited capital who build only one or two houses at a time. For much of the work, they hire other people on a per-job basis, usually, and they do some portion of the work themselves. In this way they make the most of their time and reduce their costs. While the mason is constructing the foundation, they can be cleaning up the grounds. While the carpenters are framing the house, they might be painting the windows and trim.

The steps and the sequence of steps necessary plan and construct the house, secure the mortgage, and deal with the subcontractors are all discussed and illustrated throughout this book. This portion of the work, the contracting, requires no particular skills other than the ability to deal with people and the persistence necessary to complete the paper-work details.

Construction requires skills and experience that vary depending upon the particular job in-volved. Some of the work you will be unable to do because the work is limited to licensed craftsmen.

These are people who have passed tests given by the local building department. They have a license to practice their craft.

WHAT A BUILDER DOES

Most of us have a gross misconception of the nature of the work or service provided by a builder. A builder is a general contractor. He is the manager who brings money, the land, the architect, and the various craftspeople together. He is the overall superviser of the job.

When a builder works within a municipality, the building department of that municipality pro-tects him (and the home buyer) against physical failure. The building department inspects and ap-proves the building plan before a work permit is issued and construction can begin, inspects the ex-cavation before permission is granted to pour the footings, inspects the foundation and walls (Fig. 1-1), and limits plumbing, heating, and electrical work to licensed trades and inspects their work before the walls are closed.

Fig. 1-1. When the concrete has to be pushed a great distance, a wet mix is used. The concrete delivery chute is visible, top right.

If and when any building violation exists, the violation of the building code must be corrected before work can proceed.

The building department makes a final inspection before it issues an occupancy permit (the right for anyone to inhabit the structure). The completed building may be unattractive and it may have minor flaws.

The building might not be what the public wants. In such a case, the builder might end up not being able to sell the building. But if it has been constructed within a municipality, it will be structurally safe and sound.

While it is helpful to know one or more of the building trades, it isn't necessary to be a mason, carpenter, electrician, a plumber, or an architect to

Table 1-1. Cost Comparison.

	Purchased complete	Self-constructed
Lot	20,000	20,000
Materials	26,000	28,000
Labor	29,000	20,000
Legal fees	2,000	2,000
Builder's profit	17,000	000
Agent's profit	6,000	000
Total	$100,000	$70,000

direct the construction of a residence. The difference between the experienced builder and a beginner is mainly one of time. The experienced builder will secure faster service and a little better prices so that his building might be erected more quickly than yours. Beyond that, there is little to distinguish a first-time builder's home from that of a one-house-at-a-time builder's work. If there is any difference at all, it will be in that the professional cuts a few small corners.

Why be your own builder? One reason is the pleasure and satisfaction of living in the home you built yourself. The second reason is money. The immediate savings can run from 30 to 40 percent. The long-term savings in mortgage payments can be even greater. Assuming you do a portion of the work, roughly it can break down as shown in Table 1-1.

The difference in labor costs is what you will contribute clearing the property, painting the interior and exterior of the building, cleaning up after construction, and landscaping. You will also earn the builder's profit and save the agent's fee.

Your savings might be higher or lower. In today's world, a profit of 17 percent is not unduly high. In any case, if you add to the savings in initial cost the cost of the mortgage over the years, the total sum you may save is very impressive. And as the builder, you can also let walks and paved drives and shrubs go until a later date. This will decrease your initial costs even further.

BUILD ONE STEP AT A TIME

Houses are built one step at a time. Be it a 40-room mansion or a three-room summer cottage, the sequence of steps necessary to their construction are identical. Build one house or build a hundred simultaneously, each house is constructed one step at a time.

When you enter a modern home and become aware of its piping, wires, and heating and cooling system, you might be awed by its complexity and the tremendous amount of technical knowledge and skill that is represented by a modern home. There is no denying that it is complicated. Bear in mind that the tradesmen who constructed the building did not know nor need to know everything. Their knowledge is but a small fraction of the sum total knowledge necessary to construct a modern home.

Think of it this way. The plumber did not design or construct the boiler. He went to a boiler manufacturer and stated he had a two-bath, four-bedroom house. The boiler manufacturer, working from his experience, told him he needed an 80-gallon, hot-water tank. The manufacturer or the supply house delivered the proper size tank and the plumber connected it. The plumber or the heating specialist brought the house plans to a furnace manufacturer. The manufacturer looked up the size of the house, number of windows, the amount of insulation, and the location of the building in his chart or he had his engineer calculate the size furnace that was needed. Again, the plumber or the heating man simply connected the pipes or the hot air ducts. Neither man will connect whatever electrical wiring has to be installed. That will be done by an electrician.

And so it goes. Each tradesman does his job. No one contractor knows it all and he doesn't need to know it all.

Give any competent carpenter a set of plans and he can tell you how much lumber will be needed, how much time he needs to erect the building and how much he wants for his labor. This holds true for all the trades.

THE BUILDER'S TASK

The builder assembles the parts, he directs the chorus. He raises the money, selects and purchases the land, selects the plan for the building he wants, hires a surveyor to locate the building on the lot, hires an excavator to prepare the crawl space or basement, and hires a mason to pour the footings, building the foundation. See Fig. 1-2. Each man or group of men work in sequence. Each trade more or less follows another.

Meanwhile, you—the builder—can double in brass. While the crews are working you can contribute the muscle, the unskilled or semiskilled labor. You can help clear the land, do the exterior and interior painting, shellac floors, lay down a gravel driveway, clean up the site so that work progresses more rapidly, keep the subcontractors apprised of

Fig. 1-2. On a well-organized job, the concrete block is deposited right next to the footings (where the block will be used).

progress so they show on time, check the lumber and other material delivery, do the final cleaning, landscaping, and deal with the building department. Last but not least, you can and should run errands for the crews so they do not have to stop work for missing nails or forgotten lumber. And bring coffee and pastry that you pay for.

TIME

In theory, it is possible to go from dirt to dwelling in 30 days. It never happens. The experienced builder who does nothing but supervise allows at least 6 months to go the route. If you plan to do some work, figure that at least a year will pass before you can move in. Even if you do not plan to do any work yourself, give yourself at least a year.

Supervision. You do not have to stand over any of the crews to see that they do their jobs. You are dealing with professionals who know very well they won't get paid until the job is done and done properly. But you have to show up. The reason is self-explanatory if you know the construction business. It is seasonal and it is somewhat unpredictable. Jobs are often delayed by waiting for material delivery, inspection by the building department, and the weather.

The result is that subcontractors will sign up as much work as they dare. Then they will skip from job to job so as not to lose time or to anger any customer too much. They will put off inside work until it rains. If there is any slightly plausible excuse to leave one job and work at another they will do so. If lumber delivery is delayed to your job, they won't wait. A good portion of the builder's task is to keep the crews on the job by making certain of material delivery, timely job inspection, and so on.

You can supervise a job by appearing once or twice a day for a short period, but you cannot supervise a job by remote control. If you can only get to the job site on weekends and holidays, your job will drag and drag as the crews service the jobs that best suit their schedule.

If you can't or don't want to supervise the job, you should hire an architect. His usual fee is anywhere upwards of 6 percent of the total job costs (sometimes the price of the land is included, some-times not). The architect's job is to take over complete responsibility for the structure—from blueprint through completion. If your architect suggests a responsible builder, fire him. There is no point to paying an architect and a builder.

PITFALLS

Overbuilding. Don't overbuild. There is a normal desire and tendency to build your home as strong and as durable as possible. This is nice if you have the time and the money. But think of Cheops. His last mansion outlasted him by several thousand years. And what good did it do him.

Overbuilding is an easy pit to fall into. The argument you or your associate will make as you go along is why not. Why not ½-inch plywood when ⅜-inch plywood will do. Why not select oak floors when number one or a lesser grade will do. It doesn't take long before the supposed pennies amount to thousands of dollars, and the house will not be much stronger, longer lasting or even more attractive for having selected 12-inch block in place of 10- or 8-inch block.

The same goes for size. It's true that the larger house is not proportionally more costly, but extra rooms only mean more guests and extra storage space just means more things that will be stored. See Fig. 1-3.

If money is no problem today and in the foreseeable future, go right ahead. But if money is something you bother to count now and again, do not overbuild in size and splendor. Stick within required building codes minimums and you will have a durable, long-lasting home. Making it stronger is merely a waste of material and money.

Money. Homes are not built of sweat, blood, and guts. They are not built of bricks and stone. They are built with money. And we would be remiss if we did not pound the table and shout. If you do not and cannot with certainty secure all the money you will need to complete the house and move in—*do not start.*

If you gamble that you will somehow secure the necessary funds as the need comes up and you fail along the way, you can very easily lose everything you have put into the building and lot. If you

Fig. 1-3. A very beautiful Colonial-design home. The small dormers, the cut-stone facing, and the adjoining small room to its side add thousands of dollars to its cost.

fail before the building is completed, you will be in a terrible financial position. You won't be able to go forward because no one is going to work on the chance they will be paid. The bank that has extended a building mortgage doesn't want the building; they will foreclose and put it on the block. Only the hawks will bid on an unfinished building, and they will pay nothing beyond the bank and the subcontractor's claims. You won't even be left holding a bag.

Although we mention it last, the first and foremost requirement for the construction of a

Fig. 1-4. Girder like steel reinforcement being positioned between the foundation courses of concrete block. This might have been done at the insistance of the building department. It adds to the cost, but it does provide additional foundation strength.

home is money. If you want to be certain of succeeding in your project, don't forget it.

BUILDING CODES

In the course of reading about home construction in other books and talking to other build-it-yourself people and craftsmen in the building trades, you will encounter considerable grousing. "Building codes are ruining the industry, driving us bonkers, pushing construction costs sky-high," and more of the same.

There is no denying that building codes have

pushed the cost of construction up. But the codes have also resulted in uniformly sturdy, long-lasting buildings. The codes have kept the ignorant and dishonest craftspeople out of the business. They also have and continue to protect the ignorant do-it-yourselfers from themselves.

Plumbers and electricians have to be licensed. Buildings have to be inspected during the course of their construction. Certain basic standards have to be met. True, some of the codes are confusing. True, there is often no uniformity between the code found in one village and the next. True, some codes force the use of expensive materials. One example is the ban on the use of plastic pipe in some localities that forces the installation of the much more expensive copper pipe or galvanized pipe. And it is true that even the most lenient code results in a structure that is tremendously and wastefully over-designed, according to many architects.

On the other hand, our system of municipal building inspection is a godsend to the do-it-yourselfer. The building inspector is Big Brother to the job. You can't go far wrong when you stick to the code and your work is inspected by a man or men who know what they are doing. See Fig. 1-4.

Our buildings could be constructed for a little less than they cost now. No doubt of that. But our buildings do not often fall down by themselves as they do now and again in Europe.

HOW MUCH SHOULD YOU DO?

The prime reason for building one's own home is to make home ownership possible with a comparatively small investment of cash. It would appear to follow that the greatest savings could be secured by doing the greatest portion of the work yourself. It would appear to be so, but in practice it doesn't always work out that way. Time is the hitch.

Time is your enemy; it works against you in several ways. As soon as you become the proud owner of a building lot, you become obligated to pay the taxes levied on the lot. Whether or not the community will levy a tax on your unfinished building depends on local rules and practices. Some communities will not apply real estate tax to an

incomplete building. Others will tax the owner upon the value of the improved property based on its degree of completion.

The longer the time span between the start of construction and the actual inhabitation of the structure, the greater the sum wasted. This sum has to be paid even though you might not recognize it as a building cost.

If you have drawn some portion of your construction mortgage from the bank, you are also carrying this load during the time the building is under construction. Mortgage interest continues no matter what else is or is not happening.

You should have fire insurance on your building. The insurance rates during construction and before occupancy are higher than they will be when the building is occupied.

Few, if any, insurance companies will protect your unfinished structure against vandalism and theft. The longer the building remains in an unfinished state, the greater the risk of vandalism and material theft.

Learning the Trades. There are a number of informal schools in various parts of the country that specialize in teaching the various building trades —carpentry, masonry, plumbing—to people who plan to construct their own homes. These schools teach mainly by means of actual experience. The pupils work on actual house construction. Attending such a school, reading up on the trades, and observing the construction of other homes will provide you with excellent, valuable background information that will be of tremendous help to you as a builder. Going to school, learning the trades, and doing it all (or most of all the work) yourself is not financially practical in most instances.

Essentially, the drawback is time. You need months to learn a trade, and there are several major trades involved in home construction. Even after you have mastered a trade or skill, you won't have speed. In most cases, you will be well advised to work weekends at some job you know and do well and use the money so earned to hire an experienced craftsman to do your building.

There are exceptions. You own the lot outright. The taxes are very low. You build on weekends using your own money and are not running up a debt. Or you join six or eight other people and build an equal number of homes together as a team, thus speeding up construction.

How much should you do yourself? As much as you can without interfering with the progress of the job. To this end, we have included brief descriptions of the various trades and construction practices necessary to the building of a modern home. This will enable you to determine what you can and cannot do and seek additional information, if necessary, to facilitate your efforts.

Chapter 2

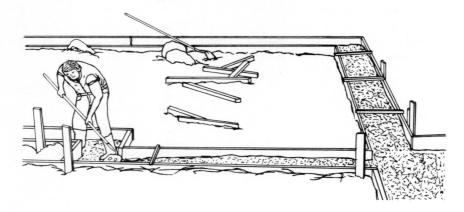

Getting Started

FOR MOST OF US, THE PURCHASE OF A HOME IS THE largest single investment we will ever make. Before you look at house plans and before you decide how many rooms you want and need, find the land. The land is crucial to all your plans. The location of the land, within or external to a municipality, determines whether or not you will have to conform to a building code and what that code will contain. The land's topography will affect your selection of building design and the difficulty or ease with which the building can be erected. The presence or absence of city water and sewer lines will affect your building costs. The presence or absence of a municipal fire hydrant will affect your fire insurance rate. The owner of a better lot (better situated, larger) is charged a higher real estate tax.

Don't buy the land at this time. Just find it and price it. Of course, by doing this you are taking a chance that someone else might buy the property ahead of you. You can prevent this by taking an option to purchase on the land. In simple terms, you give the lot owner a sum of money for which he holds the land for a specified period of time. The price of the land is agreed upon at the granting of the option and remains fixed for the life of the option. It is a simple financial arrangement, but it is advisable to have a lawyer draw up the papers.

If you are an experienced builder, you can look at a lot and estimate fairly well what it will cost you to build on it. If this will be your first attempt at building, it is much better to lose the lot or lose the option money than purchase a lot you will not be able to use or which you might have to hold for years before you can sell it.

Learn the Code. You have found your property and know its address. Go to the tax office and look the property up on the map. Assuming you are within a municipality, take note of the lot and parcel and map number. Now you can go to the building department and ask for a copy of the building code that pertains to "your" property.

Right now you are interested in the major facts. What are the major zoning restrictions? In some areas, you cannot build a private home over 35 feet in height. In other areas you cannot build a home below a specific size or your lot must have a

60- or 75-foot front on the road. Some towns limit driveway slope or pitch. All these rules will affect your home's design and construction.

Some towns require more than others. For example, White Plains, New York reputedly has one of the most demanding codes. It requires that foundations be constructed of 10-inch concrete block. Other municipalities believe 8-inch block is more than sufficient. White Plains won't permit a driveway with a slope of more than 10 degrees (a rise of 1 foot in 10). Other codes do not concern themselves with driveways at all.

Select Your House Design. Certain designs are more economical than others and certain designs are better adapted to certain topography than others. It is your task at this point to select a type and size of building that meets your needs, conforms to building department regulations, and suits the land.

Secure Plans. You will need at least six sets of blueprints. You can have plans drawn or you can secure plans from a number of other sources. Many magazines, found on local newsstands, feature homes for which you can obtain plans by sending a few dollars. There are books of plans by various companies that offer plan copies for a relatively few dollars. The Goverment Printing Office, Washington, DC 20401, offers plans.

Purchasing drawn plans has one major advantage. They are relatively inexpensive. Unfortunately, they have several disadvantages. The least is that many localities will not accept them as they are. They demand that a licensed architect approve them and, if necessary, make changes to bring them into line with local code requirements. A more telling disadvantage is that many of them are cute. They are designed to produce brilliant photographs. Economy of construction is not their strong point, but it should be your main interest.

To secure blueprints for well-designed, low-cost homes at a very low price, write to the land grant university nearest you. Address the agricultural engineering extension office. See Table 2-1.

An experienced builder or architect can look at a set of plans and tell whether the structure is relatively expensive or inexpensive to build. Bear

Table 2-1. Land Grant Universities.

Auburn University. Auburn. AL 36830
University of Alaska. Fairbanks. AK 99701
University of Arizona. Tucson. AZ 85721
University of Arkansas. Little Rock. AR 72203
University of California at Davis. Davis. CA 95616
University of California at Riverside. Riverside. CA 92521
Clemson University. Clemson. SC 29631
Colorado State University. Fort Collins. CO 80523
University of Connecticut. Storrs. CT 06268
Cornell University. Ithaca. NY 14853
University of Delaware. Newark. DE 19711
University of Florida. Gainesville. FL 32611
University of Georgia. Athens. GA 30602
University of Hawaii. Honolulu. HI 96822
University of Idaho. Moscow. ID 83843
University of Illinois. Urbana. IL 61801
Iowa State University. Ames. IA 50011
Kansas State University. Manhattan. KS 66505
University of Kentucky. Lexington. KY 40545
Louisiana State University. Baton Rouge. LA 70803
University of Maine. Orono. ME 04473
University of Maryland. College Park. MD 20742
University of Massachusetts. Amherst. MA 01002
Michigan State University. East Lansing. MI 48824
University of Minnesota. St. Paul. MN 55108
Mississippi State University. Mississippi State. MS 39762
University of Missouri. Columbia. MO 65201
Montana State University. Bozeman. MT 59715
University of Nebraska. Lincoln. NB 68503
University of Nevada. Reno. NV 89507
University of New Hampshire. Durham. NH 03824
Purdue University. Lafayette. IN 47907
Rutgers University. New Brunswick. NJ 08903
New Mexico State University. Las Cruces. NM 88003
North Carolina State University. Raleigh. NC 26707
North Dakota State University. Fargo. ND 58102
Ohio State University. Columbus. OH 43210
Oklahoma State University. Stillwater. OK 74074
Oregon State University. Corvallis. OR 97331
Pennsylvania State University. University Park. PA 16802
University of Puerto Rico. Rio Piedras. PR 00928
University of Rhode Island. Kingston. RI 02881
South Dakota State University. Brookings. SD 57006
University of Tennessee. Knoxville. TN 37901
Texas A&M University. College Station. TX 77843
Utah State University. Logan. UT 84322
University of Vermont. Burlington. VT 05401
Virginia Polytechnic Institute and State University. Blacksburg. VA 24061
Washington State University. Pullman. WA 99163
West Virginia State University. Morgantown. WV 26506
University of Wisconsin. Madison. WI 53706
University of Wyoming. Laramie. WY 82071
Extension Service. U.S. Department of Agriculture. Washington. DC 20250

in mind we are speaking of buildings identical in living space and thermal efficiency. We are not comparing apples to peaches. As a first-time builder, you can only use your common sense and follow these few rules to find your dollar-efficient home.

☐ Stay away from gimmicky houses.

☐ Use standard materials available locally.

☐ Use standard building techniques.

☐ Stick with simplicity.

☐ Remember, every turn, every extra angle costs money.

At this point, this list of do's and don'ts might not mean much. But if you drive around a few residential neighborhoods and look at the houses, you will see what is meant by simple design and complex design. If you carefully examine a dozen or so sets of prints, you will also soon see the difference between complex and simple building design.

Having Plans Drawn. With a little effort, you can find licensed architects who will draw up a set of plans for a few hundred dollars (they can do it in an afternoon). A responsible architect will come and take a look at your lot before he draws just to make certain the building physically suits the property. These will be more or less standard plans incorporating a few of your suggestions. If you want more—if you want a home that will reflect your personality—be prepared to pay lots more. If you want the architect to oversee the job, the usual fee is 6 percent or more of the total cost of the job. Often the architect will want to hire a builder to supervise construction. Thus the architect supervises the supervisor and both are on your payroll.

The "standard" plan is a plan that has been used (with small variations) successfully since the turn of the century. Unless you insist upon some outlandish variation, you will end up with an attractive, dollar-efficent, thermally-efficient, dependable home.

You can find an architect willing to simply draw plans by talking to local carpenters and contractors. They usually work with and know the no-frills architects.

Pricing the Job. You have seen the property. You know more or less what has to be done to it.

You have your plans in hand. Now you approach the various subcontractors and secure their bids. Add the bids for labor to the cost of materials and you have the cost of the house.

Contact a number of excavators, bring them to the property, or just describe it. Describe the excavation required and get their figure—in writing.

Bring your plans to the local lumberyard and have them bid on all the lumber, insulation, and roofing. They will charge $50 to $100 for the service, and they will need a copy of the plans. If possible, have them break the figures down to show how much for each item.

Do the same at the wholesale plumbing supply house. He too will need a copy of the plans.

Bring the plans to a number of carpenters. Get their bids in writing.

Bring the plans to a number of masons. Repeat the procedure.

Do the same with the heating man, the electrician, and the drywall man. You want all these bids in writing on their letterhead. You will need the figures to price the house and to show the bank when you apply for a mortgage.

You now know what the land and the building will cost you. The figure is not exact and neither is it complete. There are fees, legal expenses, mortgage costs, and finishing costs (painting, landscaping, leaders and gutters, etc.) Add 15 percent to get a ballpark figure for your total building costs. This figure does not include the cost of amortizing the mortgage over the years, the cost of taxes, heat and insurance, and everything else associated with owning one's own home. It is just the approximate cost of the building, land, and associate fees and charges you will have to meet to build and own the home you have selected.

When you know the total cost of the bulding and land, you can go to the local tax board and determine what the taxes will be on that building and property. Using the same house-cost figures, you can contact your insurance broker and learn what your insurance premiums per year will be.

Your next step is to review your financial situation. How much cash do you have? How much cash can you put down on the house and lot? How much of a monthly charge—mortgage, taxes, house expenses—you can safely carry? Remember that you also have to eat!

Now you need to know your mortgage payments. Obviously, you cannot be certain of this number because you have not yet secured a mortgage. Nevertheless you can, with a little effort, get a good working figure.

You know the total sum you will need. Subtract the cash you can put down. This gives you the sum you need to borrow. You know or you should make it your business to learn what the current new-loan mortgage interest rates in your area are. Now look up the monthly payments in an amortization table (sometimes called interest table or mortgage table). You can find copies of these tables at local public libraries and at stationery shops dealing with commercial accounts.

Here is an example. Your total costs come to $70,000. You plan to put down $20,000. You need to borrow (secure a mortgage of) $50,000. On a 10 percent, 30-year mortgage, monthly interest and amortization payments amount to $439 per month.

To this you have to add insurance, taxes, heat, and some money left for maintenance.

Can you carry this financial load without going broke? If you can't, you have got to cut your projected costs. You can try to do this several ways.

☐ Put down more cash.
☐ Get a mortgage with a lower interest rate.
☐ Change the house (less expensive fixtures, etc.).
☐ Go to a different, less costly house.
☐ Go to a less expensive lot.

Notice that we did not suggest you find a carpenter or mason who will work for less. While it is possible to find good men who will work for less than the going rate, lower labor costs are not something on which you can or should bank.

As you can see, it is possible that the very first lot you select and the very first house you choose will prove to be within your financial capabilities. On the other hand, you might have to make a dozen selections and changes before you come up with what you can afford and what you will find comfortable and enjoyable.

Chapter 3

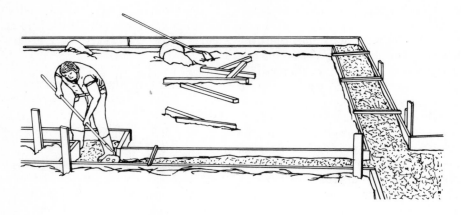

The Land

A HOME CONSISTS OF THE STRUCTURE ITSELF AND the land upon which it rests. You can throw the house away and the land will remain. The house might be destroyed by lightning, wind, or fire, but the land will remain and you can build on it again. You can err in the construction of the house and later correct your errors. For all practical purposes, the land remains the same. The land greatly determines the nature of the house that will be constructed upon it and to a great extent the cost of construction. See Fig. 3-1.

LAND VALUES

Location Comes First. The single, most important value of any piece of land, other than mineral and oil rights, is its location. You can purchase land in northern Alaska for pennies an acre. In Manhattan, you will pay millions for an acre if the land is in midtown or downtown. Some localities offer special amenities such as a view, a beach, and so on. New communities tend to have low taxes that rise dramatically and drastically.

Lot size. The larger lot (other things being equal) usually sells for more than the smaller lot. Most of us would enjoy the additional privacy afforded by a larger building lot, but the larger lot is often a luxury that costs more to purchase, more in taxes, and more in upkeep. Unless local building codes permit you to split the lot and sell off a portion, you will not be able to get your money out until you sell the entire property.

Topography. Flat land is easier and less expensive to build on. Rock-filled land can present many problems. Solid rock will make installing a septic tank and drain field almost impossible, and excavating a basement very, very expensive. On the other hand, solid rock simplifies and reduces the cost of a foundation if you are going to build on a slab, and it is not too difficult to run water and sewer lines.

Type and Condition of the Earth. If you are building on solid clay and you need to install a drain field for a septic tank, drain-field costs can be several times higher than in partial clay. If the ground is

Fig. 3-1. The cost of clearing the land of trees and shrubs is something you must always consider when evaluating property.

marshy and wet most of the year, you will have to provide some drainage. If the earth is very soft, you might have to drive piles to support your house. This can be very costly.

PERSONAL VALUES

We list the following as personal values of a piece of land because they will vary with the purchaser.

The Neighborhood. The neighborhood includes people who will be your neighbors, the schools your children will attend, the distance to shopping, employment, friends and relatives, the view or lack of a view, and driving convenience (accessible in bad weather?).

Municipal Services. Garbage collection and the quality of police and fire protection are factors. Is there a fire hydrant nearby? Its presence or absence will affect your fire insurance rate. Tax rates can be considerably different in adjoining municipalities. Is the community in a state of flux or is it old and established, with little expected or possible change? Which do you prefer?

CITY OR COUNTRY

To city-born folk, any piece of land that shows more green than concrete is the country. To a builder, city land means city water, sewer, and electricity. Any land that does not have these amenities is in the country.

Hidden Costs. City property generally costs more than country property. City real estate and school taxes are usually much more than country real estate and school taxes. The difference begins to dwindle when you add the cost of installing a water system, a sewage system, and electric power or an extended electric line on your country property. You can't simply assign a ballpark figure to such costs because they will vary with the property. Some lots might have city water and electric power lines. On others, you might have to go 200 feet to find water. At $10 to $20 a drilled foot, that can run into a bundle.

Hidden Dividends. The actual cost differential between city and country property might not be as high as the apparent figures. For example, assume that taxes and mortgage interest on the city building are estimated to be $18,000. Amortization payments are not included in this figure. If you are in the 30-percent-income-tax bracket, you will be able to save 30 percent or more of this because you can deduct the entire $1,800 from your gross income. For most of us, the higher city real estate tax is actually 30 percent less. If you are earning more, your tax bite will be proportionately less.

FINDING PROPERTY

You can ride around and look for posted For Sale signs. You can read the land offerings in the newspapers. You can go to real estate agents. If the sign or the newspaper ad reads, "brokers protected," you are going to pay a brokers fee. The asking price has been upped to take care of brokers (agents). If you go to a real estate agent, you obviously have to pay a fee. There is no getting around this. The agent is protected by law.

Agent or broker fees on unimproved land is usually 10 percent of the selling price. This can sometimes be reduced. It all depends on how badly you want the land and how badly the owner wants to sell. Your gambit is to counter the asking price with a lower offer. You will hear all sorts of stories about the land being in the family and the real estate broker being a nice guy and having needy children. If the owner wants to sell badly enough, he will lower his price, which is tantamount to not paying the commission. In any case it is a contest of wills and desires. Just don't make a counter offer so low you get chased from the property.

Avoiding the Agents. Avoiding agents calls for time and effort that is not always rewarded. Locate the land you want. Go to the city tax office and find the name and address of the owner of record. Contact him or her directly. It calls for a lot of work, but you might get lucky. You might find the owner receptive. On the other hand you might find that the land is part of an estate that is in litigation and will remain in litigation for years to come because none of the heirs can agree to anything.

CLOSING THE DEAL

These steps that are generally taken can vary in detail from one transaction to the next, but basically they remain the same.

You and the seller—with or without an agent as an intermediary—have come to an agreement on price and terms. You, the buyer, will give the seller several hundred dollars (always in check form) as earnest money to prove you are serious. The earnest money pays for the seller's trouble should you decide to cancel the deal.

The seller then furnishes you or your lawyer with a copy of the deed. This is a legal description of the property, its location, and restrictions and easements that may be in force.

You, your lawyer, or a title guarantee company searches the title. This means going to the county clerk's office and reviewing the records. It is here that all claims, liens, and judgments against the property are registered. This might be an exhaustive search or a casual search. If it is accomplished by the title guarantee company, it is part of the service rendered for the fee they will receive for guaranteeing the title.

Your lawyer now draws up a purchase offer that states clearly the terms and conditions of the sale (assuming there are no encumbrances), who will pay the agent (if involved, and how much), how much will be paid at this point, and when the balance will be paid. If there are any conditions to be met by the buyer and or seller, they too must be listed. Verbal agreements aren't worth the air with which they are formed. One condition might be that the deal be closed in 60 days or so. Another that the seller settle a tax claim, remove some obstruction, or whatever. Everything that you and the seller agree upon must be clearly spelled out.

It is also very important that you receive a plot plan; this is a legal map of the property. You need the plot plan to check the land as described in the deed against the survey made by a licensed surveyor. An error of a few inches doesn't matter. If there is a discrepancy of more than that, it must be cleared up before you purchase the land. The seller should have a copy of the plot plan.

If he will not pay to have the land resurveyed, pay the charge yourself. You need the plot plan to secure a building permit, to secure a mortgage, and to check on the legal boundaries of the property you are considering. When you build, you need to have the surveyor's stakes in place in order to make certain your house is correctly positioned.

Earnest money is not binding. Should the seller have a change of mind the money can be returned. If you change your mind, you can ask for your money back, but the seller is not obligated to return it.

The purchase offer is a legal, binding agreement. Sometimes called a deposit, its signing is usually accompanied by the changing of hands of some 10 percent of the price of the land. If either party backs out, the money is forfeited. Thus it is advisable to work through an escrow agent. This can be a lawyer or bank. Monies are held by the escrow agent until the deal is completed. At that time the money is paid over to the seller and agent, if there is one. The advantage is that should the seller back out (for any reason whatsoever), you will not have difficulty retrieving your deposit or forcing the conclusion of the deal.

When all the conditions of the deal have been met, the transaction is completed. The deed changes hands and the fact is recorded with the county clerk. You are now the owner of record.

CAUTIONS

Land swindling is one of the oldest games known to man, and today it has moved into the realm of big business. This is not to condemn every giant corporation in the land-selling business, but many perfectly legal land-sale transactions are crooked.

The Rip-offs. The most insidious rip-off is the time payment plan. It's $50 down $50 more a month and you are the proud owner of one splendid acre in a wonderful vacation retreat or leisure-time hideaway. Look at the figures carefully and you will see that you will be hard pressed to live long enough to pay off the debt. Look carefully at the fine print and you will see that you do *not* own the property until it has been paid for in full. You are buying it on a chattle mortgage deal just as you would purchase an automobile. Default on your auto payments and the sheriff can repossess your car wherever he finds it. Default on your property and you lose it all.

When you actually own property and default on a mortgage payment, the mortgage holder cannot simply dispossess you. He has to foreclose and that is an expensive, legal process. Only then can the court put up the property for public auction. If there is any money left after paying off the claims, you receive the balance.

Then there is the invisible costs ploy. You see pictures of beautiful pools, tennis courts, etc. You might imagine that these facilities are open to you as a land owner, but there is a fee or they are not paid for as yet. People owning property in the vicinity will be assessed to pay for these amenities. One variation is the disappearing road trick. You see roads in the brochure, but they are only in the artist's imagination. You and the other dupes are going to have to ante up land improvement cost—roads, sewers, water lines.

Your only protection is to never purchase without an on-site examination; never purchase without a plot plan to make certain you are getting what you are being shown; secure a full list of all costs, present and future; buy outright or not at all; specify what you will and will not pay in your purchase offer.

EASEMENTS AND COVENANTS

An easement is a privilege granted in writing by a landowner. Generally, easements are recorded in the deed. Typically, an easement will give the local power and light company the right to traverse your property with their lines.

If the easement is in the deed, you are stuck with it. The only way you can eliminate it is to secure permission from the recipient to revoke it. Some easements are not written, but they exist legally none the less. For example, if the man in the property behind yours can only reach the public road by traversing your property, he has this right; it is called the right of access.

A covenant, as used in real estate, is a written agreement between a land seller and buyer specifying certain conditions and obligations. You might argue that they are not legal, and I will agree with you, but they do exist. They are used to regiment and standardize structures and people in certain limited communities—for better or for worse.

One such covenant is used by the developers of a beautiful mountain area outside Denver. Buy land there and you must build within their specifications, must leave a specified percentage of the land untouched, permit them to inspect the inside of your home at their convenience, limit the number of your guests, contribute to their club house, and behave with decorum. Fail to comply and you will be replaced.

HIDDEN COSTS

The nature of the soil and the presence or absence of rock and water all affect the cost of construction. Marshes cause the most serious problems. See Fig. 3-2.

Soft Soils. The presence or absence of surface water does not always indicate the absolute presence or absence of soft soil. In some instances

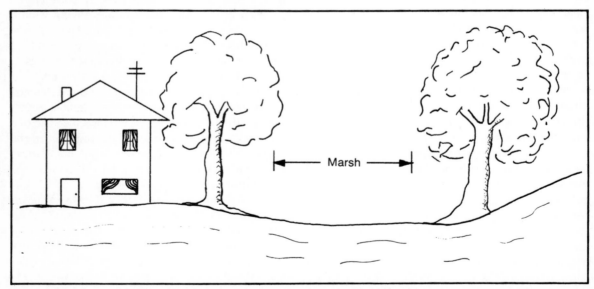

Fig. 3-2. Beware the hollow. Unless you can drain this type of area through a public sewer or there is still lower land to which you can direct the water, it will never be thoroughly dry.

Table 3-1. Load-Bearing Capability of Various Soils.

Soil types	Tons per sq ft
Solid rock	25
Hard pan	10
Rocks or gravel	6
Coarse sand (compact)	4
Stiff clay	4
Fine sand (dry)	3
Fine sand (damp)	2
Medium clay	2
Soft clay	1

the natural flow of a creek or rainwater runoff has been blocked and what you see is surface water atop firm soil. Simple drainage might solve the problem. In other cases, there is no or little visible water, but the earth feels soft and springy underfoot. In either case you can only be certain by testing. Simply digging a few feet into the earth will give you an approximate evaluation of the soil. If it isn't firm—meaning you can't make more than a slight mark with your heel—you need an engineering evaluation. Bear in mind that the topsoil is always soft. You are interested in the subsoil. See Table 3-1.

You might be able to secure free information from the local building inspector or you might have to consult a local foundation construction company. The city might insist that you pay for soil tests. If there is any doubt as to the load-bearing capability of the soil, you better find out now. If you have to go to driven piles, the cost of house construction can go up 25 percent to 30 percent. If you build on soft soil without proper foundation, your building will settle and its walls will crack.

Soil Testing. In most instances, it is unnecessary to hire a professional service to perform a soil test for a residential structure. While it is true that even a small building can weigh a total of 50 to 75 tons, the actual load per square foot of footing is very low. For example, assume that a building is 35 by 50 feet. This makes for a total footing length of 170 feet. If the footing is 1½ feet wide, the total footing area is 170 × 1.5, which gives you 255 square feet of footing area in contact with the soil. Dividing 75 tons by 255 square feet gives you .299

tons per square foot. Even soft clay that is rated at 1 ton per square foot can safely handle three times more weight.

Remove the top layer of dark top soil to reveal the lighter-colored subsoil. Try to dig your heel into the subsoil. If you cannot make more than a slight indentation, you at least have medium clay underfoot.

If you are uncertain as to the results of this simple test, you can secure soil-testing services by checking local telephone directories under Drilling and Boring, Soil Testing, and Test Boring.

The cost of the test will depend upon the difficulty of access and the number of test drillings that have to be made. Fees vary with the individual company and the depth to which they have to drill to be certain of uniform soil. You can expect costs to run to several hundred dollars.

Water. The presence of water does not always mean soft soil. Often the land is blessed or cursed with a small spring. Sometimes the spring flows only after a rain. In some locations, the ground is rock hard, but floods after a rain. See Fig. 3-3.

Unless you are at the bottom of a depression or valley, springs can be piped out and away. Rainwater can be redirected. If you must have a basement or cellar, you can waterproof it and provide sufficient drainage to keep it dry. The wiser solution is to forego the cellar.

Storm water can present a more serious problem. If you are going to build on the bank of a stream, you should learn whether or not the stream overruns its banks and, if so, how often and how far. See the local county engineering office.

Some brooks are dry most of the year and then flood in the spring. The same is true of some low-lying meadows. It all bears study.

Rock. Some areas have no rock to speak of. In others, rock is everywhere visible. In still other places, there is and there isn't rock. See Fig. 3-4. The rock might be visible at one point, present and invisible at another point, or absent. The only way you can be certain is to dig a hole or try to drive a length of pipe into the earth. See Fig. 3-5.

The presence of rock almost always increases

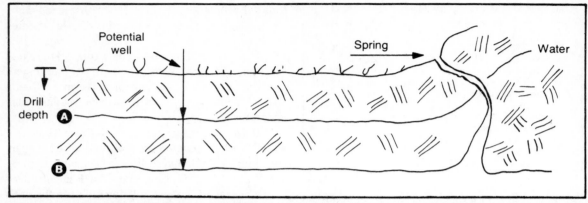

Fig. 3-3. Water might be found in the area marked A or you may have to drill down to area B. The presence of a small spring above your land doesn't guarantee water at a shallow depth.

the cost of construction. The actual cost increase depends upon the nature of the rock, the position of the rock in relation to the projected building, the design of the building, and the location of the services (if any) in relation to the building.

When and if possible the rock is avoided and ignored. In some instances, this can be accomplished by simply moving the projected house to another portion of the lot. Rock outcroppings could be permitted to remain and later could be converted into rock gardens and the like.

Large boulders can be disposed of by burying them. A power shovel is used to dig a large hole.

The boulder is pushed into the hole, covered with earth, and forgotten.

If there is just a few feet of solid rock in the way, you can hire a man with an air hammer to split the rock and break it into pieces small enough to be hand-carted away. This is easy when the rock is flawed and cracked. It is difficult to do with just an air hammer when the rock is very hard and solid.

If the entire area is solid rock or giant boulders, the cost of a standard basement or cellar becomes prohibitive. If the rock is hard it will blast easily. If the rock is soft, it will not respond well to dynamite. Lots more effort will be required and

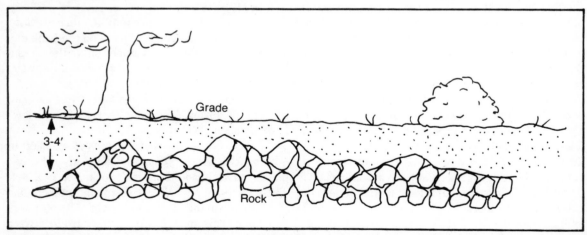

Fig. 3-4. Rock is where you find it. The presence of large trees and shrubs is no indication that there isn't bedrock lying in wait for you.

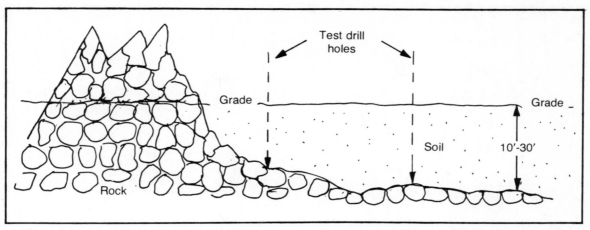

Fig. 3-5. A visible outcropping of rock might fall away beneath the grade. You have to make test drillings (holes) to be certain.

probably considerable air-hammer work too.

In any case, rock removal is done on the basis of so much per cubic yard removed. Within a municipality, blasting can only be done by a contractor licensed for the work. He must carry an insurance policy that, as you can imagine, carries a very high premium. Outside of a municipality anyone can blast, but it is extremely dangerous work for an amateur.

The practical alternative is to forego the cellar or basement. Use the rock or the boulders, if they are large enough, either as the support for footings or as the base for a slab foundation. The rock is washed clean and the concrete is poured directly on the stone. If the surface of the rock is pitched, steel pins are used to lock the footing to the rock. See Fig. 3-6.

There is no alternative to running service lines over rock other than to cut channels in the rock and insert the pipe in the channels (Fig. 3-7). The water pipe has to be below the frost line. The sewer pipe can be a little higher. You can, however, reduce the depth of the trench or channel by insulating the pipes. Ordinary rock wool insulation can be wrapped around the pipe and held in place with wire. The soil placed atop the pipe and insulation

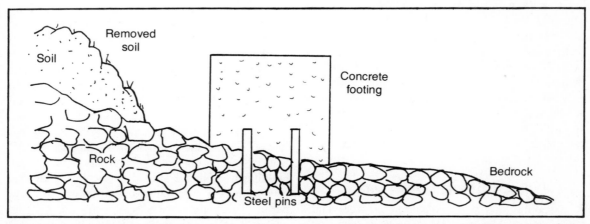

Fig. 3-6. You can build directly on bedrock. Just clean it before pouring your footings. If the rock is pitched, pin the footing to the rock with steel rods as shown.

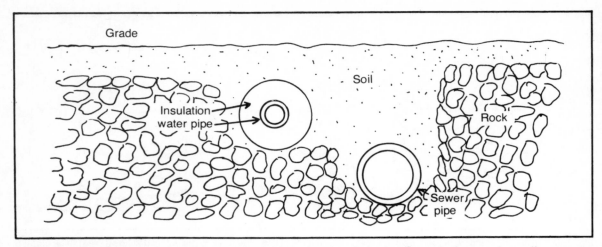

Fig. 3-7. Never run a copper (or galvanized) pipe adjoining a cast-iron drain pipe. Separate them as shown. If you cannot position the water line below the frost line, insulate it.

will keep the latter in place when the wires rust through.

Rock and Septic Tanks. Rock and septic tanks don't mix. You can build atop solid rock, but you cannot place a septic tank above ground. It has to be below ground for the waste from the house to enter the tank by gravity, and the tank has to be protected from frost.

Rock and Drain Fields. Assuming that your tank can be submerged beneath the soil but the logical position for the drain field has to be on exposed bedrock, the solution in such instances is to cover the exposed rock with a layer of soil several feet thick. The perforated drain pipes are placed in trenches in this layer of soil and covered with more soil.

The results will be satisfactory but, as you can imagine, you will need considerable soil. For example, if your drain field is to cover an area of 30 × 30 feet and you cover this area to a depth of 3 feet, you have 30 × 30 × 3 = 100 cubic yards of soil. It can't be any old muck; it should be somewhat sandy soil for best results.

CESSPOOLS AND SEEPAGE PITS

A cesspool is simply a deep hole in the ground into which household sewage is directed. Because both bacterial action and percolation of the liquid into the soil takes place in what is effectively a single tank, the cesspool is not very effective for very long. Its walls become clogged. Few municipalities permit cesspools anymore.

A seepage pit is a deep pit in the earth. The effluent from a septic tank may be emptied into a seepage pit. Properly constructed in permeable soil with a low water table, the seepage pit can effectively replace a drain or leaching field.

SERVICE LINES

There is rarely a problem beyond simple costs when installing gas, electric, and water lines. They can run up hill and down and the electric lines can be installed above or below the earth. Sewer lines are another story. The bottom of the toilet bowl, the shower, and tubs must all be higher than the center of the sewer main by a distance of at least ¼ inch to the foot. See Fig. 3-8. This is necessary for the soil and waste to flow by gravity into the sewer main.

Sewer mains are generally positioned so that this is accomplished with normal building. When it is not possible, one solution consists of raising the building by making the foundation walls higher than usual. Another solution involves the use of a soil pump. The pump automatically lifts the soil the proper height from where it flows by gravity into the city sewer main. See Figs. 3-9 and 3-10.

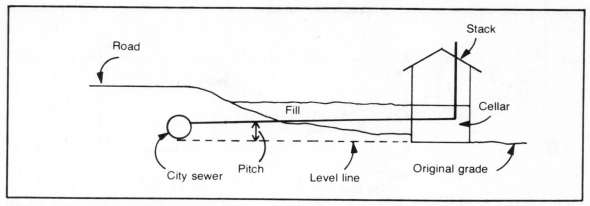

Fig. 3-8. The bottom of the sewer pipe at your home must be higher by a minimum of ¼ inch to the foot than the point of connection to the city sewer main.

Septic Tank Elevation. If the house sewer has to drain into a septic tank and drain field, the building must be higher than the tank and the following drain field. The same consideration must be given to the elevation of each as described for the house in relation to the city sewer main. The soil pump can also be used to move soil from a "low" building up to a higher septic system.

WELL AND SOIL SYSTEMS

When your property is out of reach of the city water main, you have to install a well or go dry. The cost of the well will depend upon the depth to which it has to be drilled and the nature of the soil through which the drilling has to be done. There is presumably underground water everywhere in this country, but some of it can be 200 feet down. The simplest way to get an approximate cost is to approach a local well-drilling company. They will or should know what wells have been successfully drilled near the property you are interested in and their depths and costs.

Septic tanks and their associate drain fields are

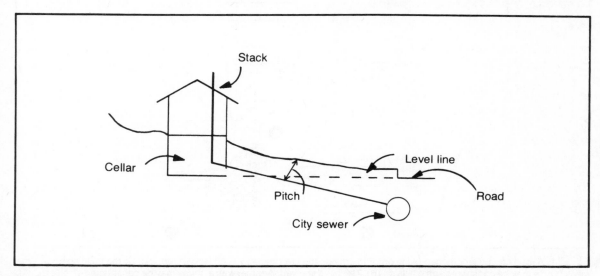

Fig. 3-9. To provide the necessary house sewer-line pitch, you will have to raise the building as shown.

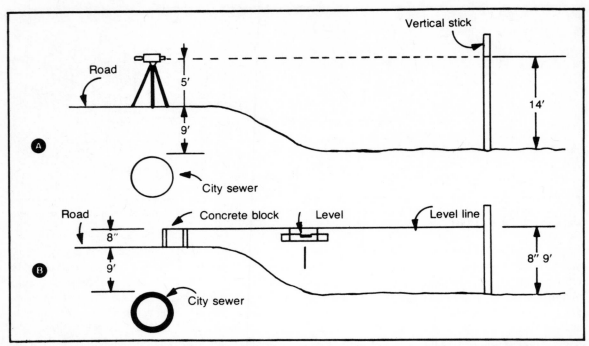

Fig. 3-10. A transit (A) can be used to determine the elevation above a given point in relation to the city sewer main. The distance the sewer is beneath the road is provided by the city building department. A simple line level (B) can be used to determine the elevation of a given point in relation to the city sewer. The line (tight string) is moved up and down until the level's bubble is centered. Then you know the line is perfectly horizontal.

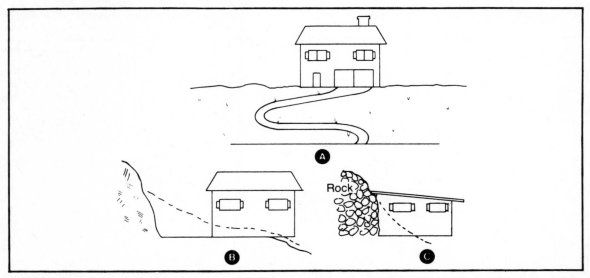

Fig. 3-11. A road can be lengthened (A) in order to provide the low driveway pitch (angle) required by the building code. One way a house may be constructed on a hillside (B). The hill is shelved. Another way a house may be constructed on hillside (C). The hill is made a portion of the building.

Fig. 3-12. A simple way to find the pitch of a hill. You know the line is level when the line-level bubble is centered. Knowing the height of the string above the grade, and the length of the string, permits you to calculate pitch.

another expense city property purchasers do not have to meet. In most instances, their construction and maintenance present no problems. Keep in mind that it is difficult to make drain fields work properly when and where the earth is soaked all the time. Drain fields are also difficult when the soil is hard clay and impossible where there is nothing but bedrock. When conditions are right, they do not require much space and can go for 20 years with little more than biannual cleaning by a commercial tank-pumping company.

BARGAIN LOTS

In your search for property on which you can build a home, you will possibly come across a number of bargain lots. They are bargains because the asking price is considerably lower than that asked for comparable lots. The reason for the lower price is not always obvious, but there always is a reason. In some cases, the lot is:

☐ Considerably lower than the nearest city sewer line, necessitating the cost and problem of a soil pump (it quits when the electric power quits).

☐ All rock and you have to blast to install the service lines.

☐ Undersize and you cannot legally build on it.

☐ Slated for condemnation by the county for an access road or county building.

☐ Difficult to build on due to local topography.

If you can find a solution to the problem or problems, you have found a bargain. If you can't find solutions, you are wasting your money. See Figs. 3-11 and 3-12.

NO-MONEY-DOWN LOTS

It is sometimes possible to purchase a building lot with very little or no cash down. Sometimes you can get the seller to agree to a subordinate mortgage with little cash down and the balance in monthly payments.

A subordinate mortgage is a second mortgage. In the event of default, the property is put up for auction. From the monies resulting, the first mortgage holder is paid off first. The second mortgage holder is paid off next and the owner gets what is left, if there is anything left.

In certain instances, a bank will lend a prospective homebuilder money on the lot as well as the building. In such cases, the borrower must have a very strong financial position. In other words, it is easy if you are otherwise rich.

Chapter 4

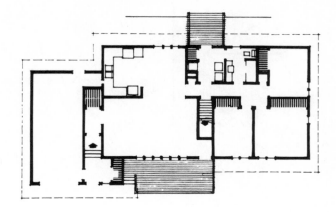

Reading Blueprints

LIKE IT OR NOT, YOU CANNOT BECOME AN EFFEC-
tive builder/contractor until you learn how to read
and understand a blueprint. The "print" is the language of the building trades. It is the shorthand by
which the architect communicates with the building
department, the bank, and all the craftspeople.

Prints are essentially simple. What makes
them appear complex at first inspection is that they
contain a lot of information. In a sense it is as if five
stories were written on the same page, one atop the
other. In such cases, the stories would be difficult
to read. If different color ink was used for each of
the stories, reading would be greatly eased. This is
what is done in a print. Different lines are related to
different subjects. If you pay attention to just one
set of lines or symbols at a time, understanding is
greatly simplified.

THE BASIC SYSTEM

Figure 4-1 shows an isometric drawing of a small
building with a gable roof. We can see the roof, the
front, (designated A) and one side (designated B).

Figure 4-2 shows a plan view of the same
building. The roof is not shown. The view looks
directly downward.

There is no distortion and all the lines are
drawn to scale. In this case, ⅛ inch on the drawing
equals 1 foot. *To scale* means that if a dimension is
not indicated on the drawing you can "scale" it off.
In other words, measure the drawing itself and
multiply the distance by 96 to get its actual size. (1
foot (12 inches) divided by .125 or ⅛ inch gives you
96.) Thus it is not necessary to indicate every
dimension on a print.

In Fig. 4-2, the drawing is actually 5 inches by
3.75 inches. As the scale is ⅛ inch to the foot, the
drawing represents a building that is 40 feet by 30
feet overall. These figures are noted to the outside
of the lines representing the building.

Symbols have been added to Fig. 4-3 to indicate the doorway (it is swinging inwards) and the
windows. Windows are drawn on all four walls of
the building and a second door, a rear door, has
been added to the rear wall.

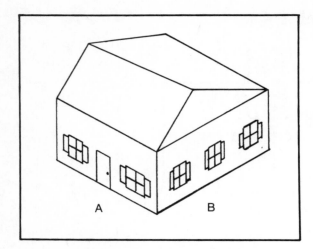

Fig. 4-1. A simplified isometric drawing of a small building. Its front elevation is marked A and its side is marked B.

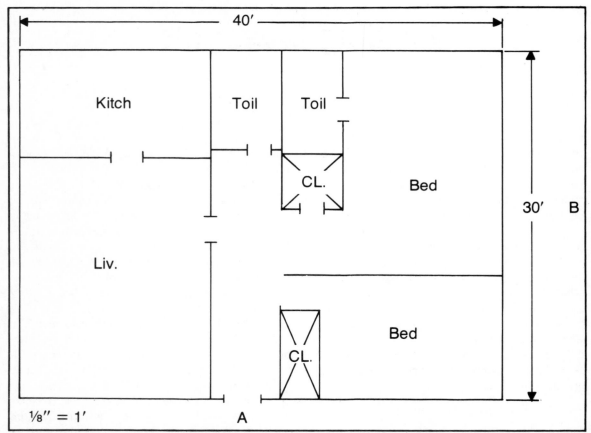

Fig. 4-2. A plan view of the building. Note where the A and the B sides of the building are. Note how they relate to the same sides in the isometric drawing. In this drawing, you are looking straight down into the building. The various rooms are marked off with lines. The overall, exterior dimensions of the building are shown. The building is 30 feet deep and 40 feet long.

28

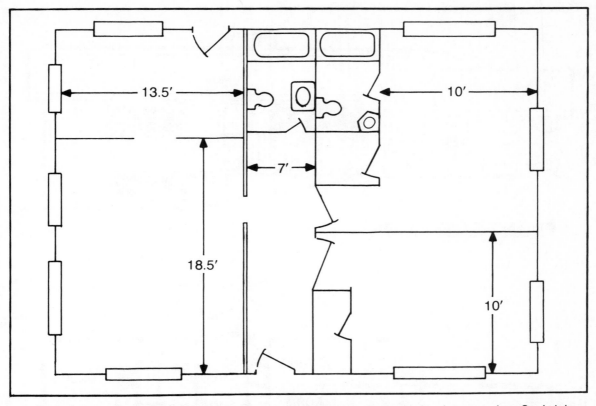

Fig. 4-3. A plan view of the building. In this drawing, interior dimensions have been added to show room sizes. Symbols have been added to show doors, windows, and toilet fixtures.

These doors and windows have been carefully positioned. If, as is this case, no dimensions are given, you can determine their size by scaling them. Measure the symbols representing the doors and windows and then multiplying (by 96 but only in the case of prints drawn to the same scale). The same can be done to determine the position of the doors and windows.

In Fig. 4-3, symbols have been added to indicate the position of the toilets and tubs. Note also that room dimensions add up to less than the overall building dimensions. This is due to the thickness of the walls; they are generally computed at being 6 inches thick.

Figure 4-4 shows a simplified print of a moderately simple building constructed on a slight slope. No dimensions are provided.

Note the front elevation. This is how the com-

pleted building will appear when viewed from a position in front of the building.

Note how the stairs are indicated in the floor plan and how the kitchen cabinets are indicated. The broken line encircling the building indicates the edges of the roof.

Figure 4-5 shows a house plan developed by the Forest Products Laboratory of Madison Wisconsin and designed by the Forest Service, U.S. Department of Agriculture. Copies are available on request for a small fee.

To mentally align the second floor in respect to the first floor, bear in mind that the stairs shown in each view are one and the same. This plan carries more details than the previous plans, and the symbols used are a little different. Otherwise, all the plans are read the same.

Figures 4-6, 4-7, and 4-8 show additional

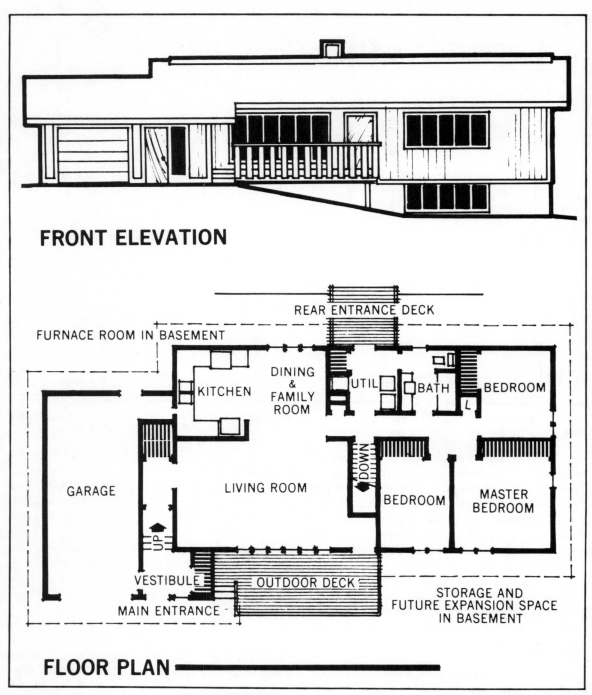

FRONT ELEVATION

REAR ENTRANCE DECK

FURNACE ROOM IN BASEMENT

KITCHEN

DINING & FAMILY ROOM

UTIL

BATH

BEDROOM

GARAGE

LIVING ROOM

DOWN

BEDROOM

MASTER BEDROOM

UP

VESTIBULE

OUTDOOR DECK

MAIN ENTRANCE

STORAGE AND FUTURE EXPANSION SPACE IN BASEMENT

FLOOR PLAN

Fig. 4-4. The front elevation of a small building constructed on a slope and a plan view of the building. No dimensions are given. The arrows indicate the directions of the stairs. Courtesy U.S. Department of Agriculture.

House Plan no. FS-FPL-2

This home (Plan FS-FPL-2) was developed for a large family of up to 12 children at a reasonable cost. It is 24 by 36 feet in size and is one and one-half stories. The first floor has 864 square feet, consisting of three bedrooms, a bath, and a living-dining-kitchen area. The second floor contains about 540 square feet and consists of two large dormitory-type bedrooms. Each is divided by a wardrobe-type closet which, in effect, contains space for two single beds on each side. The plan was developed by the Forest Products Laboratory of Madison, Wis., and is one of a series of low-cost houses of wood being designed by the Forest Service, U.S. Department of Agriculture.

AREA = 1404 sq. ft.

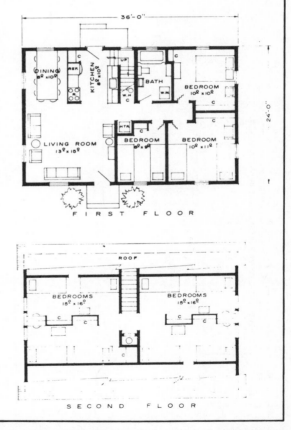

Fig. 4-5. A small-house plan. This one differs from the previous plans in that the positions of beds, tables, etc., are indicated. Courtesy University of Connecticut.

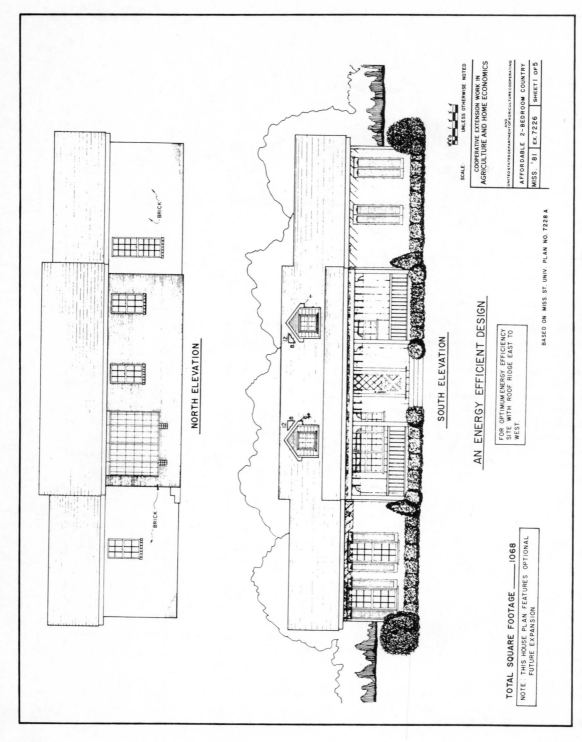

NORTH ELEVATION

BRICK

BRICK

TOTAL SQUARE FOOTAGE _____ 1068

NOTE: THIS HOUSE PLAN FEATURES OPTIONAL
FUTURE EXPANSION

SOUTH ELEVATION

AN ENERGY EFFICIENT DESIGN

FOR OPTIMUM ENERGY EFFICIENCY
SITE WITH ROOF RIDGE EAST TO
WEST.

SCALE: UNLESS OTHERWISE NOTED

COOPERATIVE EXTENSION WORK IN
AGRICULTURE AND HOME ECONOMICS
AND
UNITED STATES DEPARTMENT OF AGRICULTURE COOPERATING

AFFORDABLE 2-BEDROOM COUNTRY

MISS. '81 | EX.7226 | SHEET I OF5

BASED ON MISS. ST. UNIV. PLAN NO. 7228 A

Fig. 4-6. Two elevations of an energy-efficient design home with 1068 square feet of living space. Courtesy, U.S. Department of Agriculture.

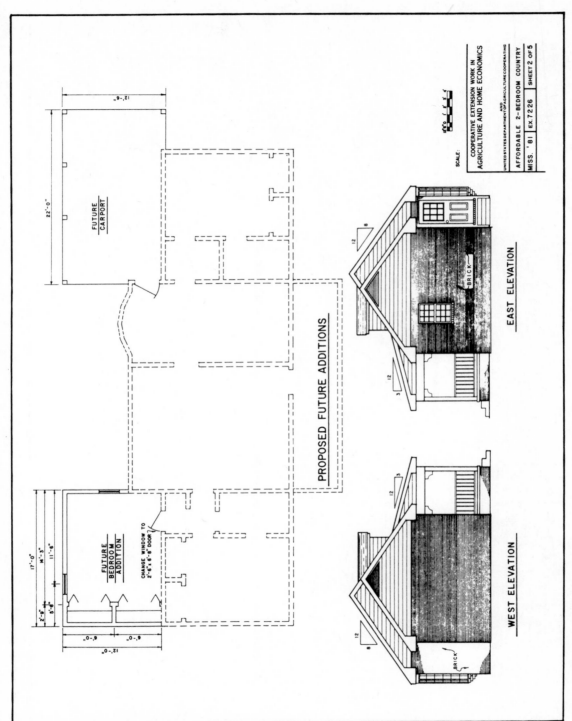

Fig. 4-7. Side elevations of the building.

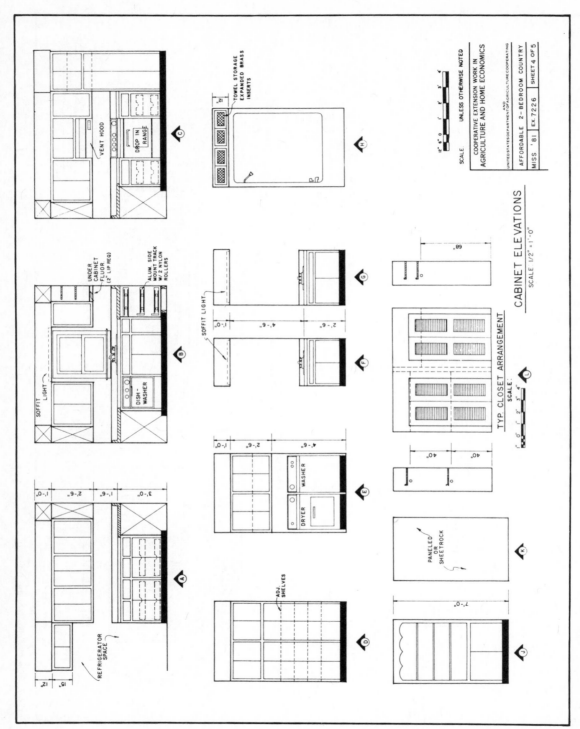

CABINET ELEVATIONS
SCALE 1/2" = 1'-0"

TYP. CLOSET ARRANGEMENT

Fig. 4-8. Interior details.

buildings in more detail. Figure 4-9 details show lights, switches, fans, and outlets. Figure 4-10 shows a wall section (how it may be constructed) and two foundation designs.

ARCHITECTURAL SYMBOLS

A building consists of more than just floors and walls. It also includes windows, doors, lights, toilet fixtures, and any number of other pieces of equipment and furnishing. All these things must be described and positioned. This is accomplished with a minimum amount of space and effort through the use of almost universally accepted symbols. The position of the symbol pinpoints its location in the building. The details of the symbol describe its construction, type, or nature.

There are common symbols for almost everything (Figs. 4-11 through 4-14). There are symbols indicating earth, rock, gravel, sand, concrete, and flagstones. There are symbols indicating windows, doors, and screening. There are symbols indicating plumbing fixtures and a system of connecting lines indicating how and where the pipes are to be run. There are symbols for hot- and cold-water pipes, low-pressure steam, high-pressure steam, sprinklers, and more. There are symbols that indicate heat ducts and registers. There are electrical symbols that show where the switches will go, where the outlets will go, and how the connecting wires should be run.

Generally, with a little thought all symbols can be understood. All it takes is some study.

CHECKING THE PRINT

The building department must pass on the design before they will permit you to erect the building. While this is true if you are building within a municipality, the building department personnel do not assume responsibility for any errors in the print or for errors in the design.

Possible Print Errors. Let us assume that the building in question is 40 feet overall. The rear of the building is divided into three rooms, plus a hallway. Consider just the widths of the room and hall (i.e., the dimensions that run parallel to the length of the building, 40 feet overall). Room and

hall dimensions are 12 feet, 12 feet, 5 feet and 10 feet. Together these dimensions add up to 39 feet.

At first glance, nothing appears to be in error here. The building is going to be 40 feet. But there are also five walls that form the rooms and hall. A standard wall is close to 6 inches thick. Therefore 2½ feet of the length of the building is going to be taken by the walls. The print is off by 1½ feet in the dimensions we have discussed. Either the building's length has to be increased by 1½ feet or this dimension must be taken from one or more of the rooms.

If such an error is caught in the print stage, no harm is done. Permitted to go to construction, considerable waste can result for such an error. Time will be wasted because the carpenters might not spot the errors until they are framing. Then they have to come to you to get your decision to enlarge the building or reduce one or more rooms. If a room is to be reduced in size, which one? If you have planned on specific furnishings for a room, you might have a problem. For example, you cannot squeeze a refrigerator. A reduction of 1½ feet is awkward. An increase in size by a similar amount can also prove troublesome. You want to work in modules of 2 feet because that is the multiple of lumber and building materials most often used.

If you have ordered kitchen cabinets for a room of a specific size and the room has to be increased in size, you might have to put up with unattractive open spaces alongside your cabinets. The possible, troublesome variations of dimensional errors on prints are endless. Fortunately, such errors are few and far between, but remember that prints are drawn by people and people do make mistakes.

Other errors to look for are misplaced doors, stairs, windows, and the like. In the case of stairs, you should check to make certain the stairs shown on the first floor will actually terminate where they are shown on the second floor print. This is done by scaling. This consists of simply measuring the drawing to locate the stairs on the print. In a sense, you are placing the second floor print atop the first floor print to see if the stairs line up.

The doors might be misplaced in the sense that they are not going to be where you would like them

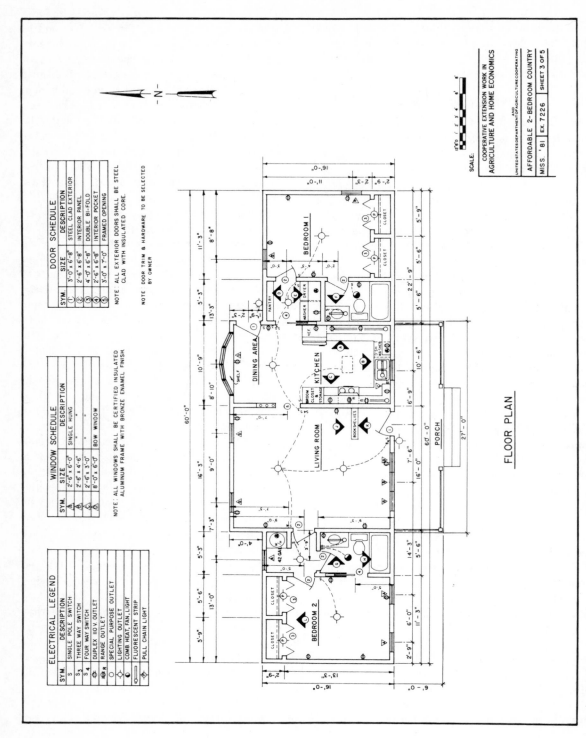

Fig. 4-9. Floor plan of the building. Note the electrical symbols.

36

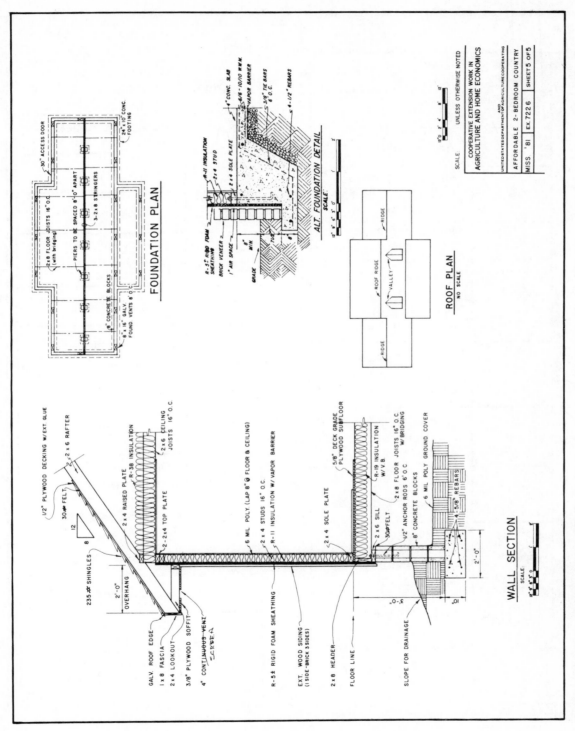

FOUNDATION PLAN

30" ACCESS DOOR
24"x10" CONC. FOOTING
PIERS TO BE SPACED 8'-0" APART
3-2x8 STRINGERS
2x8 FLOOR JOISTS 16" O.C. (with bridging)
8" CONCRETE BLOCKS
8"x16" GALV. FOUND VENTS 8' O.C.

ALT. FOUNDATION DETAIL
SCALE:

4" CONC. SLAB
6/6 - 10/10 W.W.M.
VAPOR BARRIER
4-1/2" REBARS
3/4" TIE BARS 8' O.C.
R-11 INSULATION
2x4 STUD
2x4 SOLE PLATE
R-5± RIGID FOAM SHEATHING
BRICK VENEER
1" AIR SPACE
GRADE
8" MIN

ROOF PLAN
NO SCALE

ROOF RIDGE
RIDGE
VALLEY
RIDGE

WALL SECTION
SCALE:

1/2" PLYWOOD DECKING W/EXT. GLUE
2x6 RAFTER
R-38 INSULATION
2x4 RAISED PLATE
2x4 CEILING JOISTS 16" O.C.
2-2x4 TOP PLATE
30# FELT
6 MIL POLY (LAP 8" @ FLOOR & CEILING)
2x4 STUDS 16" O.C.
R-11 INSULATION W/ VAPOR BARRIER
5/8" DECK GRADE PLYWOOD SUBFLOOR
R-19 INSULATION W/V.B.
2x8 FLOOR JOISTS 16" O.C. W/ BRIDGING
6 MIL POLY GROUND COVER
2x4 SOLE PLATE
2x6 SILL
30# FELT
1/2" ANCHOR RODS 6'-0" O.C.
8" CONCRETE BLOCKS
4-5/8" REBARS
235-# SHINGLES
OVERHANG
2'-0"
GALV. ROOF EDGE
1x8 FASCIA
2x4 LOOKOUT
3/8" PLYWOOD SOFFIT
4" CONTINUOUS VENT SCREEN
R-5± RIGID FOAM SHEATHING
EXT. WOOD SIDING (1 SIDE-BRICK 3 SIDES)
2x8 HEADER
FLOOR LINE
SLOPE FOR DRAINAGE
12
8
2'-0"
8'-0"
10"

SCALE   UNLESS OTHERWISE NOTED

COOPERATIVE EXTENSION WORK IN
AGRICULTURE AND HOME ECONOMICS
AND
UNITED STATES DEPARTMENT OF AGRICULTURE COOPERATING

AFFORDABLE 2-BEDROOM COUNTRY
MISS. '81 | EX.7226 | SHEET 5 OF 5

Fig. 4-10. Construction details of the building.

□	Interconnection box
⊗	Exit light
◇	Annunciator
◀	Regular telephone (add note to designate jacks)
◁	Interphone for office communication
TV	T.V. outlet
▨	Master power service panel
▮	Lighting distribution panel (fused or circuit breakers)
(_)	Switch leg indicator connects lights to switches
○ AB	Any switch, outlet, or electrical device as motors, electric compressors, air conditioners, or others should be assigned a symbol with an explanation given in the key to the symbols.
◓ AB	
□ AB	

⊖ WP	Weatherproof duplex receptacle outlet
⊖ GR WP	Grounding type weatherproof duplex receptacle outlet
⊖ S	Receptacle outlet with switch
⊖ R	Range outlet
⊖ 220	220 volt outlet
◓ DW	Special—must be explained in the key to the symbols
⊖J	Junction box
⊖	Lighting outlet
⊡	Square recessed light (size varies)
⊡	Rectangular recessed light (size varies)
⊙	Round recessed light (size varies)
⊠	Fluorescent light
⊏O━	Fluorescent light
⊖L	Lampholder
⊕L PS	Lampholder with pull switch
⊕P	Pull switch light (same as above)

Fig. 4-11. Electrical symbols. (Continued on page 39.)

(Continued from page 38.)

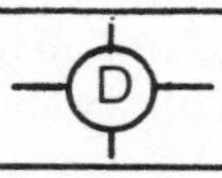 (D)	Drop cord
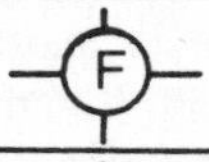 (F)	Fan
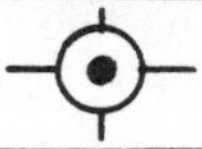 (●)	Floor lighting outlet
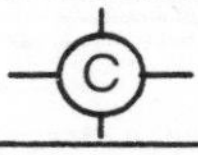 (C)	Clock outlet
 CH	Chime
 Bell	Bell
 Buzzer	Buzzer
 Combination bell and buzzer	Combination bell and buzzer
 ●	Push button
 D	Electric door opener
 M	Maid's signal plug
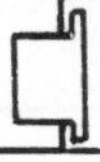 Recessed intercom	Recessed intercom

S	Single pole switch
S	Single pole switch
S₃	Three way switch
S₄	Four way switch
S_D	Automatic door switch
S_P	Switch with pilot light
S_WP	Weatherproof switch
S₂	Double pole switch
S_I	Switch for low voltage system
– – – – –	Low voltage wire
MS	Low voltage master switch
 R	Relay equipped lighting outlet
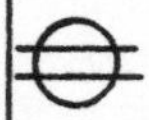 3	Duplex receptacle outlet
	Receptacle outlet other than duplex
	Split wired receptacle outlet
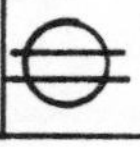 GR	Grounding type duplex receptacle outlet

39

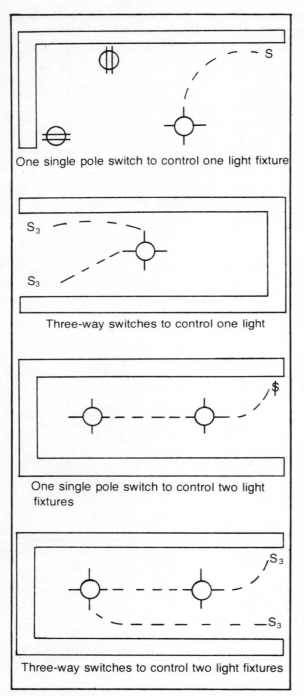

One single pole switch to control one light fixture

Three-way switches to control one light

One single pole switch to control two light fixtures

Three-way switches to control two light fixtures

Fig. 4-12. How the symbols are used to indicate connections and controls.

to be for reasons of passage or planned furniture positioning. Perhaps the side to which they open is not correct. If so, now is the time to make the change.

Windows might be missplaced from your point of view or needs. You might want the window in the child's bedroom to be higher to preclude them leaning out. You might want the windows farther apart to facilitate the installation of shutters or closer to make them attractive without shutters. If there are, for example, three windows in a wall—two in one room and one in another—you might want to change them around. You might prefer two windows in the now single-window room.

Building Department Errors. In the main,

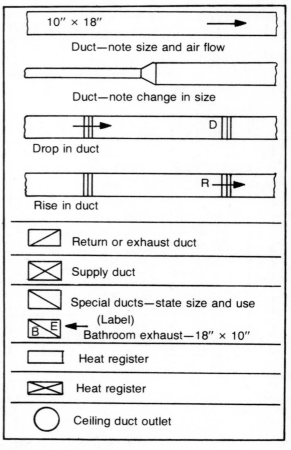

Fig. 4-13. Hot-air duct symbols.

40

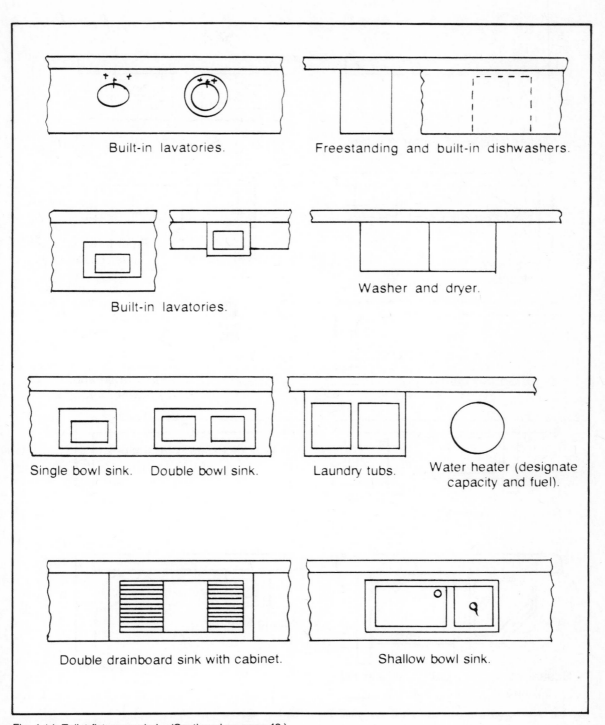

Built-in lavatories.

Freestanding and built-in dishwashers.

Built-in lavatories.

Washer and dryer.

Single bowl sink. Double bowl sink.

Laundry tubs.

Water heater (designate capacity and fuel).

Double drainboard sink with cabinet.

Shallow bowl sink.

Fig. 4-14. Toilet fixture symbols. (Continued on page 42.)

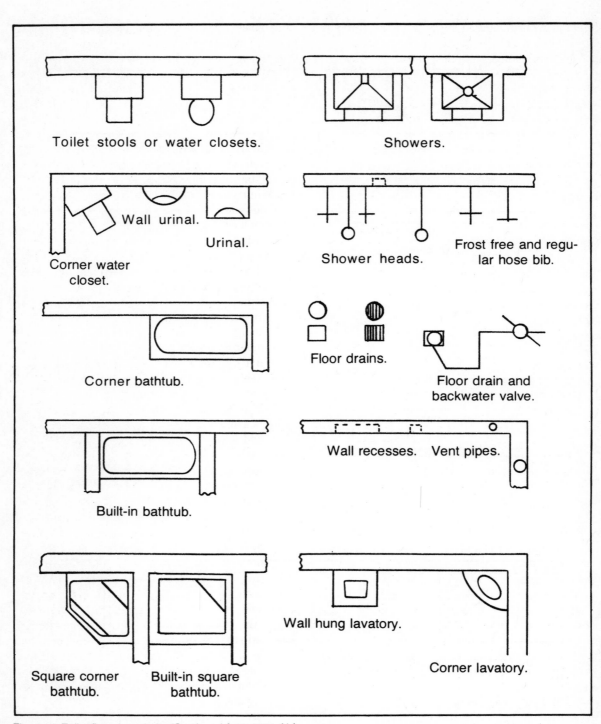

Toilet stools or water closets.

Showers.

Wall urinal.

Urinal.

Corner water closet.

Shower heads.

Frost free and regular hose bib.

Corner bathtub.

Floor drains.

Floor drain and backwater valve.

Built-in bathtub.

Wall recesses.   Vent pipes.

Square corner bathtub.

Built-in square bathtub.

Wall hung lavatory.

Corner lavatory.

Fig. 4-14. Toilet fixture symbols. (Continued from page 41.)

building departments do not stand behind *their* errors. When a building department reviews and approves a building application, you can assume that all is kosher. If the inspector says it is acceptable, it is acceptable. In some cases it ain't so. Assume that your architect or you specified the use of 2 × 8s for a specific stretch of floor and that everyone else on the block was using 2 × 10s for the same application.

If the department passes on your application, do not assume that the requirements have been reduced or that, because they passed on it, there is nothing the department can do (they said okay so they are now stuck with it). It is not so. If an inspector spots the variation on the job, you will be forced to make the correction. Their stand is simple and unassailable. The law is the law.

In most instances, you will be told how you can correct the violation. Perhaps you can do this by adding more lumber, more bracing, and so on. If the violation is minor, it can be overlooked with a warning. If the violation is serious—if it is clearly going to endanger the structure—you have to make the change. If you don't the building department has the legal power to apply a daily fine on your structure until you do.

EVALUATING DIMENSIONS

You have a print in front of you on your desk. At first it is gibberish but, as you study it, the proposed building's outline and main features become clear. You can see where the living room will be, how you will be able to walk into the kitchen, the bedroom, the hall, the basement, and so on. With a little effort you can imagine what it will be like to live in the building when it has been completed. But will you have sufficient space?

You have the floor plan. With a little math, you can quickly compute the total living space (just how many square feet there will be). Most commercial plans provide this information. It is a convenient yardstick for comparing one home design to another.

Let us say that you now live in a modest apartment and it has 800 square feet of living space. The plan you are reviewing offers 1300 square feet of living space. That is quite an increase. Why question it? The reason is that all living spaces are not alike. Square footage doesn't by itself tell the entire story.

There are a few rules of thumb that will enable you to quickly eliminate undersized rooms. For example, no bedroom should be smaller than 8 by 9 feet. No living room should be less than 10 by 12 feet. No hall should be less than 3 feet wide. No main staircase should be less than 36 inches wide. Cellar stairs can be narrower.

Minimum dimensions don't mean much. For example, do you actually know what an 8-by-9-foot bedroom looks like or what a minimum living room is like when it is filled with a few pieces of furniture? To fully appreciate the dimensions of the rooms and halls illustrated in the blueprint, you have either to visit rooms of equal size or lay out the room somewhere. This can be done with string on the floor of a larger room or a front lawn. Until you are actually within the confines of a specific space, the numbers mean very little.

Furniture. You can get more furniture to fit comfortably in one large room than in two small rooms with an equal amount of floor space. It is possible to be more comfortable in an apartment than in a somewhat larger house because there are fewer and larger rooms, but less private because there are fewer rooms. Put another way, you will have more work and living space if you construct your kitchen as an adjunct to your dining room than if you separate the kitchen from the dining room. This is especially true if you install a swinging door between them. The wall and the door obstruct more space by far than the space they actually stand on.

Another factor to consider is your present furniture in relation to your projected home. Will it fit? You can check this by actually measuring your furniture and then "laying it out" on the house plan. Follow the scale given for the drawing and use the same ratio to "fit" your furniture onto the plan. For example, if you have a bed that is 7 feet long and the plan scale is ¼ inch to the foot, then the bed you draw or cut out of paper should be 7 × ½ inch or 1¾ inch long and proportionally wide.

This is still not a true indication of the space you will have. Bear in mind that there must be walk spaces between the pieces of furniture.

Then you need to consider the problems you or the moving men might encounter bringing the furniture into the building. If you have a piano, you have to be certain that the front door will be wide enough to accept the piano. If you have a long couch, you have to be certain you can get it to pass down a long hall. This is especially important if there is a turn along the path you want the couch to take.

The same problem might crop up with a staircase. If the stairs are a straight run, see if there will be sufficient clearance at the ends. With some home designs, the stairs terminate at a very small landing leading to a number of doors. You cannot get a long piece of furniture to go up the stairs and make the turn into one of the rooms. If the stairs have a turn, the large pieces of furniture might not be able to get past the turn. These are things that must be checked out before you start to build. They are things the architect rarely considers because—unless he is designing especially for you—he designs for someone with average-size furniture.

Chapter 5

Selecting the House

YOU ARE STRIVING TOWARDS A NUMBER OF GOALS and operating under a number of constraints. The results must, by circumstance, be a compromise, but a compromise is not necessarily a midpoint between conflicting demands. You will want to, and probably need to, favor one goal over another and give in more to one pressure than another.

You are seeking to construct the best possible house for the least amount of money. Within the constraints of minimum costs, you are seeking maximum energy efficiency. In addition, you want a home that suits your needs and, to a lesser extent, suits your taste. Meanwhile, back at the building department office, you have to keep the inspector happy by conforming to the building code.

SPACE EFFICIENCY

Of all the enclosed spaces known to man, a ball is the most efficient (Fig. 5-1). It has the smallest surface for the largest interior area. Unfortunately, a ball is an uneconomical shape to build from wood and stone. The next best shape from the same point

of view is an octagon. During the late 1800s a number of octagonlike buildings were constructed. One is still standing in Yonkers, New York. The design did not become widely used because of the cost of making all the joints and the waste of material that accompanied the carpentry work.

The next best shape, the cube, is eminently practical. It has only four corners and encloses the maximum area possible with a straight-sided building (other than an hexagon or octagon).

A cube with a flat roof is the most space efficient. Unfortunately, a flat, level roof doesn't shed water or snow. It must be pitched. This can be accomplished with one single pitch or slope—which makes it a shed—or two pitches, which makes for a gabled roof.

The cube with the gable roof is a most efficient building form. The basic design has been with us for ages. The true or almost true cube is achieved with a two-story structure commonly called a Colonial. Variations include an overhang in front, making the floor plan a bit more rectangular than square, and

Fig. 5-1. The ball (A) provides the maximum interior volume for the minimum of exterior surface, but it is not a practical shape for a home. The octagon shape (B) solves the problem of enclosing a circular area with straight boards. Some were constructed during the 1800s, but the cost of the carpentry makes them prohibitive to construct now. The cube (C) is the best compromise between the problem of building with "straight" material such as boards and timbers and enclosing a maximum volume of space. The cube is used where there is little rain and little snow. To solve the snow and rain problem a pitched roof (D) is used. The Colonial is simply a two-story cube varied a bit in dimensions to make it more attractive.

adding dormers to the pitched roof.

Two Floors Versus One. The cost advantage of two floors over one is obvious. Under the same roof and upon the same piece of ground, you have two floors and almost twice the living space afforded by a single floor. You lose the space devoted to the stairs and you need to furnish higher walls, but the cost of the second floor is far less than half the cost of the first floor alone.

The Argument Against a Cellar. For years, cellars were a standard portion of the majority of private homes constructed in this country. In the heyday of coal stoves, they were necessary to store the tons of coal that would be burned over the

winter. Coal dust and ash made the cellar a dusty, dirty place. You wouldn't want the coal furnace next to your living quarters.

Today, few people install coal-burning furnaces in their homes. They depend upon oil, gas, wood, or electricity for heating. These heating systems are clean and safer at ground level than they would be in the cellar below ground level.

A cellar is essentially an expensive storage place. The heating equipment and the laundry equipment require no more than 200 square feet of floor space. There is, of course, the counter argument that the balance of the cellar can or will be used for a playroom. True. But if your goal is to secure a home at minimum cost, a playroom is a luxury. Having a cellar adds several thousand dollars to the cost of construction. Finishing a playroom can cost even more.

When you excavate, you run the risk of striking rock or water; it's bad news in either case. Banks do not view cellars as living space. If your bank allows, for example, $3 per cubic foot for above-ground, full ceiling-height living space, it might allow only $1 to $1.50 for each below-ground cubic foot of living space. When you construct a cellar, you proportionally decrease the overall financing you can secure in relation to the total cost of the building.

The Ranch Versus the Colonial. Some find abhorent the thought of walking up and down stairs. Others prefer the two-story home because there is little chance of anyone walking in on an unmade bed. No one tramps through upstairs rooms the way they tramp through ground floor rooms. But consider the relative space efficiency of the two basic designs (Fig. 5-2).

Ignoring space lost to inner and outer walls and stairs, a full Colonial with 2400 square feet of living space and no cellar has an exterior wall area (ignoring fenestrations—windows, doors, etc.) of 2800 square feet. This building would have a floor area of 30 by 40 feet (1200 sq. ft. each floor).

To secure an equal floor area in a ranch, you would need a building 40 by 60 feet overall. It would have an exterior wall area of 2000 square feet. This amounts to 800 feet *less* exterior wall area. The roof of the Colonial need only be 1200 square feet (we are ignoring pitch for simplicity). The roof on the ranch would need to be 2400 square feet. That is 1200 square feet more roof is needed with a ranch than with a Colonial with the same floor area. And more important, you need a much larger lot for the ranch.

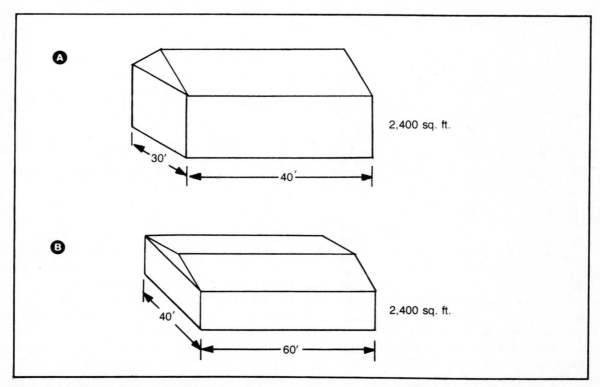

A

2,400 sq. ft.

30'

40'

B

2,400 sq. ft.

40'

60'

Fig. 5-2. Comparing the material and land efficiencies of two popular home designs. Both contain close to 2400 square feet of living space. Compare the dimensions of the Colonial (A) with the dimensions of the ranch (B).

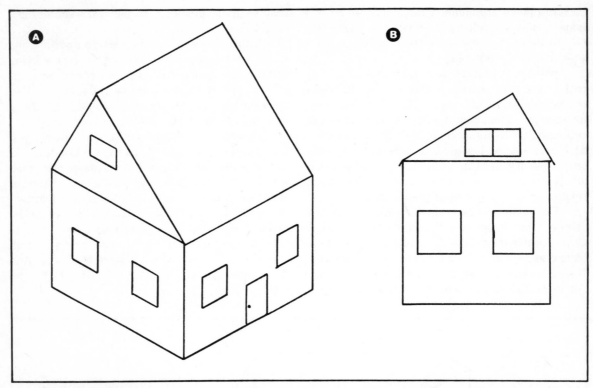

Fig. 5-3. The Cap Cod design (A) is space efficient because it is a cube. To take care of rain and snow, its roof is pitched. To utilize some of the attic space, the roof pitch is increased beyond that needed for run-off, and the space is used for living area. The salt box (B) is the same Cap Cod with an off-center roof.

Salt Boxes. A salt box is a 1½-story building with an off-center gabled roof. When the roof is evenly divided down the middle, it is called a Cape Cod or a cottage. See Fig. 5-3. The gimmick here is a compromise. These structures are normally erected in heavy-snow country where a steeply pitched roof is a necessity to prevent snow buildup. Because the roof must be steeply pitched, why not pitch it some more and fit a room or two under the eaves. Salt boxes, Cape Cods, and cottages are space efficient only when they are above a minimum physical size.

Costs Versus Space. The common thought of people building for the first time and seeking to cut costs is to think small. The smaller the building the less it will cost. True, but bad thinking nonetheless.

Banks will not lend money on tiny houses.

Very few people want tiny, one-bedroom houses. Try to build below what is a popular size for your locality and time period and the banks will not finance it, and you will be hard pressed to sell it should you somehow manage to build it.

Many of the costs of building are relatively fixed. They don't vary or vary much with a change in the size of the building. For example, your legal costs remain the same. The cost of the survey remains the same. The cost of excavating is only fractionally higher. The same is basically true for heating, electrical, and plumbing (unless you added bathrooms).

The big change would be in material and labor, but it would not be proportional to the gain in floor space and the gain in mortgage money. For example, you are planning a small Colonial with overall dimensions of 32 by 32 feet. This works out to about

2000 square feet of living space (less the 4 by 10 feet you need for the staircase). Figuring 20-foot high exterior walls and no windows or doors (for simplicity) this building would have a total exterior wall area of 2560 square feet. If you enlarge the floor plan to 32 by 40 feet, the exterior wall area would be increased by approximately 12.5 percent. Living space, however, would be increased 25 percent because the single floor area would now be 1280 square feet or 2560 square feet (less stairs) for two floors. There would also be the additional cost of the enlarged floors, cellar or crawl space, and roof. Nevertheless, all these additional costs would not compare to the 25 percent increase in living space.

TYPES OF FOUNDATIONS

Your choice of foundation will, in many instances, determine the type of house you can build.

Pier Foundations. With pier foundations, the structure is raised above the earth on a number of masonry piers (Fig. 5-4). This is the most

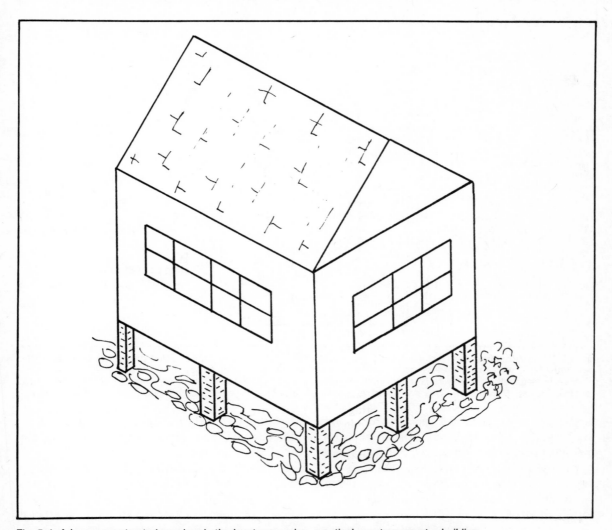

Fig. 5-4. A house constructed on piers is the least expensive, practical way to support a building.

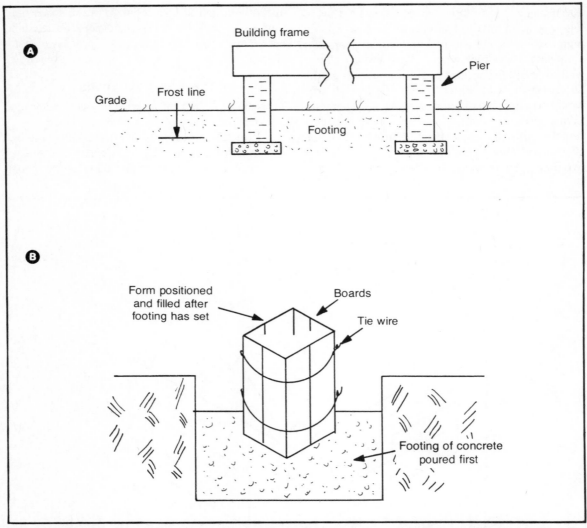

Fig. 5-5. Basic considerations in designing and constructing piers (A). The footing must be below the frost line, the tops of the piers must be at the same elevation, and the piers must be properly positioned beneath the house frame. In firm soil the concrete footing for the pier may be poured directly into the excavation (B). When the concrete has set, a form can be used to construct the pier. Pour the form very slowly and reinforce it securely because wet concrete develops tremendous pressure.

economical way to construct a small building, and is very useful for small buildings. The bottom of each pier must rest on firm subsoil a few inches or more below the frost line for the area (Fig. 5-5). The piers can be made of poured concrete, concrete block, brick, or field stones laid up in mortar. See Fig. 5-6.

Pier foundations are fast, easy to construct but

allow the wind and small creatures to get beneath the building. The only tools you need to excavate for piers is a shovel and a pick.

The Slab Foundation. The slab foundation is simply a slab of poured-in-place concrete. Its thickness depends upon its size, the nature of the underlying soil, and the load it will carry—whether it will be a one- or two-story frame or concrete-block

Fig. 5-6. A typical pier constructed of concrete block on a cast concrete base. Base dimensions are predicated on the nature of the soil and the weight of the building.

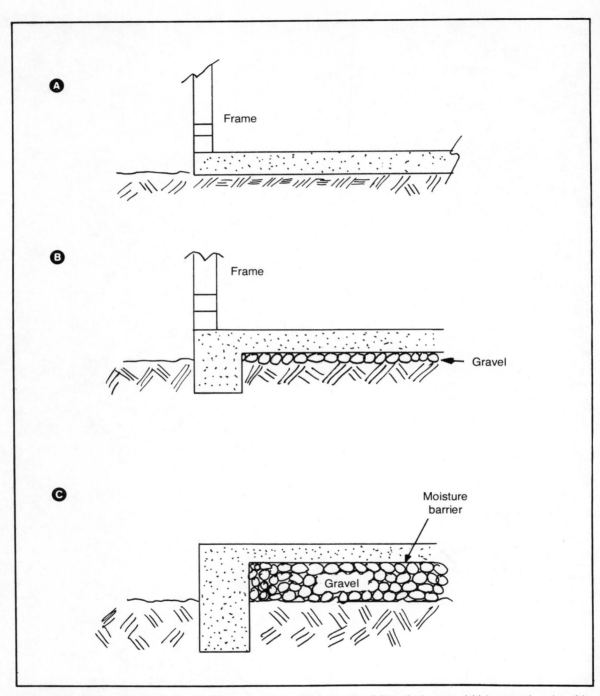

Fig. 5-7. A very simple slab foundation (A) that can be used on hard, dry subsoil. Note the increased thickness at the edge of the slab (B). When there is a possibility of ground moisture, the slab is insulated with a sheet of plastic (C). In cold climate, the slab is insulated as shown in D.

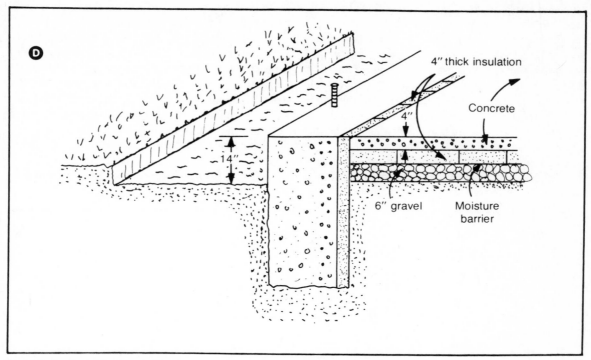

Fig. 5-7. Continued from page 52.

structure. To save on concrete, the entire slab does not have to be made in one thickness. Only the edge needs to be made thicker (Fig. 5-7).

The slab is the most practical and, next to the pier foundation, the most economical foundation thus far devised. Worm proof, rot proof, fire proof, and practically wear proof, the slab has the added advantage of the potential to store heat. The slab is a natural for use in a passive solar heating system.

In the hot, dry Southwest, the slab can be poured directly on the subsoil. Elsewhere in this country, it is necessary to provide drainage that consists of a layer of crushed stone beneath the slab. In cold areas—and when the slab is to serve as a heat storage unit—the slab is insulated.

The slab foundation can be used beneath a wooden structure or a masonry structure. Once the building is completed, the slab is not visible and the building looks just like any other building.

There is, however, one drawback to the slab. There is no give to concrete. Unless you lay down resilent tile, carpet, or a wood floor atop the con-crete, walking feels hard. In warm regions, most homeowners put down ceramic tile and a few small throw rugs here and there.

The Full Cellar. The full cellar or basement makes sense only when the terrain calls for it. An example is if your building is going to back up into a steep hill. In such cases, the cellar or basement ends up half above ground. To build on a slab under such conditions would be to end up with the house backed tightly against the hill. To excavate and construct a full-depth cellar on flat ground is to spend a lot of money for storage space (Fig. 5-8).

Perimeter Foundations. Sometimes called a crawl-space foundation or partial cellar founda-tion, the perimeter foundation is a masonry wall that follows the outline of the building. It is con-structed exactly like a full cellar except that it is far less deep.

Perimeter foundations are selected by people who somehow feel that no house is normal without a space below it. It is also used to lift the first or ground floor a foot or more above the grade line.

That is something not easily done with a slab. See Fig. 5-9.

Its real value, and the only time the perimeter foundation should be used is to correct for terrain problems. For example, there is a mass of bedrock poking up in the center of the area in which you want to position the building. It is far less expensive in most instances to construct a perimeter foundation and lift the building a few feet than to cut the rock down an equal number of feet.

In another instance you might want to build on the side of a hill. Rather than cut a deep shelf into the hill to give the rear of your building clearance, you lift it on a perimeter foundation.

Bear in mind that the earth within the foundation must be sealed to prevent moisture from entering the building. Sealing can be accomplished by sloshing a couple of inches of concrete over the earth or doing the same with blacktop. This consists of crushed stones mixed in tar and is spread hot with the aid of a rake.

The crawl space must be ventilated and the underside of the building must be insulated.

Wood Foundations. In recent years, a new

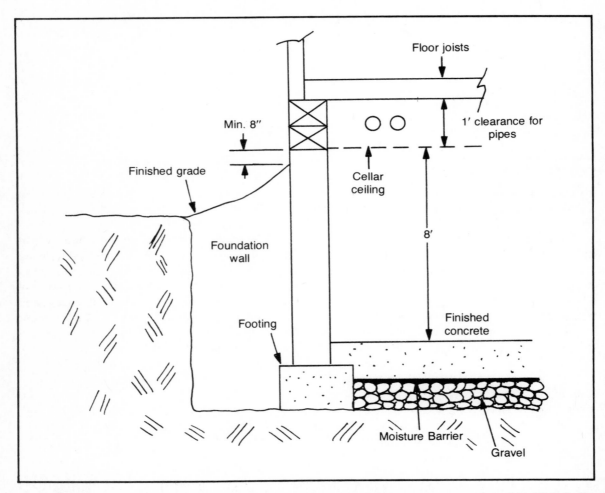

Fig. 5-8. When you are planning a full cellar, you have to make the height allowances shown to get an 8-foot-high finished cellar ceiling.

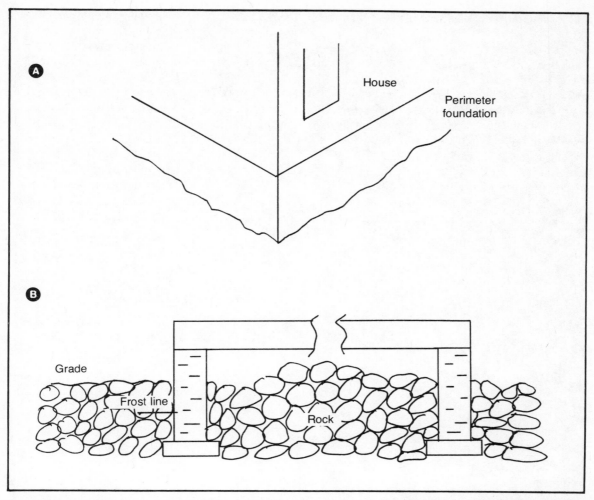

Fig. 5-9. Two simplified views of a perimeter foundation. Drawing A shows how the foundation will appear from outside the building. Drawing B shows how the interior might look and how the perimeter foundation might be used to circumvent the problem in bedrock.

type of foundation material has been developed: wood. Previously, wood was not permitted to rest upon the earth. In fact, standard construction practices calls for at least 12 inches of clearance between the grade (surface of the earth) and the lowest timber of a structure. The reason is that wood rots quickly in the presence of earth. Once wood rots it invites termites that further destroy it.

The wood used for foundations is chemically treated to resist rot. Instead of making the foundation of the building from poured concrete, the treated wood is laid in the foundation trench and a wood foundation is constructed of 2-×-4-inch studs just as a standard wall might be constructed. See Figs. 5-10A, 5-10B, and 5-10C.

Pile Foundations. When and where the earth is too soft to support any of the foundations previously mentioned, the only solution is to go to piles. They consist of tarred poles driven into the earth or metal tubes driven into the earth and later filled with concrete. This is accomplished with powered equipment that huffs and puffs and with

Fig. 5-10A. Foundations of wood. Here the earth has been excavated and the workman is finishing the spreading of a layer of gravel.

Fig. 5-10B. The foundation wall, constructed of treated 2 × 8s and plywood, is simply stood up in place. The workman is caulking the joint between two of the prefabricated panels.

B

Fig. 5-10C. An exterior view of the wood foundation. Bracing holds the wall up temporarily. Courtesy American Plywood Association.

C

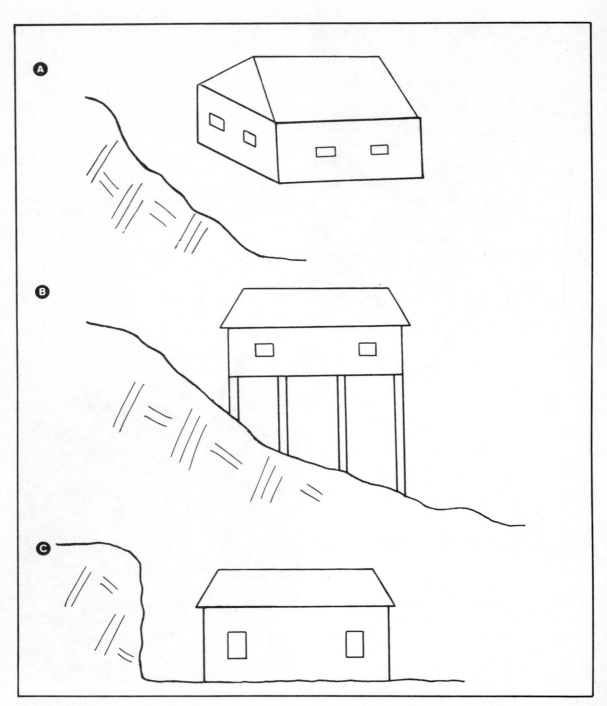

Fig. 5-11. Three ways to erect a house shown on a hillside: (A) the house and the hill, (B) the house can be raised on piles, etc., or (C) the hill can be shelved (cut back).

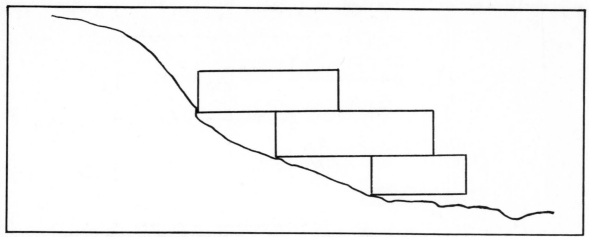

Fig. 5-12. Another way to erect a house on a hillside is to step it. Build it in several sections.

great wailing on the part of the builder. Piles and pile-driving can be very costly. In any case, the piles are driven into the earth until they no longer respond to measured blows. Then they are cut flush with the earth. A concrete footing is then poured on top of the pile ends and the building erected on the footing.

MATCHING THE HOUSE TO THE LAND

When you have a level lot to work with, all options are go. You can select any building design you prefer and build it without problems or penalties. When the land is pitched or uneven, you have to match the structure to the land or pay a premium in labor and materials.

Stepped House Designs. One of two basic designs can be used successfully on sloping land. One is the split or split-level building. The other is called stepped.

Figure 5-11(A) shows the outline of a hill and the outline of a ranch-like building. Part (B) of Fig. 5-11 shows a solution to the problem; the building rests on a number of tall piers. In (C) of Fig. 5-11, another solution is shown by cutting deeply into the side of the hill.

Figure 5-12 shows another solution to the problem; the building is stepped. Without going into the pros and cons of this solution, there are places where this stepped design (we have seen buildings with four steps) is practical.

The Split. The split is a stepped building design, but it differs in that the distance between floors is roughly half that of a full floor. Figure a standard height differential of 9 feet between floors (the usual distance is roughly 4½ feet). Figure 5-13 shows how the split can be accommodated to front-to-rear changes in grade elevation and side-to-side changes.

The Forced Split. The forced split is neither here nor there; it is forced upon the land. It can be done and is done in any number of ways. Most often the garage and entryway are on one level—ground level. The playroom is to the side of the entryway and down 4 feet or so. When you go from the entryway to the living room, kitchen, or whatever, you go up half a flight of stairs and then turn to go above the playroom. Now a second set of short stairs can lead you to the area above the garage. See Fig. 5-14.

One variation raises the entryway and the adjoining playroom by 4 feet or so. You go up external stairs to enter the building. From there you have a short staircase leading to the area above the playroom and a second set of steps leading to the area above the garage.

When the terrain calls for a split, the split is often the most efficient design in terms of material, costs, and living space. When you "force" the split,

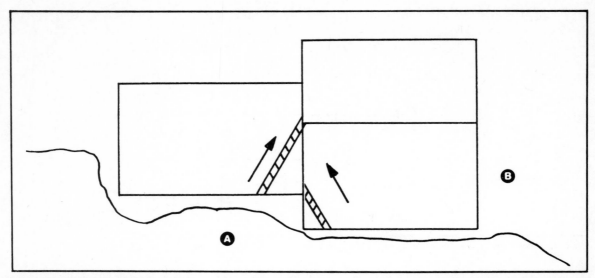

Fig. 5-13. The basic split. Viewed from A, this would be a side split. Viewed from B, this would be a front-to-back split. It's advantage is that it utilizes a hillside with a minimum of construction cost and effort.

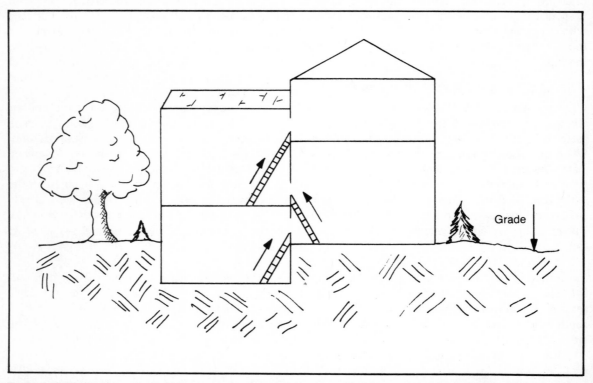

Fig. 5-14. This is the "forced" split. Because there is no natural slope, you, in effect, construct one by excavating for a portion of the building.

very often it doesn't look attractive and it is usually more expensive in material and labor than a Colonial. Bear in mind that every break in a wall and every change in building design costs money. Boards have to be cut (causing waste), joints have to be made and sealed, and so on. The simpler the building is structurally, the less it costs to build.

Selecting the property is the single most important decision you need to make when building your own home. Selecting the correct building design for the property is the second most important decision on the road to building your own home. Take your time. Weigh all the factors carefully. Go look at completed houses.

Chapter 6

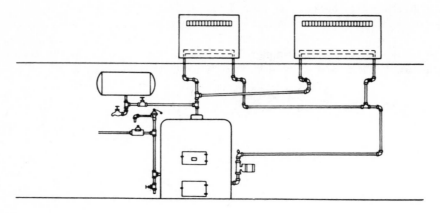

Heating and Plumbing

YOUR CHOICE OF HEATING FUELS AND EQUIP-ment will depend to some extent upon your location. Oil is available almost everywhere, but gas and wood are not. The cost of heating by electricity is exorbitant in many parts of the country. Solar heat is present everywhere, but not in the same strength everywhere.

OIL HEAT

Oil has a proven history of dependability. Newer and better heating furnaces are now available for cutting the cost of heating by oil.

Oil, Hot Water. With the oil-and-hot-water system, water is heated in the furnace and driven by a pump through the radiators. Water holds heat very well so that heating is fairly even.

Oil, Hot Air. With the oil-and-hot-air system, air is heated and driven through the building. It is rarely used.

The oil-and-hot-water heating system is the most expensive to purchase and install. Its thermal efficiency is roughly on par with that of gas heat.

Oil's major drawback is its inefficient hot wash-water heating arrangement. The burner goes on during the summer to make hot water. Not only is this wasteful, but it acts to heat up the house. Some oil-burner owners install a gas-fired hot-water heater and turn their oil system off in the summer.

GAS HEAT

The gas-heating unit costs less to purchase, much less to install, and about the same for heat as other systems. It has the advantage that its ducts can be converted to air-conditioning in the summer (you need to add a refrigeration unit, of course). It can be used for hot-water area heating, but it is seldom used this way.

Almost always, gas heating is used with hot air. Its chief advantage is its low initial cost. Its major disadvantage is the hot air. As the thermostat switches on, you get a hot current of air followed by a noticeable cooling period. This is most annoying on very cold days. You need a separate water heater with a gas-heating system.

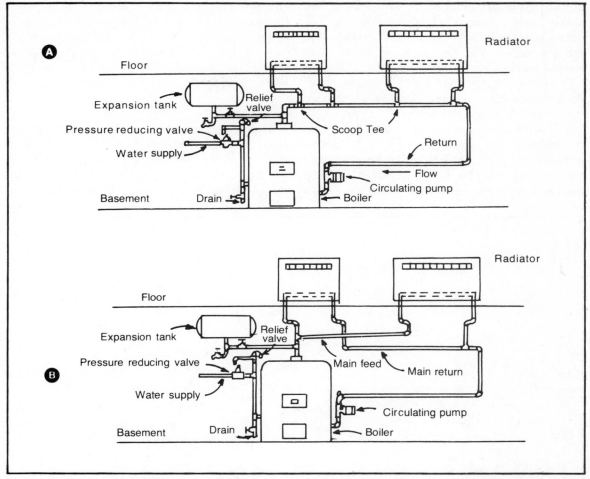

Fig. 6-1. A basic hot-water heating system. Drawing A shows the single-pipe system. Drawing B shows the two-pipe system. Supposedly, heat distribution is better with the two-pipe system.

There are two basic types of hot-air systems; high pressure and low pressure. The high-pressure system costs less. It uses smaller ducts. To compensate, air velocity is increased, and you can sometimes hear the air rushing about.

WOOD AND COAL HEAT

In some areas, the cost of wood for burning is roughly the same as the cost of an amount of oil that will produce an equal amount of heat. Despite this, you can heat your home for considerably less with wood. Roughly a cord of dry hardwood which might

sell for about $130 can produce as much heat as 100 gallons of Number 2 oil.

The explanation lies in where and how the heat is generated. The oil is burned in the furnace to heat water that is piped through radiators, which in turn heat the space surrounding them. The wood is burned in a stove that sits in the center of the room it heats. Little heat is lost between the wood stove and yourself. Lots of heat is lost between the furnace and yourself.

Drawbacks. It is now possible to purchase a wood-burning stove made so tightly that you can control the rate of burning with great accuracy. One load of wood will last all night. But that is it. You cannot go away for a weekend and leave the wood fire unattended. You have to manually feed and clean a wood stove.

The same holds true for a coal-burning stove. An added problem is more dust. Coals produce much more dust than wood.

If you want to heat your home with a wood- or coal-burning stove, you must plan for it. You need a free-standing stove, and it has to be positioned more or less central to the house. Open-air paths for the air to circulate must be provided. You cannot just plop the stove down in a corner as an afterthought. The heat will be confined to that corner and the balance of the house will be cold. Nevertheless, as an adjunct source of heat and pleasure, a wood-burning stove is a practical, sensible investment.

FIREPLACE

A dream involving a home usually includes a fireplace. You picture yourself and loved ones sitting on a cold winter evening before a snapping fire, logs blazing, chestnuts roasting, and a kettle singing on its hob. It is a lovely picture. Unfortunately, it is

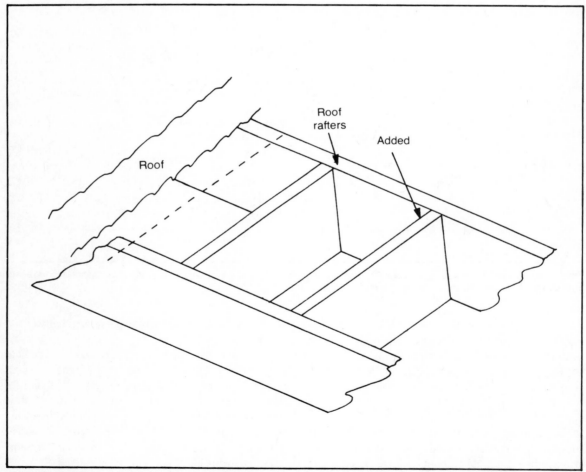

Fig. 6-2. If you frame out the roof and ceiling rafters, as shown, you can introduce a wood-burning stove chimney at a later date with little difficulty.

expensive to create in more ways than one.

A fireplace adds at a minimum, an easy thousand dollars to the cost of a home. Positioned within the building it occupies valuable floor space. Placed exterior to the building, a fireplace might occupy scarce land.

A fireplace—next to an open fire—is the least efficient way known of heating a house. As much as 90 percent of the heat produced by the wood fire goes up the chimney. At the same time, a fireplace is a thermal opening in the wall of your building. Brick and stone are not good insulators. You lose considerable heat through the brick wall. In addition, you lose hot air that goes up the chimney. This loss is considerable when the fire is going, and it is not inconsequential when the fire is not going and the damper is closed.

Still another problem with a fireplace is that it unbalances your heating system. Generally, the heating thermostat is positioned in the living room where the fireplace is located. Heat from the wood fire pushes the thermostat up and that promptly turns off the heating system. This means you have to turn the thermostat up when the fireplace fire is going and then remember to turn it back down when the wood fire is out.

The solution to the problem of providing efficient heat, keeping building costs down, and still having an open fire is the freestanding, wood-burning stove. It is thermally efficient because it provides the building with some 90 percent of the heat available from the burning of the logs. There are models that have doors that can be swung open so that you and your family can enjoy all the pleasure of a wood fire. Most important to your basic aim, the freestanding fireplace can be installed after your home is constructed.

To facilitate future installation of a stove, frame an opening in the ceiling, as shown in Fig. 6-2, and mark the area. At a later date, you can easily cut through and install the necessary chimney.

SOLAR HEATING

The sun is just beginning to rise on solar heating. When it has arisen, every new home constructed in this country, as well as many commercial buildings, will be mainly heated by the sun. When done properly, solar heating is eminently practical. Homes as far north as Boston (and even farther) have been constructed that rely upon the sun for 80 percent to 90 percent of their heating.

Passive Heating. The passive system of solar heating is the only practical one developed to date. Active systems require moving parts. Essentially they consist of a collector, a storage device, and radiators (Fig. 6-3). The sun strikes the collectors. Fluid within the collectors is warmed and pumped to the storage tank. As needed, warm fluid is pumped from the tank through the radiators.

The argument for this system is that the heat in the tank will carry the house through cloudy days. This is true. In order to prevent winter freeze-up, some sort of antifreeze must be used. To store several day's worth of heat, a giant tank is required, and it must be insulated. To move the fluid you need pumps and controls. No tank is ever large enough to provide heat through all cold weather contingencies.

Passive solar heating has only one moving part. It is an insulated window shade that is raised and lowered every day and night. See Fig. 6-4.

The system consists essentially of a heat storage medium. Almost always it is a large, concrete slab. The type of slab upon which a house is constructed does nicely. The slab is exposed to the sun through a large window. At night, the shade is pulled down to keep the heat indoors.

There is also a roof overhang that can be considered a part of the system. The house is so positioned and the overhang affixed to the house so that only low-angle sunlight can enter the large window or windows. In addition, the house is oriented with its heat-collecting windows directed so that the summer sun does not enter the building. In this way, the interior of the building benefits by the desirable heat of the sun in the winter and is shielded from the undesirable sunlight in the summer.

With the general exception that most of the large windows are located on the sheltered side of the building, and that there is an unusually large

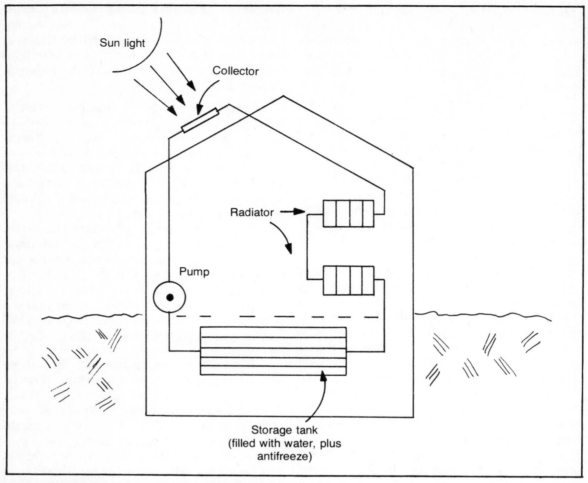

Fig. 6-3. Principle parts of an active solar heating system.

roof overhang on that side of the building, the passive solar home is quite similar to all other buildings.

With this arrangement there are days when a homeowner has to resort to his conventional heating system for heat. This difficulty has been solved by the elimination of the overhang and its replacement by an external, movable window shade. The new design incorporates sufficient glass to provide the required heat even on fairly cloudy days. The shade or window covering is electrically powered and mounted outside the sun window. In this way, it is possible to easily regulate the quantity of sunlight entering the building and so maintain a desirable temperature.

One additional feature of a passive solar home is a heat collector or storage arrangement. In most designs, the heat-storage unit consists of no more than an unusually thick concrete floor. Whereas a standard home constructed on a slab foundation might have a 4-inch-thick slab with thickened edges to bear the load of the walls, the passive solar home, depending upon a slab for heat retention, will have a 6-inch-thick slab. Slab composition, however, will be identical; the same ratios of sand to cement and stone will be used.

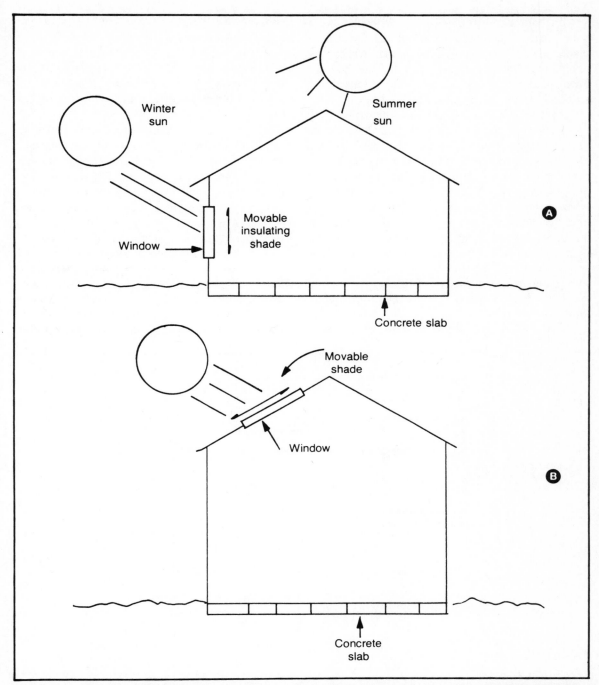

Fig. 6-4. Two types of passive solar heating systems. In design A, only the low winter sun can enter the building through the window to heat the concrete slab floor. In design B, the sun is admitted any time the external, movable shade is pulled up. Generally, this shade is electrically powered.

In both a conventionally-heated house and a solar-heated house, it is important that the slab be insulated. In the solar-heated home, where the foundation slab is to be warmed by the sun, the need for insulation between the slab and the underlying earth is even more important.

In the standard home, the foundation slab temperature is always a fraction lower than the air or room temperature because the slab itself is never heated directly. In the conventional home, there might be a rug or vinyl tile or even wood flooring atop the slab. In a passive solar home where the slab is exposed directly to the source of heat (the sun), the slab becomes warmer than the air in the room. If the room temperature is 75 degrees Fahrenheit, the slab's temperature might be 85 degrees Fahrenheit. Heat transfer—the movement of heat from one substance or area to another—depends upon their temperature difference.

The rate of heat movement rises rapidly with temperature differences. That is why, for example, a hot cup of coffee becomes lukewarm very quickly, but will remain lukewarm for a much longer time. The heat loss rate from a sunlight-heated slab to the earth below will be several times greater than the heat loss from an identical slab at a lower temperature.

Other devices are sometimes used to store heat from sunlight. One system consists of a masonry wall installed parallel to the sunlight coming in through the sun-collecting window. This sounds strange, but in practice the masonry wall serves as a room divider, countertop support, and the like. When designed properly, it doesn't look like a sore thumb protruding out of the floor.

Another device used to store heat from sunlight consists of water-filled cylinders made of translucent plastic. These are filled with water, sealed at both ends, and positioned vertically within the reach of the sun's rays. The sunlight enters the building, strikes the cylinders, and heats the water.

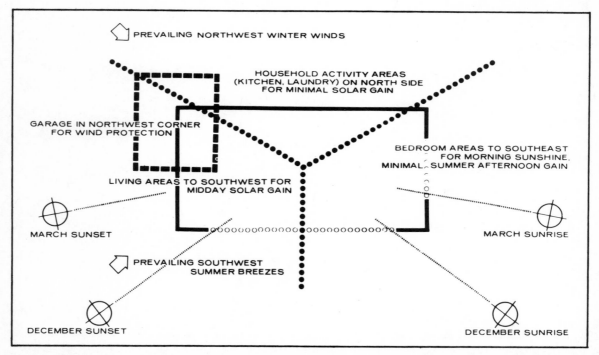

Fig. 6-5. Optimal home orientation for solar heating and weather protection in northern latitudes. Courtesy U.S. Department of Agriculture.

Vegetation placed around the south side of the house traps cold northern winds.

Vegetation planted around the north side of the house protects the house from cold winter winds.

Fig. 6-6A. Placement of vegetation. (Continued on page 70.)

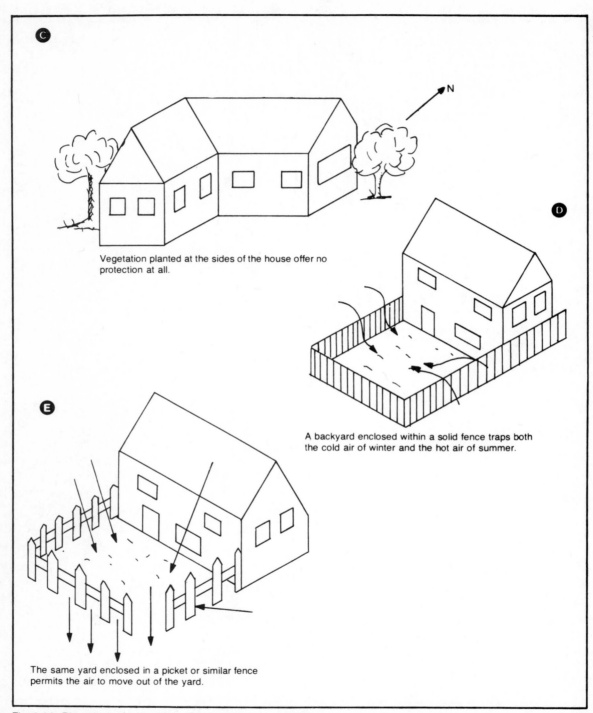

Vegetation planted at the sides of the house offer no protection at all.

A backyard enclosed within a solid fence traps both the cold air of winter and the hot air of summer.

The same yard enclosed in a picket or similar fence permits the air to move out of the yard.

Fig. 6-6A. Placement of vegetation. (Continued from page 69.)

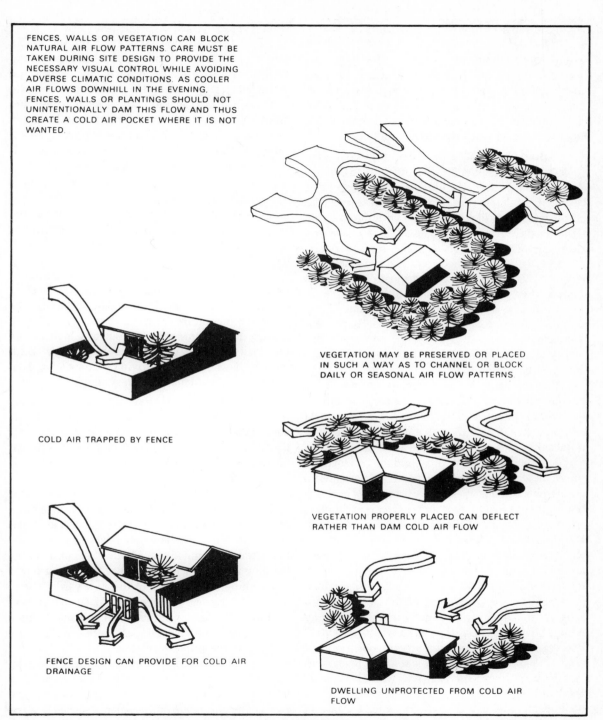

FENCES, WALLS OR VEGETATION CAN BLOCK NATURAL AIR FLOW PATTERNS. CARE MUST BE TAKEN DURING SITE DESIGN TO PROVIDE THE NECESSARY VISUAL CONTROL WHILE AVOIDING ADVERSE CLIMATIC CONDITIONS. AS COOLER AIR FLOWS DOWNHILL IN THE EVENING, FENCES, WALLS OR PLANTINGS SHOULD NOT UNINTENTIONALLY DAM THIS FLOW AND THUS CREATE A COLD AIR POCKET WHERE IT IS NOT WANTED.

VEGETATION MAY BE PRESERVED OR PLACED IN SUCH A WAY AS TO CHANNEL OR BLOCK DAILY OR SEASONAL AIR FLOW PATTERNS

COLD AIR TRAPPED BY FENCE

VEGETATION PROPERLY PLACED CAN DEFLECT RATHER THAN DAM COLD AIR FLOW

FENCE DESIGN CAN PROVIDE FOR COLD AIR DRAINAGE

DWELLING UNPROTECTED FROM COLD AIR FLOW

Fig. 6-6B. Effect of wind flow on various arrangements of fence and plantings. (Courtesy, U.S. Department of Agriculture.)

When the sun sets, the water reradiates the heat it has absorbed. Water has just about the highest specific heat (ability to absorb heat) of any substances known. The columns of water therefore can hold considerably more heat than you might think. The system of water-filled cylinders is generally used to convert a standard home to passive solar heating (at least partially, if not totally).

Solar Home Costs. The basic cost of a solar-heated home is somewhat higher than that of a conventional house. The large sun windows must be double or triple glazed and the house must be better insulated. The solar home with the external shade costs even more because of the shade and attendant mechanism. The cost difference between all three, however, is not great and can amount to no more than a small percent at most. This is soon compensated for by the savings in fuel.

In theory, a well-designed solar home (Figs. 6-5 and 6-6) will not consume more than 10 percent as much fuel as will a conventional home. But theory alone does not define the rate at which the heat will be required.

For the sake of discussion, let us assume a building that requires 100,000 Btu per hour during the winter because of its size and geographical location. Assume further that you have incorporated sufficient sun windows and a heat-storage slab to keep the interior of the building comfortable through the coldest winter expected. There are no problems when the sun shines every day. There are few problems if the sun shines every other day. What about a week of clouds? Will you need the full 100,000 Btu of artificial heat by the end of the week? Are week-long sunless days common in your area?

The building that is solar heated as described here needs only 10 percent of the conventional, artificial heat over the average year. Can you get by with a heating system that has less than 100,000 Btu capacity? This is an important question not quickly answered. It depends upon how many sunless days can be expected and how well the house is insulated. The better insulated the house the longer it can remain without heat from sunlight. Mass of the storage slab and how much discomfort you are willing to accept are other factors.

If you are willing to risk a few uncomfortable days a year, you can stint on the back-up heating system and save a bundle. If you do, the overall cost of the solar home will be that much less or nearly that much less than the conventional home, and there will be the additional savings in fuel through the years. A practical compromise arrangement could be made with either a wood-burning stove, a coal-burning stove, or electrical heating.

The stove and its chimney costs about a thousand dollars. This compares to $10,000 or so for a conventional oil, hot water system. While the stove cannot heat an entire building, it can provide all the heat that is required in its immediate vicinity.

An electrical heating system is much more expensive than a wood-burning stove, but the electrical system is automatic and easily adjusted to the desired temperature. The drawback to the electrical heating system is the inordinately high cost of electricity in most sections of the country. Still, with the basic solar heat providing most of your heat energy, you wouldn't need very much electricity.

The Envelope House. The envelope house (Fig. 6-7) is another variation of the passive solar-home design. Visually, it is probably the most attractive. From a thermal point of view, it is probably just as efficient as any of the two designs previously discussed.

The cost of an envelope house is almost twice that of a conventional building. The reason is obvious when you examine an envelope house. Basically, the envelope house consists of a standard insulated building over which a second larger building is constructed. The larger building might be anything from a few feet to a few yards larger, and it will have one or more walls made up mainly of windows. In effect, the inner building sits within a greenhouse. The dead airspace between the walls serving as the prime insulator.

Specific designs vary. Some will have an airspace completely around the inner structure. Others will limit the green house to one or more sides. The advantage of this solar design is that the earth in the airspace can serve as a sunroom,

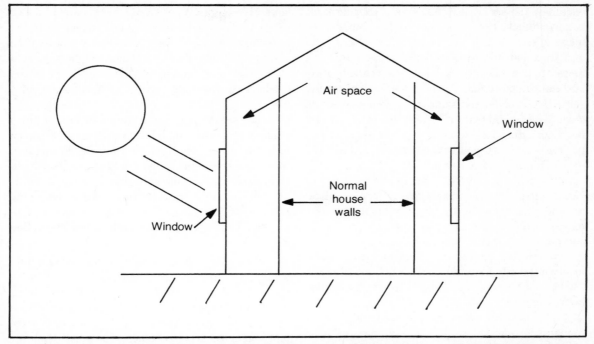

Fig. 6-7. The major parts of an envelope house. Actually, it is a house constructed, more or less, within a green house.

greenhouse, or even a garden. The overall effect is one of graciousness and beauty, but it is not inexpensive.

ELECTRICAL HEAT

Electrical heat provides the cleanest, most accurately controlled form of heat presently known. Also the equipment required for electrical heating of a home is far less expensive and more dependable because—with the exception of small radiant heaters—electrical space-heating systems work at relatively low temperatures. There is almost nothing to wear out.

Operating Costs. The drawback to electrical space heating is cost. If you do not happen to live in an area where the electricity is very inexpensive—and there seems to be a decreasing number of these areas—the cost of home heating with electricity is prohibitive. Because the need for heat is as regular as winter, the cost can add up to astronomical figures over the years.

To secure an approximate comparison of the cost of the various fuels, you can use Table 6-1 as a guide. The cost comparisons are approximate because no correction is made for the efficiencies of the various systems used with the different fuels.

Using Table 6-1, assume that your home requires 68,000 Btu per hour on a cold winter's day to maintain the interior temperature at 70 degrees Fahrenheit. The average oil-fueled heating system is about 50 percent efficient. Because you require twice as much heat in the furnace, it works out to an even 136,000 Btu (we picked easy numbers for our

Table 6-1. Heating Values of Various Fuels.

Fuel	Quantity	Btu
Coal	ton	25,000,000
Oil (No. 2)	gallon	136,000
Gas (manufactured)	cu ft	500-550
Gas (natural)	cu ft	1,000-1,100
Gas (butane)	cu ft	3,200
Gas (propane)	cu ft	2,519
Electricity	KW hour	3,412
Wood	cord	12,500,000

example). To secure 136,000 Btu in your furnace, you would have to burn 1 gallon of No. 2 fuel oil an hour.

An electrical space-heating system is much more efficient. Generally, electrical space-heating systems are more than 75 percent efficient. For the same house under the same conditions you would need 1.333 × 68,000 or 90,650 Btu of electricity per hour. Because electricity produces 3412 Btu per kilowatt hour, you would draw 90,650 ÷ 3412 or 26.56 kilowatts per hour.

If you are paying $1.30 per delivered gallon of No. 2 fuel oil, the cost of heating your home with oil for one hour would be the price of 1 gallon of fuel (discounting the electricity required by the burner and pump, and equipment maintenance).

If the cost for electrical power, at the same location the oil can be purchased, is $.12 kilowatt, the cost of heating your house electrically for one hour would be 25.56 × .12 or $3.19.

This is only an approximate method for determining the relative costs of various fuels. For an exact comparison, you need to know fairly closely the actual efficiency of the system. In addition, in the case of costing electrical heat, you need to determine whether or not the power company reduces the rate when the house is heated by electricity.

Electrical Heaters. An electrical heater consists of a resistance wire connected to the source of electricity. There are many designs with two basic variations: high temperature and low temperature. The high temperature devices are called radiant. They get red hot and their use is almost always limited to portable units. The low temperature units do not produce visible heat. They are usually permanently installed in ceiling and baseboard units.

BASIC PLUMBING SYSTEM

When you are connected to a city water main, the city provides water under pressure. It is your responsibility to run a service pipe from your home to the city's pipe. The city makes the actual connection.

Inside the building, the pipe is "split" into several branches. One branch supplies cold water to the sinks and tubs and another branch goes to the hot-water heating system, and then is piped to the sinks, tubs, and showers. There might also be a cold water line, feeding a spigot that leads to the garden or garage, and a line to the furnace. See Fig. 6-8.

The waste-disposal system consists of pipes leading from the sink, lavatory, and toilet to an in-house sewer main or main drainpipe. From there the waste flows out to the city's sewer line. Note that drainpipe traps are almost always vented. This is done to prevent the trap from emptying and to permit fresh air to circulate within the drain system, helping to eliminate odors and gases. See Fig. 6-9.

Pipe Size. At a minimum, the service line would be ¾ inch in size, and larger if the house is large or the pressure is low. The main feed lines within the building should be ¾ inch, with branch lines no less than ½ inch. Only the last foot or so of pipe can be reduced to ⅜ inch. The small diameter pipe is needed to conveniently connect the fixtures.

Drainpipe sizes vary with the fixture to which the pipe is connected. Table 6-2 lists recommended drainpipe diameters for various fixtures. Very often the drainpipes will be connected to a stack. This is simply a drainpipe stood on end for construction convenience. A minimum of 2 inches for waste stacks and 3 inches for soil stacks (toilet discharge) is the standard. We suggest you use nothing less than a 4-inch stack (and following main sewer pipe) for soil removal. See Tables 6-3, 6-4, and 6-5.

Fixtures. In plumbing terms, fixture applies to sinks, tubs, showers, and the like. The types, colors, designs, and price of fixtures cover a very wide range. There are marble tubs with gold-plated faucets at one end of the scale and plastic tubs with brass faucets on the other end. In between there are probably a hundred different designs to choose from. See Fig. 6-10.

To determine which fixtures you like best, you can look at the displays at the local plumbing supply shops, write to any of the fixture manufacturing companies that advertise regularly in homeowner magazines and visit some of the larger building

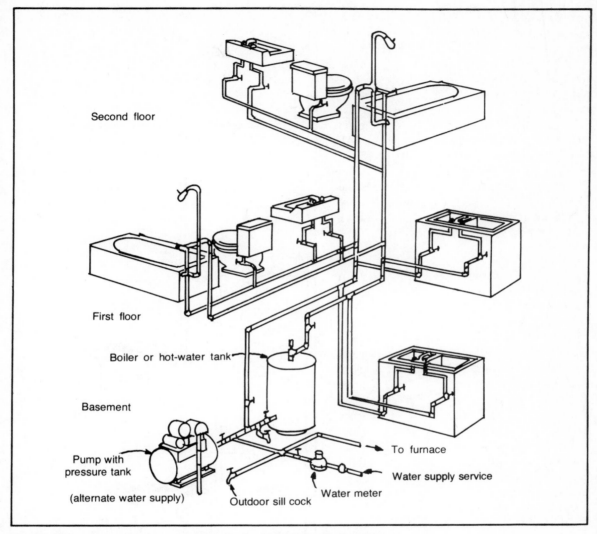

Second floor

First floor

Boiler or hot-water tank

Basement

Pump with
pressure tank

(alternate water supply)

Outdoor sill cock

Water meter

To furnace

Water supply service

Fig. 6-8. Major parts and their arrangements in a residential plumbing system.

supply yards. Figure 6-11 is typical of some of the photos you can secure by writing to the manufacturers. They will also furnish color brochures.

Bear in mind that any fixture, except a tub and built-in shower, can be removed and replaced in less than half a day. Don't hesitate to specify the lowest-priced fixtures to keep your initial costs down.

Valves and Clean-outs. The only thing you need to know about valves is that you need gate

valves in the main lines (they do not reduce water pressure as much as compression valves) and valves in front of every fixture. In other words, you want to be able to shut off the water supply at each fixture and not have to go to the basement and shut off the main valve every time you need to change a washer. Valves only cost a few dollars and it is short-sighted policy to stint on them.

Clean-outs are plugs fitted to the drainpipe at various intervals to permit you to clear the line in

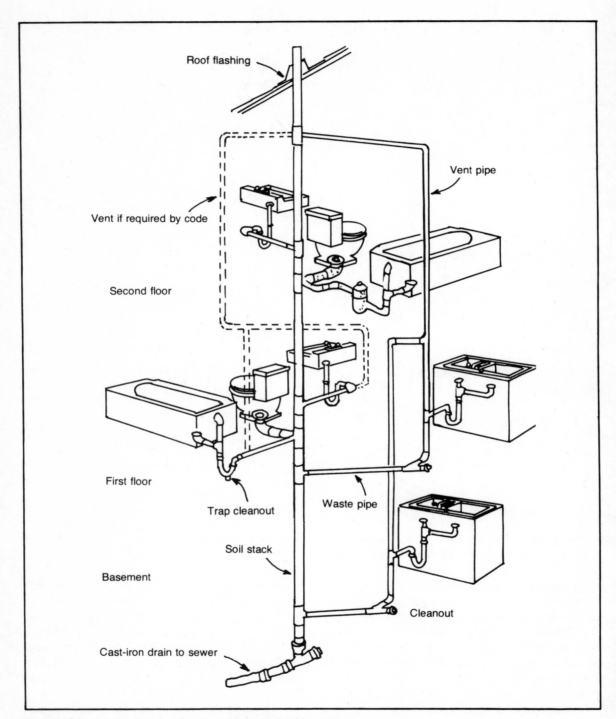

Fig. 6-9. Soil, drain, and vent piping in a residential plumbing system.

Table 6-2. Maximum Capacity of Drainpipes.

Maximum capacity of various diameter drainpipes at various pitches as measured in fixture units. Table may be used for branches, house drains, and sewers.

Maximum Fixture Units Allowed

	Pipe Diam.	Fixtures on Same Level			Fixtures on 2 or More Levels		
		⅛-in. Pitch	¼-in. Pitch	½-in. Pitch	⅛-in. Pitch	¼-in. Pitch	½-in. Pitch
No toilets	1¼	1	1	1	1	1-2	1-2
	1½	2	2	3	2	2½-5	3½-7
	2	5	6	8	7	9-21	12-26
	2½	12	15	18	17	21	27
	3	24	27	36	33-36	42-45	50-72
No more than 2 toilets	3	15	18	21	24-27	27-36	36-48
Any number of toilets within fixture unit capacity	4	82	95	112	114-180	150-215	210-250
	5	180	234	280	270-400	370-480	540-560

case of a blockage. They must be positioned when the pipe is assembled because there is no practical way of installing them afterwards. Be certain to specify brass plugs because the cheaper iron plugs often rust in place.

Material. The water service pipe should always be copper. The interior water lines can be plastic. It is far less expensive than copper. If your local code doesn't permit using plastic pipe, it is a toss up as to which the plumber will install for less—copper or galvanized iron. If you are going to do your own plumbing, it is no contest. The copper is far, far easier to work. Incidentally, copper, having less internal water friction, can be used one size smaller than galvanized pipe. Never run less than ¾ inch for the service line. See Tables 6-6 and 6-7.

Indoors the drainpipe can be of plastic or copper. When and where the drain runs beneath the

Table 6-3. Estimated Fixture-Unit Values.

Estimated fixture unit values. Each unit is equal to a flow of 7½ gallons of water *out* of each fixture.

Fixture	Fixture Unit Values*
Bathtub (with or without shower)	2
Dishwasher (home)	2
Drinking Fountain	1
Kitchen Sink	2
Lavatory	1
Laundry	2
Service Sink	2
Shower (separate, each head)	2
Washing Machine	2
Water Closet (tank)	3
Water Closet (flush valve)	6
Bathroom Group (tank)	6
Bathroom Group (flush valve)	8

*Values are for total discharge, hot and cold. For either hot or cold discharge by itself, use 75% of the total fixture unit value.**

Courtesy Copper Development Association.

Table 6-4. Minimum Pressures and Flow Rates for Plumbing Fixtures.

Type of Fixture	Minimum Required Pressure	Desired Flow Rate
Lavatory faucet	8 psi	3 gpm
⅜ sink faucet	10	4.5
½ sink faucet	5	4.5
Bathtub faucet	5	6
½ laundry tub	5	5
Dish washer	8	5
Clothes washer	8	5
Shower	10	5
Toilet tank	10	3
Toilet flush valve	15	15-40
Sill cock plus 50' Garden hose	30	5

Table 6-5. Average Quantity of Water Used At One Time.

Fixture or Appliance	Gallons
Bathtub	30
Shower bath, 5 min.	15
Lavatory	2
Kitchen sink, 1 meal	3
Dishwasher, 1 load	4
Clothes washer, 1 load	40

concrete in the building, or a driveway outside the building, always use cast iron. On the run to the sewer, you can use Transite, plastic, or vitrified clay. Although more expensive, the clay will probably last longer.

DOMESTIC HOT-WATER SYSTEM

Domestic hot water is the water used for washing,

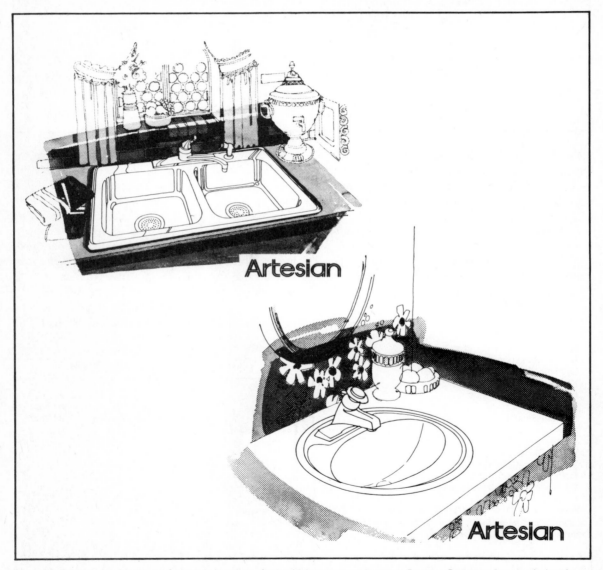

Fig. 6-10. Typical plumbing manufacturer's handouts from which you can select your fixtures. Courtesy Artesian Industries.

Fig. 6-11. A simple, low-cost bathroom finished with tile. Courtesy American Olean Tile Company.

Table 6-6. Minimum Diameter
Copper Tubing for Use With Fixtures.

Fixture	Copper Tube Size, inches
Drinking Fountain	3/8
Lavatory	3/8
Water Closet (tank type)	3/8
Bathtub	1/2
Dishwasher	1/2
Kitchen Sink	1/2
Laundry Tray	1/2
Service Sink	1/2
Shower Head	1/2
Sill Cock, Hose Bibb, Wall Hydrant	1/2
Washing Machine	1/2
Flush valve, toilet	1

The 3/8-inch tubing should never be more than 2 feet long.

Courtesy Copper Development Association.

Table 6-7. Minimum Galvanized Pipe for Supplying Fixtures.

	Pressure at the Water Main		
Application	High 85 psi	Medium 50 psi	Low 35 psi
Water service	3/4	3/4-1	1-1¼ inch
Bath or shower	1/2	1/2	1/2 inch
Lavatory	1/2	1/2	1/2 inch
Flush tank, toilet	1/2	1/2	1/2 inch
Flush valve, toilet	1	1	1¼ inch
Water heater	1/2	1/2	3/4 inch
Kitchen sink	1/2	1/2-3/4	3/4 inch
Laundry tub	1/2	1/2-3/4	3/4 inch
Clothes washer	1/2	1/2-3/4	3/4 inch
Dish washer	1/2	1/2-3/4	3/4 inch
Sill cock	1/2	1/2	3/4 inch

cleaning, and cooking. It is distinguished from hot water that might be used in the heating system. Your problem is to determine the type and capacity of the system that best suits your needs and your pocketbook.

Computing Hot-Water Demand. Table 6-8 lists the approximate quantities of hot water used by various household appliances and fixtures. With a little effort, it is easy to figure the total times the dishwasher will be used each day and the probable number of showers, hot tubs and the like taken by members of the family and guests each day. Adding the gallons per device per use will give you the total quantity of hot water required per day. That is not all the data you need. You also need to know when the hot water is taken and how much at each time.

It is much too expensive and inefficient to provide a constant flow of hot water at a rate equal to the peak demand. The practical solution is to provide just enough capacity, plus a reserve, to satisfy peak demand. This is done with a tank system. The domestic hot water heating system can only bring a comparatively small quantity of water up to temperature at a time, but it works to keep the tank filled with hot water.

Your problem is to determine how much hot water you need in that tank and just how fast the heater must replenish that water that is removed.

First determine when the greatest quantity of hot water will be used. Will it be over a period of time or all at once? If, for example, it is the custom of your family to shower every morning, and there are five of you, you are going to need 5 × 15 gallons (75 gallons of hot water in just as much time as it takes five people to shower). To provide this quantity of hot water, you will need a 100-gallon tank. For one thing, you cannot get 75 gallons of hot water out of a 75-gallon tank because as hot water is

Table 6-8. Estimate of Hot-Water Requirements.

Number Bathrooms	Number Bedrooms	Laundry	Size (in gallons)
1	1 or 2	No	30
		Yes	40
2	3 or 4	No	40
		Yes	50*
2	4 or 5	No	50
		Yes	75*
3	4 or 5	No	75
		Yes	100*

Table 6-9. Electric Hot-Water Heater Performance.

HIGHBOY MODELS

Heating Unit Wattages

		30	30	40	40	52	52	66	66	82	82	120	120
Tank Cap. Gals		30	30	40	40	52	52	66	66	82	82	120	120
Elements		1	2	1	2	1	2	1	2	1	2	1	2
Hgt. of Heater		44⅞	44⅞	58½	58½	58⅜	58⅜	58½	58½	58½	59½	61¾	61¾
Jacket Dia.		17¾	17¾	17¾	17¾	19¾	19¾	22¼	22¼	24¼	24¼	28¼	28¼
N.E.M.A. Standards 230 V.A.C.	Upper		1000		1250		1500		2000		2500		3000
	Lower	1500	600	2000	750	2500	1000	3000	1250	4000	1500	6000	2000
Max. UL. Approved 230 V	Upper		6000		6000		6000		6000		6000		6000
	Lower	6000	6000	6000	6000	6000	6000	6000	6000	6000	6000	6000	6000

LOWBOY MODELS

Heating Unit Wattages

		20	20	30	30	40	40	52	52
Tank Cap. Gals		20	20	30	30	40	40	52	52
Elements		1	2	1	2	1	2	1	2
Hgt. of Heater		31½	31½	29½	29½	31½	31½	39¾	39¾
Jacket Dia.		17¾	17¾	22¼	22¼	24¼	24¼	24¼	24¼
N.E.M.A. Standards 230 V.A.C.	Upper		1000		1000		1250		1500
	Lower	1000	600	1500	600	2000	750	2500	1000
Max. U.L. Approved 230 V	Upper		6000		6000		6000		6000
	Lower	6000	6000	6000	6000	6000	6000	6000	6000

drawn, cold water enters. You also need the larger tank to take care of aging. Tanks lose efficiency with time. At the same time, you can use a tank with a comparatively slow recovery system because the system has 24 hours to catch up.

On the other hand, your family might take its showers at different times of the day, but use the clothes washer a great deal of the time. According to Table 6-8, a clothes washer takes 40 gallons of hot water. Although this is not stated in the table, the washer takes about 30 minutes to run through its cycle. Roughly, you would need a 75-gallon tank with a recovery system capable of bringing some 40 gallons of water up to temperature every hour.

Table 6-10. Btu Output of Various Fuels.

Electricity	3413 Btu/kilowatt hour
Natural and mixed gases	800 to 1200 Btu/cubic foot.
Sewage gases	600 to 800 Btu/cubic foot.
Lp gases	2500 to 3300 Btu/cubic foot.
Number 2 heating oil	140,000 Btu/gallon.
Number 4 heating oil	148,000 Btu/gallon.
Number 5 heating oil	152,000 Btu/gallon.

Table 6-11. Gas-Fired Hot-Water Heater Performance.

Tank Cap. Gal.	Heat Input in Thousand Btu's				Rec. 60° Rise G.P.H.	Rec. 100° Rise G.P.H.	Approx. Ship. Wt. (lb.)
	Nat.	Mxd.	Mfd.	L.P.			
30	45	45	45	——	63.0	37.8	
30	——	——	——	38	53.1	31.9	116
40	45	45	45	——	63.0	37.8	
40	——	——	——	38	53.1	31.9	150
50	50	50	50	——	70.0	42.0	
50	——	——	——	45	63.0	37.8	225
30	36	36	36	36	50.4	30.2	128
40	38	38	38	——	53.1	31.8	
40	——	——	——	36	50.4	30.2	190

(Left margin label for Table 6-11: HIGHBOY for upper rows, LOW-BOY for lower rows)

81

Types of Water Heaters. If you opt for gas-fired, hot-air heat, your best choice from a cost and efficiency point of view is a gas-fired hot water heater. If you go to oil, the hot-water heating unit is generally part and parcel of the space-heating furnace. Installing a gas-fired heater for summer use in such cases has its advantages of lower operating costs and the reduction of waste heat in the furnace room.

In areas where electricity is comparatively inexpensive, the electrical heater is your best bet. It is the safest. To determine relative operating costs, compare your various energy costs with the figures in Tables 6-9, 6-10, and 6-11.

Chapter 7

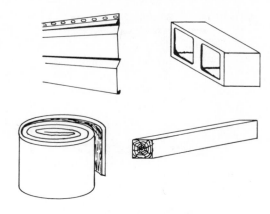

Building Materials

IT MIGHT SEEM THAT HAVING REACHED THIS POINT in your selections and decision making that there is little else to do before picking up your tools and getting down to work. That's not so. There are still more decisions—important decisions—to make. For example, consider the windows you are going to use. Their number has already been determined. They are indicated on the house plan you have selected or have had drawn for yourself.

Standard, double-hung windows (Fig. 7-1) of wood sell for about $80. The same size window in a casement design might sell for three and four times as much. On one hand, you have 10 windows at $800. On the other hand, you could spend $2400 and more for windows for the same house. You can point to almost any item of building material used in a home and come up with a dozen different types, grades, and prices. Just remember that the most expensive item is not necessarily the best.

You must choose between wood and stone and between a wood-frame house and a concrete block house. There are advantages and disadvantages to using certain materials; some are real and some are imagined.

Thermal Efficiency. Wood is a better insulator than stone. Surprisingly, the block house has some advantages. Concrete has mass. It holds heat and it holds cold. During winter, the concrete will retain some of the sun's heat. In the summer, the concrete will retain some of the night's cold. The building's mass slows thermal change.

Appearance. A block house does not have to look like a block house. The outside can be stucco. The major visual difference is the greater wall thickness, visible at the windows (Figs. 7-2A and 7-2B).

Rot and Fire. Other than repainting the window frames every four years, there is no maintenance to the outside of a block house. You can't say as much for the conventional wood-frame building sided with a wood that requires painting. Concrete does not have to be painted. It is impervious to the weather. A good stucco job can last 25 and more years. It is almost impervious to the weather.

There are homeowners who tire of the color of the concrete or stucco home and paint it. This is a mistake. Concrete and stucco, which is a layer of concrete, soak up paint like sponges. Once painted,

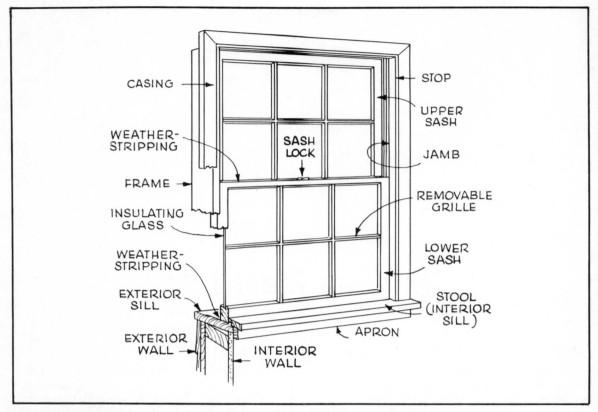

Fig. 7-1. The major parts of a standard, double-hung window. Courtesy Andersen Corporation.

the building has to be repainted every 4 years or so because the paint deteriorates and fades.

Some homeowners opt for a clear finish on their exterior. This looks beautiful for a year or two, but the varnish invariably breaks down in spots, and rot sets in, which doesn't harm the wood but discolors it. To keep a clear-finish home looking good, you have to go over the wood at least every two years.

Special Woods. To secure a natural wood exterior that will hold its beauty through the years, you have to go to pale cedar or cypress for your siding. These woods are sealed and stained to produce a light brown color that is beautiful. The cost is several times greater than for ordinary wood siding.

Cost Comparison. No general guide or rule of thumb can be given to compare the costs of the two types of building materials. A lot depends upon the location of the job, the distance to a supply of block, the market price for lumber, and (to some extent) the design of the desired house. A simple one- or two-story Cape Cod or Colonial on a slab present one set of problems and costs. A complex split presents different construction problems sometimes more easily solved with wood than with stone.

The only certain way to compare costs of building in wood or stone is to get bids on the job. You can also make lists of the required materials, price the materials, and estimate the labor required to get a ballpark number. For an actual figure, you have to request bids.

CONCRETE

Concrete is made by mixing sand, small stones, water, and cement together to form a mud. The

Fig. 7-2A. A wood buck used as a temporary construction guide for a window opening in a concrete block wall.

relative proportions of the materials used determines the strength of the concrete and its price. To determine the quantity of concrete you will need for any given construction project, compute the volume required in cubic feet and divide by 27 to get cubic yards. Concrete is sold by the cubic yard. Add 15 percent for quantities under 5 cubic yards and 10 percent for quantities of over 5 yards to take care of waste (concrete that sticks to the chute and tools).

Order or price the concrete mix you need from Table 7-1 or tell the supplier the purpose of the concrete. Do not order concrete stronger than required. It is simply a waste of money.

Mix or Buy. There are two ways to secure concrete. One way is to purchase the ingredients and mix them together yourself (Fig. 7-3). The other way is to purchase ready-mixed concrete. The yard delivers the concrete already mixed with water and drops it off into your form by a chute.

Hand mixing is fine when all you need is half a yard or so. Companies charge a premium for delivering less than a good-size load, so there is a financial advantage and a convenience to mixing small quantities of concrete by yourself. When you run to more than a cubic yard, you run into trouble. It is a lot of work to mix, haul, dump, and take care of the in-place fresh concrete. You cannot plop a little today and a little tomorrow. Even with the use of a chemical, bonding will not be as good as the same piece of concrete poured as a unit.

Fig. 7-2B. A wood buck used as a construction guide for a door opening in a concrete block wall.

Table 7-1. Concrete Mix Formulas.

Mix	Description
1 part cement 2-¾ parts sand 3 parts stone	The strongest mix. Used for swimming pools, watertight construction where there is exposure to the weather as for example, walks and drives.
1 part cement 2-¾ parts sand 4 parts stone	Moderately strong. Used for walls and foundations normally not directly exposed to the weather.
1 part cement 3 parts sand 5 parts stone	Weakest of the three. Used for heavy construction, thick slabs, massive foundations, thick retaining walls, dams, and the like.

Fig. 7-3. Small quantities of concrete are fairly easily mixed by hand if you work with a large pan. Here a shovel is used to open a bag of cement.

Most important is that the ready-mixed concrete will cost you less. The reason is the nature of concrete. To make 1 cubic yard of 1:3:5 concrete, you need 22 cubic feet of stone, 13 cubic feet of sand, 4.5 cubic feet of cement, plus 4 cubic feet of water. That is a total of 43.5 cubic feet of material (27 cubic feet make up 1 cubic yard). The reason is that the sand fits into the voids between the stones, the cement fits into the voids between the sand, and the water slips into the spaces remaining. When you add the cost of the individual materials necessary to make the concrete, mixing your own costs more than purchasing the ready-to-use concrete.

CONCRETE BLOCK

Your primary decision—the size of the block—will be determined by your local building code. You can then compute the number of blocks fairly quickly with a reasonable degree of accuracy.

The face dimensions of the standard block is a nominal 8 by 8 by 16 inches. Its actual dimensions are 3⅝ by 7⅝ by 15⅝ inches. The block is designed

Fig. 7-4. This window has been set in a concrete block wall and the joint between the wood frame and the block has been sealed at an angle with mortar. The block has been parged (plastered) with a single coat of mortar cement, and then roughened so as to facilitate the adherence of the second, final coat of mortar cement.

to be positioned with the aid of a band of mortar ⅜-inch thick, thus bringing the overall block dimensions to its nominal size.

The fastest way to determine the number of blocks needed for a given wall is to work in inches usng a pocket calculator. The standard block has a face of 128 square inches (8 × 16). Find the wall's square area in inches and divide the area by 126.

For example, assume the desired wall is to be 35 feet long and 10 feet high. That multiplies out to 350 square feet. Multiplying by 144 brings the figure to 50,400 square inches. Dividing by 128 gives us a total of 393.75 block. To this figure, add 3 percent for waste to get the actual count.

Fenestrations. If there are to be windows and doors and other fenestrations in the wall, simply find the area to be left open and subtract that from the total. When there are to be fenestrations, it is advisable to use 5 percent as a waste figure because of the cutting that will be necessary. See Fig. 7-4.

Costs. You can price the block out easily enough at the masonry yard. As for labor, many masons will give you a per-block labor figure that should include the necessary mortar.

Finishing Block. The word finish is probably a poor choice for use with concrete block. Once the block has been positioned and the joints have been tooled (made smooth), nothing else needs to be done externally. If you prefer, the block can be left as is. This used to be done years ago; now the block is covered with a layer of mortar (cement and sand) and is called stucco.

Internally, where there is no need for insulation, the block wall can be given a layer of plaster as a finish. When insulation is required, furring strips of wood are nailed to the block wall. Insulation is positioned between the strips. The strips are next covered with Sheetrock and the Sheetrock joints are taped (covered and made smooth).

Costs. The cost of the stucco is far less than the cost of wood shingles or any other siding normally used on a wood-frame house. The cost of the insulation remains the same, as does the cost of Sheetrock and taping. The only additional cost of finishing the interior of a concrete block house—over the cost of finishing the interior of a wood-frame house—would be the labor and cost of the furring strips, plus possibly some additional cost for window and door frames because they need to be several inches wider.

FRAMING LUMBER

There are no decisions to be made concerning concrete block. You use the smallest block the building code will allow. There is no point in using anything larger. Lumber is not disposed of quite as easily.

The Least Expensive Lumber. In some localities, the yards will only stock the least expensive framing lumber available locally. In other yards, they may offer a choice. For example, they might stock poplar as well as the more common fir. Poplar costs less, but it is softer and weaker than fir.

If your code will permit you to make an equal replacement, then poplar is your best bet. On the other hand, the code might specify larger-size lumber when switching from construction-grade fir to construction-grade poplar. In certain positions such as studs, the poplar might be acceptable. As floor joists over a span of say 10 feet, you might have to go from a 10-×-2 fir to a 12-×-2 length of poplar. Depending on relative prices, the switch may or may not result in a savings.

Prefabs. Some lumberyards stock or can secure prefabricated flooring joists. With these you save on labor and on material because they are stronger than the framing timbers they replace. But is there a dollar savings? You cannot tell until you price it all out.

Pricing. Most but not all lumber is sold by the board foot. To find the total cost of any piece of lumber sold this way, you need to compute the number of board feet it contains.

Very simply a board foot is a board 1-foot wide, 1-foot long, and 1-inch thick. It is no matter that the board might actually be less than 1-foot wide and 1-inch thick. It was this size when it was first cut from the log. Later, smoothing and seasoning reduced its size, but you still are charged for the full dimensions.

A 2 × 10 is actually 1⅝ × 9⅝ inches, but when

you purchase a 2 × 10, 10 feet long, you are billed for 20 board feet.

A modern 2 × 4 is actually 1⅝ × 3⅝ inches in cross section. When you purchase a 2 × 4, you are billed on the basis of 2/3 foot per running foot. This works out to 5.3 board feet to every 8-foot long 2 × 4.

To determine how many 2 × 4s, how many rafters, and how many flooring joints you will need, you have to sit down and go over the plan, figuring that these timbers are positioned normally on 16 inch centers. Then add the doubles you will need alongside windows, doors, floor openings, and attic openings.

The easier way is to bring the plan to the lumberyard and have them bid the entire job. The trouble with this plan is that they will charge $50 or $100 for the work, and they will want to bid for all the lumber. The reason is that they make most of their profit on the trim. Generally, they are not anxious for the framing timber business. Getting all your lumber from one source simplifies purchasing and record keeping, but it precludes shopping around for some of the individual items. It also costs you money.

Aged Lumber. Wood that has been left to the weather often develops a light grey patina. This does not reduce the strength of the board or its ability to hold paint. Beware, however, of boards that have rested on the earth for any length of time. The areas that have turned black have rotted and must be discarded. Most often the rot has traveled the length of the wood and the board should be discarded.

SHEATHING

Sheathing is the material you place over the frame of the building and the material with which you deck the roofing timbers. Sheathing serves several purposes. It braces the frame and it provides a solid wall. With some designs, the sheathing serves as a nailing base for shingles and other siding. In other designs, the sheathing itself might also serve as the siding. See Fig. 7-5.

Any number of materials are being used as sheathing. Your choice will depend upon price and

the attendant labor. Some sheathing is easier to install than others. You will have to price them out to make your decision.

Boards. Yellow pine or Southern pine is most often used because it is strong but not too attractive—which holds its cost down. The boards should be tongued and grooved. The wide boards are better because you need fewer boards and there is less waste. Bear in mind that the finished width (in place) of the 4-inch tongued and grooved board is only 3¼ inches. The finished width of the 6-inch board is only 5¼ inches. You will be charged as if the boards are fully 4 and 6 inches in width. If the boards are nailed horizontally across the studs, figure 5 percent waste. If the boards are installed at an angle, which provides greater frame rigidity, figure that 10 percent will be lost in the cutting. No frame bracing is needed with board sheathing.

Gypsum Board. Sometimes called exterior Sheetrock, blacktop, or plasterboard, gypsum board sheathing is rotproof, fireproof, and can withstand considerable wetting. Commonly manufactured in 2-×-8-foot sheets, ½ inch thick and tongued and grooved along its long edges, it is quickly and easily nailed in place. Frame corners must be braced. The gypsum has very little insulating value and requires special nails to hold shingles. Nevertheless, it is the least expensive of modern-day sheathing. Its poor insulating qualities can be easily offset by using more insulation between the studs.

Insulating Sheathing. Light in weight, easily applied, sheathing made of polystyrene, polyurethane, isocyanurates and Styrofoam (a Dow trademark) have R ratings ranging from 3 to 8. This is their plus. On the negative side, corners must be braced and the sheathing is combustible. This presents a fire and smoke hazard if not properly installed.

Plywood. Construction-grade plywood is probably the most used sheathing, although it is not the least expensive in material cost. It goes up fast, requires no corner bracing, and takes ordinary nails very well. Use ⅜-inch panels and take care to stick with building designs that are multiples of the standard 4-foot width of the panels. If you don't, a

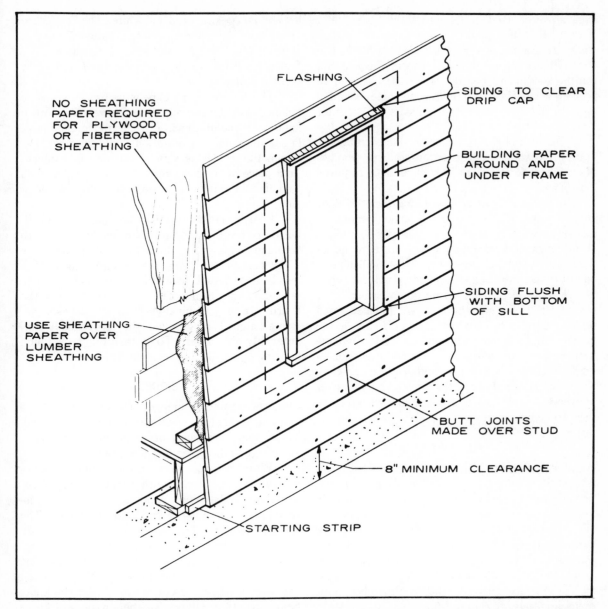

Fig. 7-5. Sheathing, building paper, and clapboard (bevel) siding are applied over a wood building frame. Note how the siding butts up against the frame of the window.

considerable quantity of plywood can be wasted.

Subflooring. Your prime decision is choosing the type of finished floor surface you want. If you are going to install a wood floor, you must lay down a subfloor. If you are going to use carpet or tile,

omit the subfloor. The floor you lay down is the only floor.

Subflooring can consist of square-edged, 1-inch boards nominally 4 or 6 inches wide. They are spaced about ⅛ of an inch apart and can be laid at a right angle or 45 degrees across the floor joists. Bear in mind that the 4-inch boards are 3⅝ inches wide, and that the 6-inch boards are only 5⅝ inches wide. Figure an additional 5 percent waste if you run the subflooring boards straight across, and 10 percent waste if you run them at an angle. Running them at an angle supposedly makes for a firmer floor.

The alternative to the square-edged subflooring is plywood. Use construction-grade plywood ⅜ of an inch thick. It is more expensive, but it requires less work.

In the above we are assuming that the floor joists are spaced the usual 16 inches on centers. If this spacing is increased by using larger floor joists or prefabricated floor joists, you have to go to thicker plywood. Just how much thicker will depend upon the increase in spacing and your local code.

When you plan on laying down carpeting or resilient tile, you can eliminate the finished wood flooring and lay your carpet or tile directly on the subflooring (which becomes the one and only flooring). In such instances, you cannot use square-edged boards or ⅜-inch plywood. You have to go to a nominal 1-inch plywood floor and an even thicker plywood panel if your floor joists are spaced more than 16 inches apart.

FLOORING

Wood-strip flooring is the most popular flooring. It is beautiful, long lasting, and easily maintained. Some seven different kinds of wood are commonly used to make flooring. They are maple, oak, beech, birch, pecan, fir, and pine. The first five are hardwoods and most desirable. The last two are softwood and are only used when and where low cost is the major consideration. Maple is used most often for sport surfaces. Oak is first choice for residential use. See Fig. 7-6.

Grades, Widths, Waste. The seasoned lumber is machine cut into tongue and grooved strips, graded, and packed into bundles. Each bundle is tagged with the specific number of *nominal* square feet of flooring contained. No bundle contains pieces less than 9 inches long.

There are four grades of unfinished oak floor-

ing and two colors—red and white. The first grade is called Clear, the second is called Select & Better. The third is called No. 1 Common. The fourth grade is No. 2 Common; this grade may contain a mixture of red and white boards.

The better, more expensive grades come in bundles with longer pieces and have fewer or no knots or discolorations. The cheaper grades have knots and some discoloration. The difference between the grades is almost entirely appearance. Your place of purchase should be able to show you samples of the flooring so you can make your decision.

Boards ¾ of an inch thick are most often used, but there are thinner hardwood flooring boards to be found. Widths range from 1½ to 3¼ inches. The wider boards cost more, but require considerably less labor to install. In addition, there is less waste with the wider board. There is waste because the boards are only nominally 1½ to 3¼ inches wide. Being tongued and grooved, they are actually considerably narrower. To determine how much flooring you will need, consult Table 7-2.

SIDING

Siding is the outermost layer of material placed on a building. Years ago, wood was the only siding used. Today there are many other materials that have advantages other than just low price.

Wood Siding. Made in the form of strips of various widths, some with tongue and groove, some simply beveled, wood siding is always fastened atop sheathing of one kind or another. The wider boards have less waste, go up faster, but are more expensive. If you use expensive cedar you can seal and stain, which is easier than the painting needed for pine. If you purchase the cheapest wood-strip siding, be certain to shellac the knots before painting. Otherwise their rosin will bleed through.

Wood siding might appear simple to install, but it takes skill and experience to fit the boards properly and make tight joints. We don't suggest a beginner try their hand at installing wood siding.

Plywood. If you prefer, you can eliminate the sheathing completely by using plywood for your

Guide to Hardwood Flooring Grades

A brief grade description for comparison only.

NOFMA flooring is bundled by averaging the lengths. A bundle may include pieces from 6 inches under to 6 inches over the nominal length of the bundle. No piece shorter than 9 inches admitted. The percentages under 4 ft. referred to apply on total footage in any one shipment of the item. ¾ inch added to face length when measuring length of each piece.

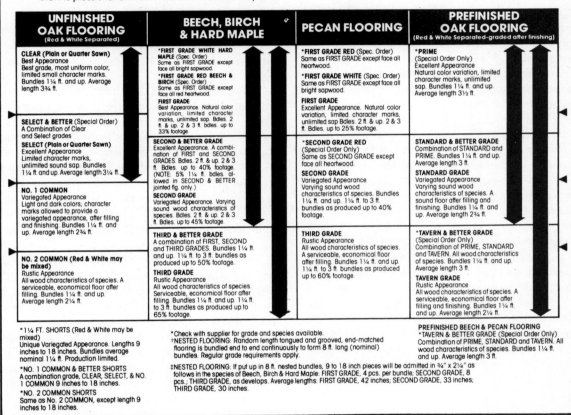

UNFINISHED OAK FLOORING (Red & White Separated)	BEECH, BIRCH & HARD MAPLE	PECAN FLOORING	PREFINISHED OAK FLOORING (Red & White Separated—graded after finishing)
CLEAR (Plain or Quarter Sawn) Best Appearance. Best grade, most uniform color, limited small character marks. Bundles 1¼ ft. and up. Average length 3¾ ft.	***FIRST GRADE WHITE HARD MAPLE** (Spec. Order) Same as FIRST GRADE except face all bright sapwood. ***FIRST GRADE RED BEECH & BIRCH** (Spec. Order) Same as FIRST GRADE except face all red heartwood. **FIRST GRADE** Best Appearance. Natural color variation, limited character marks, unlimited sap. Bdles. 2 ft. & up. 2 & 3 ft. bdles. up to 33% footage.	***FIRST GRADE RED** (Spec. Order) Same as FIRST GRADE except face all heartwood. ***FIRST GRADE WHITE** (Spec. Order) Same as FIRST GRADE except face all bright sapwood. **FIRST GRADE** Excellent Appearance. Natural color variation, limited character marks, unlimited sap Bdles. 2 ft. & up. 2 & 3 ft. Bdles. up to 25% footage.	***PRIME** (Special Order Only) Excellent Appearance. Natural color variation, limited character marks, unlimited sap. Bundles 1¼ ft. and up. Average length 3½ ft.
SELECT & BETTER (Special Order) A Combination of Clear and Select grades **SELECT (Plain or Quarter Sawn)** Excellent Appearance. Limited character marks, unlimited sound sap. Bundles 1¼ ft. and up. Average length 3¼ ft.	**SECOND & BETTER GRADE** Excellent Appearance. A combination of FIRST and SECOND GRADES. Bdles. 2 ft. & up. 2 & 3 ft. Bdles. up to 40% footage. (NOTE: 5% 1¼ ft. bdles. allowed in SECOND & BETTER jointed flg. only.) **SECOND GRADE** Variegated Appearance. Varying sound wood characteristics of species. Bdles. 2 ft. & up. 2 & 3 ft. Bdles. up to 45% footage.	***SECOND GRADE RED** (Special Order Only) Same as SECOND GRADE except face all heartwood. **SECOND GRADE** Variegated Appearance Varying sound wood characteristics of species. Bundles 1¼ ft. and up. 1¼ ft. to 3 ft. bundles as produced up to 40% footage.	**STANDARD & BETTER GRADE** Combination of STANDARD and PRIME. Bundles 1¼ ft. and up. Average length 3 ft. **STANDARD GRADE** Variegated Appearance Varying sound wood characteristics of species. A sound floor after filling and finishing. Bundles 1¼ ft. and up. Average length 2¾ ft.
NO. 1 COMMON Variegated Appearance. Light and dark colors; character marks allowed to provide a variegated appearance, after filling and finishing. Bundles 1¼ ft. and up. Average length 2¾ ft.	**THIRD & BETTER GRADE** A combination of FIRST, SECOND and THIRD GRADES. Bundles 1¼ ft. and up. 1¼ ft. to 3 ft. bundles as produced up to 50% footage. **THIRD GRADE** Rustic Appearance All wood characteristics of species. Serviceable, economical floor after filling. Bundles 1¼ ft. and up. 1¼ ft. to 3 ft. bundles as produced up to 65% footage.	**THIRD GRADE** Rustic Appearance All wood characteristics of species. A serviceable, economical floor after filling. Bundles 1¼ ft. and up. 1¼ ft. to 3 ft. bundles as produced up to 60% footage.	***TAVERN & BETTER GRADE** (Special Order Only) Combination of PRIME, STANDARD and TAVERN. All wood characteristics of species. Bundles 1¼ ft. and up. Average length 3 ft. **TAVERN GRADE** Rustic Appearance All wood characteristics of species. A serviceable, economical floor after filling and finishing. Bundles 1¼ ft. and up. Average length 2¼ ft.
NO. 2 COMMON (Red & White may be mixed) Rustic Appearance. All wood characteristics of species. A serviceable, economical floor after filling. Bundles 1¼ ft. and up. Average length 2¼ ft.			

*1¼ FT. SHORTS (Red & White may be mixed) Unique Variegated Appearance. Lengths 9 inches to 18 inches. Bundles average nominal 1¼ ft. Production limited.

*NO. 1 COMMON & BETTER SHORTS A combination grade, CLEAR, SELECT, & NO. 1 COMMON 9 inches to 18 inches.

*NO. 2 COMMON SHORTS Same as No. 2 COMMON, except length 9 inches to 18 inches.

*Check with supplier for grade and species available.

†NESTED FLOORING: Random length tongued and grooved, end-matched flooring is bundled end to end continuously to form 8 ft. long (nominal) bundles. Regular grade requirements apply.

‡NESTED FLOORING: If put up in 8 ft. nested bundles, 9 to 18 inch pieces will be admitted in ¾" x 2¼" as follows in the species of Beech, Birch & Hard Maple: FIRST GRADE, 4 pcs. per bundle; SECOND GRADE, 8 pcs.; THIRD GRADE, as develops. Average lengths: FIRST GRADE, 42 inches; SECOND GRADE, 33 inches; THIRD GRADE, 30 inches.

PREFINISHED BEECH & PECAN FLOORING *TAVERN & BETTER GRADE (Special Order Only) Combination of PRIME, STANDARD and TAVERN. All wood characteristics of species. Bundles 1¼ ft. and up. Average length 3 ft.

Fig. 7-6. A guide to hardwood flooring. Courtesy National Oak Flooring Manufacturer's Association.

Table 7-2. Computing Required Wood Flooring.

Desired floor area in square feet				
Plus	55%	when using	¾ × 1½"	flooring
Plus	42½%	when using	¾ × 2"	flooring
Plus	38½%	when using	¾ × 2¼"	flooring
Plus	29%	when using	¾ × 3¼"	flooring

Includes allowance for side and end matching, plus an additional 5% for normal waste.

siding. Plywood is manufactured in thicknesses of ⅜ to 19/32 of an inch and in panels 4 × 8, and 10 feet. Whether you can use the "thin" siding or have to go to the "thicker" siding depends on your local code. Without the sheathing, even the thicker plywood siding still offers a considerable savings in labor and material. The plywood is offered in a number of surfaces—bare, prefinished, smooth, stirated, etc.

Building paper is not needed when the plywood is used over sheathing, when the joints are shiplapped, or when the joints are covered by battens. When square-butt joints are used and the panels are applied directly to the studs, building paper must be used.

Application of single-layer plywood siding is uncomplicated. The sheets are marked 16 inch O.C. or 24 inch O, indicating the maximum stud spacing permitted with that particular sheet.

Hardboard Siding. Hardboard is a kind of wood made by reducing chips of wood to fiber and then molding the fibers into a board with the aid of high pressure. Hardboard siding is made in lapboard and panel dimensions. Both are available in range of thicknesses of ⅜ through 9/16 of an inch. The lapboards are 16 feet long and come in widths of 6, 8, and 9 inches. The panels are 4 × 8 and 9 feet.

A large range of surface textures are available including smooth, wood-grained, V-grooved, and imitation wood shingle. The lap and panels can be obtained unpainted, primed, and or painted in any of a number of colors. The paint is guaranteed for 5 years and the board itself is guaranteed for 25 years.

The lap siding can be applied over sheathing or directly to the studs (which cannot be more than 16 inches on center). The same may be done with the panels. In both cases, it is advisable to brace the corners when the sheathing is not rigid. It is also advisable to cover the studs with a continuous moisture barrier to prevent moisture from the interior of the building reaching the hardboard.

SHINGLES

Shingles can be a form of siding. They differ only in dimensions and in that shingles are never fastened directly to the studs. They are always fastened atop sheathing of one kind or another.

Asbestos Cement. Called siding shingles, because they are not used for roofing, asbestos cement shingles are durable, reasonably attractive, and can withstand the elements for many, many years. They do lose their color and they do get dirty. Some homeowners wash them down. Most just let the shingles turn dark grey.

The most-used size shingle is 12 × 24 inches and 5/32 of an inch thick. Given the recommended exposure, you need 57 shingles to cover 100 square feet of wall surface.

Asbestos shingles are fireproof, have almost no insulating value, but are the least expensive of all the shingles used for siding. You need a special shingle cutter to cut them, and building paper strips must be positioned under them.

Shakes and Shingles. Shakes and shingles are alike in that both can be used for roofing as well as siding, and both are usually made of wood (generally cedar). Shakes have a rough texture on one or both sides. Shingles have machine-cut surfaces that can be smooth or grooved.

Most building codes prohibit the use of shingles or shakes when the building includes a wood-burning fireplace. Codes that do permit fireplaces require special protective devices to prevent sparks from landing on the roof.

Neither cedar shingles nor shakes need to be painted. Left bare they can resist the weather for 50 to 100 years, but they will darken with time and sometimes warp. If there is considerable shade, moss will grow on the cedar and eventually destroy the wood.

Shingles and shakes are expensive and time consuming to apply. They are nailed in place one at a time and require cutting and fitting at corners and fenestrations.

Grades and Dimensions. Shingles come in four grades and lengths ranging from 16 to 24 inches. The top grade has no knots. The bottom grade has loose knots. The longer shingles cost more, but you need fewer of them. In place, one grade will last just as long as another, and appearance is just a matter of taste.

Shakes range in length from 15 to 24 inches and are graded according to method of manufacture (hand split, taper sawn) and butt thickness. The thicker, rougher shakes provide the more rustic appearance.

Prepainted Shingles. Prepainted shingles can be purchased simply primed or with one or two coats of paint following the prime. If you want painted shingles, the best compromise is the primed shingles. Priming seals the wood. If you apply paint directly to unprimed shingles, the wood soaks up copius quantities of paint.

ALUMINUM SIDING

Aluminum siding has been available for 30 years. So far, some 10 million homes have been sided with aluminum.

Aluminum doesn't rust in the ordinary sense. Its baked-on paint finish lasts from 20 to 40 years, depending upon the grade you purchase. Aluminum doesn't rot, split, warp, or crack.

Many Styles. Aluminum strip siding is made in many colors, finishes, two gauges and most often in a single width of 8 inches. See Fig. 7-7. The two gauges are called thick and thin. The thick gauge is 0.24 of an inch thick. The thin gauge is 0.019 of an inch thick. The difference in price and insulating qualities are small. If you are planning to work alone, opt for the thick gauge because it is stiffer and easier to handle.

In addition to the single-width, 8-inch panel, there is the double-4, which is one 8-inch panel with a crease down the middle so that it looks like two 4-inch lengths of clapboard. There are also clapboardlike panels with 5-inch exposure, 9-inch exposure and two bevel edges to give the appearance of two strips of bevel-edge siding.

For vertical application, aluminum siding is available in the same number of colors and finishes and is manufactured in 10-, 12-, and 16-inch board and batten strips, plus V-groove styles.

All siding is sold on the basis of exposure. Thus a box marked 2 squares will cover 200 square feet of wall. Some companies make their siding 13 feet long and others make their siding 12½ feet long. A box holding double-4 or single-8 panels will cover equal amounts of wall area.

Insulation. The aluminum panel by itself has an R value of only 1.24. When you back up the panels with polystyrene insulation, plus two layers of reflective aluminum foil, you get an R factor that reaches 6.0. The insulation fits into the space behind the aluminum panels. See Fig. 7-8.

Installation. The installation of aluminum panels is relatively simple. The soft metal can be cut with a pair of tin snips or a power saw. The end of one panel slips into either a clip or the end of another panel, depending upon the system the manufacturer uses. The only point to bear in mind is that the panels *hang* from their nails. The nails are not driven home; they are spaced a fraction of an inch to permit the panels to expand and contract with temperature changes. Panel edges fit into J-channels or starter strips or other preformed accessories. See Fig. 7-9.

The Hard Part. The tough part is covering the trim with metal. The trim includes the windows, door frames, the fascia, and the soffit.

Coil stock, which is a roll of sheet aluminum, is cut to size and then bent to shape on a brake. This is a sheet-metal bending device. The cut and shaped pieces of metal are nailed in place atop the trim. This protects the trim from wear and eliminates the need to paint the wood.

Soffit and fascia are covered with preformed strips of metal (bent and perforated as required). This is easier than covering the trim, but still lots more difficult than simply applying the siding. See Figs. 7-10, 7-11, and 7-12.

For more information on aluminum siding and its application, write to the Aluminum Association, 818 Connecticut Ave. N.W., Washington, DC 20006, for a copy of their brochure.

VINYL SIDING

Vinyl siding (to be chemically exact, polyvinyl chloride), sometimes called PVC formed-strip siding, is made by molding and extruding the thermoplastic into the required shapes. It is made in at least six pale colors and in various architectural styles and surfaces. Most common shapes are the 8-inch and the double 4-inch formats for horizontal

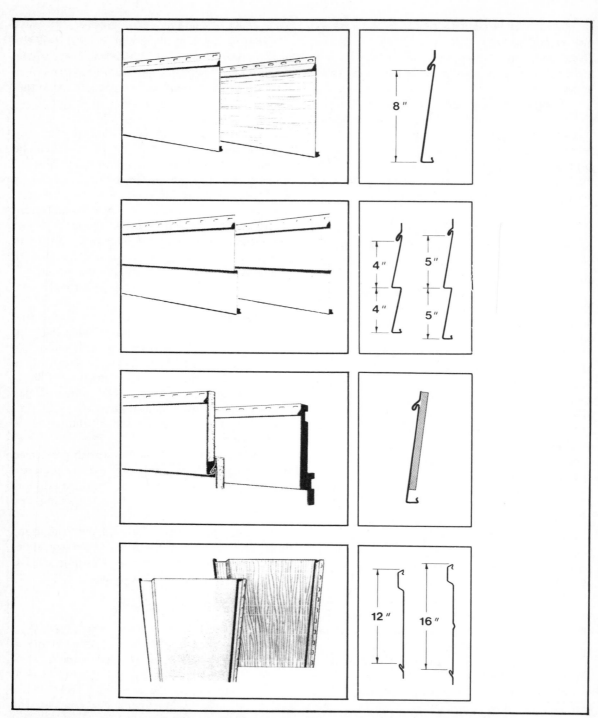

Fig. 7-7. Popular aluminum siding styles and their major dimensions. Courtesy The Aluminum Association.

application, and a number of beveled and board and batten widths for vertical application.

The panels are usually 12 feet 6 inches long when designed for horizontal use and the vertical panels are usually 10 feet long. Both are 9 inches wide. Sufficient paneling to cover 100 square feet weighs about 45 pounds, and generally the panels are boxed in quantities sufficient to cover 2 squares.

Essentially, the application of plastic-strip

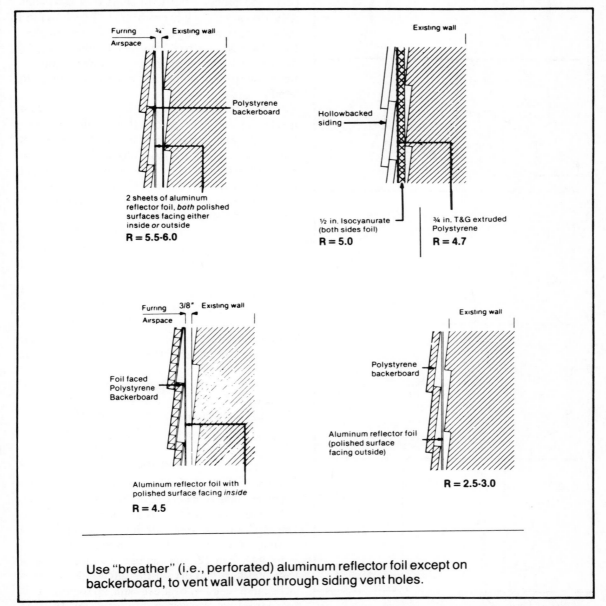

Use "breather" (i.e., perforated) aluminum reflector foil except on backerboard, to vent wall vapor through siding vent holes.

Fig. 7-8. Various combinations of aluminum siding and insulation and the resulting R factors. Courtesy The Aluminum Association.

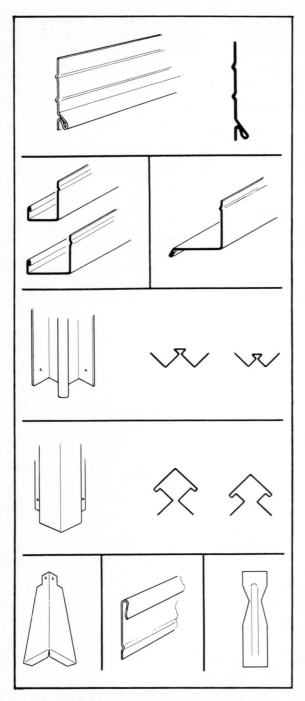

Fig. 7-9. Prefabricated accessories used to install aluminum strip siding. Courtesy The Aluminum Association.

siding to a structure is identical to the procedure and techniques used with aluminum (with a few small differences). A little more space must be provided around the nails to allow for greater dimensional changes with temperature. The panels cannot be properly cut with snips or a saw when they are very cold. It is much more difficult to form the coil stock into angles and channels to cover the trim. This can only be done when the plastic is at 70 degrees Fahrenheit or more. At lower temperatures, the plastic will crack when you attempt to bend it.

As an insulator the plastic alone has slightly greater insulating properties than aluminum alone. But strips of insulation cannot be glued to the rear of the plastic. There is too much change with temperature for the backer board to remain in place. Sheet insulation and strip insulation can be used behind the plastic siding to achieve the same R factor as is possible with insulated aluminum siding.

Aluminum is soft and can be easily damaged by a baseball or the like. Plastic will rebound without damage in warm weather, but in very cold weather a blow can crack it.

Plastic will sag in time after exposure to high summer temperatures. Plastic will burn when it gets hot enough. Plastic's color runs all the way through. Whether or not plastic siding will maintain its appearance for as long as top-grade aluminum, no one really knows.

For more information about applying vinyl siding write to The Society of the Plastics Industry, Inc., 355 Lexington Ave., New York, NY 10017.

ROOFING

When we speak of roofing we mean the material placed atop the roof deck to improve its appearance and to prevent water from penetrating the building. The pitch of your roof will determine the type of roofing you can use. When the pitch is between 4 and 8 inches in 12, you can use shingles on top of 15-pound felt, laid dry. If the pitch is less than 4 inches in 8, you had best use built-up roofing. This consists of several layers of coated felt that are completely sealed with tar and sometimes stone.

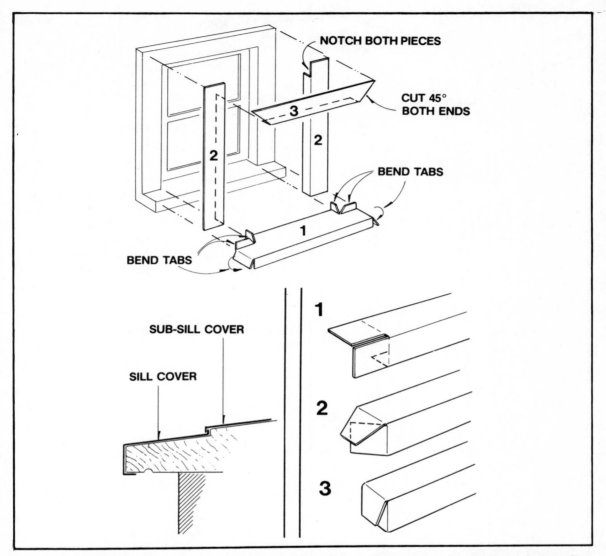

NOTCH BOTH PIECES

CUT 45°
BOTH ENDS

BEND TABS

BEND TABS

SUB-SILL COVER

SILL COVER

Fig. 7-10. The window and door trim can be covered with sheet aluminum cut and bent to size and shape. Courtesy The Aluminum Association.

Asphalt Roofing. Many materials are used for roofing—including metal, wood, and stone—but the roofing material most used (because it is the least expensive and can last 20 or more years) is asphalt-based or fiberglass-based asphalt shingles. Shingles are fire resistant and can be used on homes with wood-burning fireplaces. Shingles bearing the Underwriters Laboratories wind-resistant label can withstand 60 mph winds for at least 2 hours.

Weights. Asphalt roofing is manufactured in various thicknesses and styles, resulting in various weights ranging from 235 pounds per square to 425 pounds per square. In roofing terms, a square is sufficient shingles to cover 100 square feet of roof. In general, the heavier the shingle the more it costs but the longer it lasts. Because application repre-

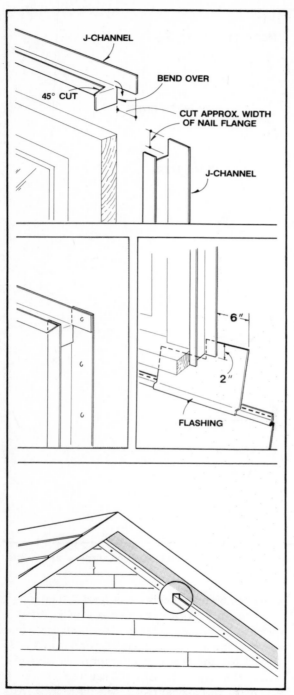

Fig. 7-11. Door frames are trimmed and the siding is brought up under a gable. Courtesy The Aluminum Association.

sents a good portion of roofing costs, the heavier shingles are the wiser choice.

Lumberyards carry asphalt roofing, but it is worth your time to locate a roofing distributor in your area. There is a good chance he will sell directly to you.

INSULATION

Glass fiber batts in 4-inch thicknesses for the walls and 6-inch thicknesses for the ceiling provide the best compromise between insulation costs and results. When you install 6-inch batts, you have to go from 2-×-4 studs to 2-×-6 inch studs. That makes for a considerable difference in lumber costs.

Usually there is no problem in making the ceiling insulation thicker, but in all insulation your savings in heat does not increase proportionately with increasing insulation. If 2 inches will cut your heat bill in half, 4 inches will not cut it in half again, and 8 inches will not reduce heating costs to ⅛. It doesn't work that way because there are other means by which heat escapes from a building. Don't attempt to seal the house completely. You must admit fresh air.

The farther north you go the more insulation you need. The farther south you go the less you need, but you always need some insulation in order to keep cool in the summer. In any case, check locally to find what is most economical in terms of heat savings and material costs in your area.

Don't forget the windows. More heat is lost through the windows than all your walls. You need double glazing (single-airspace storm window) in most areas and triple glazing anywhere you get zero or colder days. See Fig. 7-13.

Installation. The batts are always installed with the impermeable barrier facing the interior of the house. In the case of ceiling insulation, that means the barrier goes on the down side. In the case of floor insulation, the barrier goes on the up side.

There should be no spaces between batt ends and no spaces around obstructions such as gem boxes and pipes. If necessary, a batt can be cut or taken apart and stuffed into a crack. Cutting can be done with a razor knife. If you do the work

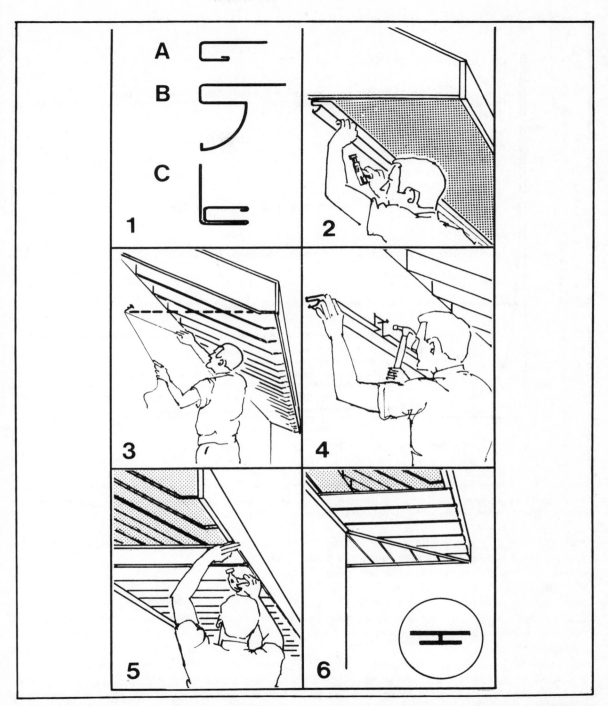

Fig. 7-12. Steps in covering the fascia and soffit. Illustration 1 shows the end views of three of the types of prefabricated accessories that are used with fascias and soffits. Courtesy The Aluminum Association.

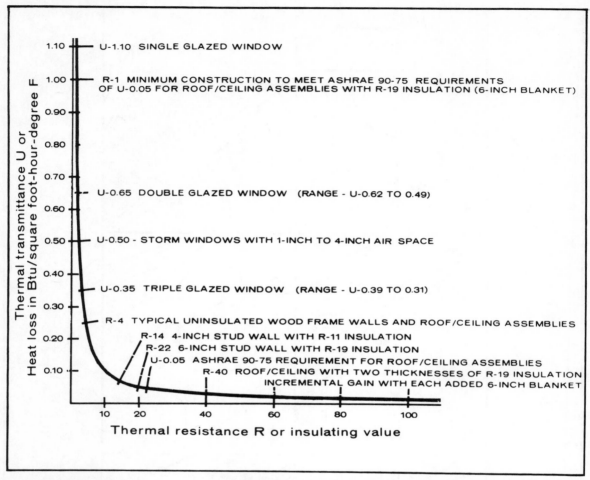

Fig. 7-13. The relationship between thermal transmittance U and the thermal resistance R of various materials. Reducing thermal efficiency below U values of 0.10 becomes increasingly expensive.

yourself—it is not at all difficult—be certain to wear gloves and do not work bare headed or bare armed. The tiny fibers of glass can be very painful.

The batts must be positioned between the studs and the joists. No portion of the batt flange should project beyond the studs or joists because that would interfere with the placement of the Sheetrock.

Loose fill insulation is not as good as the rigid insulation because the fill tends to settle and compact with time. In this way it looses much of its insulating effectiveness. Blown insulation is only used on existing structures; it is literally blown into

the spaces between the studs. See Figs. 7-14, 7-15, and Table 7-3.

CABINETS

Kitchen cabinets are available in a wide range of materials, styles, and prices. You can purchase them from specialty manufacturers, local kitchen cabinetmakers, retail stores, or you can even have a carpenter make them. Although the cabinets look "built in," they are not. They are prefabricated and slipped into place.

We caution you against obtaining the metal

cabinets. The paint chips and wears with time and refinishing is difficult.

We recommend that you forgo the cabinets and replace them with a pantry. This is an old-fashioned, walk-in closet with lots of shelves and a window. The walls of the pantry should be insulated so that you can keep the window open and keep the pantry cool without cooling the balance of the house. A simple 4-×-6-foot pantry can hold several times more cans and what not than several kitchen cabinets. It is a lot easier to find things in the pantry than in the cramped cabinets that rob the kitchen of floor space.

ELECTRICAL WIRING

Inspectors are never lax or lenient where electrical

Fig. 7-14. Rigid-foam insulation fastened to the outside of a low-energy home to restrict heat loss through the foundation.

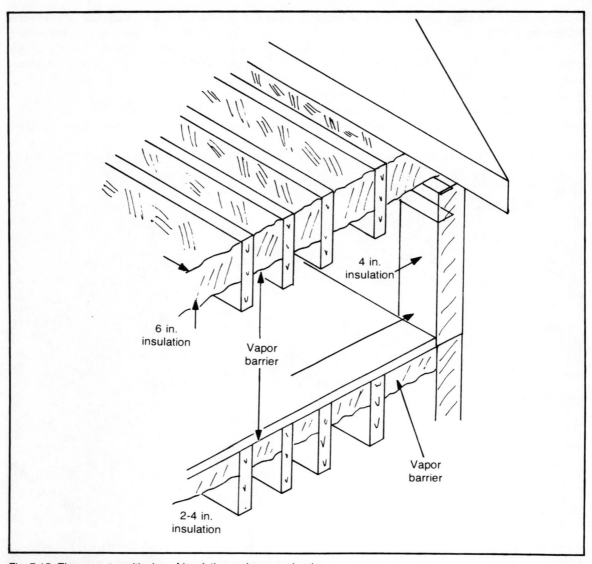

Fig. 7-15. The correct positioning of insulation and a vapor barrier.

6 in.
insulation

Vapor
barrier

4 in.
insulation

2-4 in.
insulation

Vapor
barrier

wiring is concerned. They demand the work adhere to the code to the letter of the law. Most municipalities insist that a licensed electrician do the work, and that the inspector be given the time necessary for his inspection before the walls are closed in. That means before the Sheetrock or panels are installed and the wires are hidden. Some municipalities insist that the inspector makes a second visit before the gem box covers are positioned. A gem box is a metal box in which connections are made.

Outlets. Sometimes called receptacles, outlets are female plugs or connectors that accept the male plug connected to the end of an appliance wire. We have all seen these things and have used them thousands of time, but perhaps you have never

Table 7-3. R Values of Common Building Materials.

	R
Solid concrete	.08/inch
Stone	.08/inch
Std. Concrete block	.105/inch
Light Concrete block	.156/inch
Common brick	.205/inch
Face brick	.113/inch
Stucco	.20/inch
Plastic vapor barrier	.00/inch
Building paper	.06/per single layer
Gypsum board	.879/inch
Sand plaster	.30/inch
Insulating plaster	i.50/inch
Ceiling tile	2.40/inch
Fiberboard sheathing	2.90/inch
Plywood	1.30/inch
Softwood sheathing	1.13/inch
Roll roofing	.15 per single layer
Asphalt shingles	.16 per layer
Wood shingles	.86 per layer
Tile or slate shingles	.08 per layer
Glass fiber batt	2.75/inch
Rock wool batt	3.6/inch
Glass fiber loose fill	2.2/inch
Rock wool loose fill	2.75/inch
Celluosic fiber loose	3.6/inch
Enclosed air	.25/inch
Foamglas	2.63/inch
Styrofoam batt	5.0/inch
Polystyrene batt	5.0/inch
Isocyanurate batt	5.0/inch
Single-weight glass	.13
Double glazed ½-inch air space	1.72
Metal edge insulating glass	1.85

Note: R factors vary in some materials with thickness. Generally, doubling the thickness doubles the R value, but not in all instances.

called them by either of these two names before. Outlets are generally dual; they will accept two plugs simultaneously. Some outlets combine a switch and a single outlet (the switch controlling the outlet). Some also incorporate a small light. The light goes on when the switch is in the on position.

Every outlet, single, dual, switched or multiple (four or even six), is always mounted on a gem box. The gem box is a small metal box, generally 3 × 2½ × 3½ inches in size. See Table 7-4. It is fastened with nails to the side of a stud and positioned so that its front surface is about ¼ inch shy of the front surface of the finished wall. Naturally, a rectangular hole has to be cut through the Sheetrock or the panel to accommodate the gem box. Gem boxes that will be used for floor appliances such as vacuum cleaners and the like are centered 12 inches above the finished floor. Gem boxes positioned above a countertop are usually 8 inches above the top.

Electrical cables are connected permanently to the gem boxes. The wires comprising the cables are brought into the box, skinned, and connected to the outlet. The wires are looped under the screws; take care to connect the white wire to the nickle-plated terminal and the black wire (covering) to the copper terminal. The third wire of the cable—the wire that has no insulation—is the ground wire. This goes to the ground connection on the outlet.

The wires are then folded back upon themselves, and the outlet is forced into position and held in place by two screws through its ears. When the cover plate is positioned, the gem box and the clearance space around it is covered.

The purpose of this entire arrangement is that the connections—the wires-to-the-screws connections—are made inside a metal box. If they come apart, the chance of a fire produced by an electrical spark is reduced. When and where two cables have to be connected to one another, the connection must also be made in a gem box or a junction box.

Junction Boxes. Junction boxes are metal boxes. They are designed primarily for connecting one cable to one or more cables. Today, connections are always made with the aid of wire nuts. Wires are no longer soldered and taped. The ends of the two or more wires to be joined are scraped clean, twisted together, cut at an angle, and then the insulated wire nut is run up and finger tightened. What is important here is that the correct size nut is used. There is a range of nuts available so it is no problem to match wire nut size to the number of wires and their sizes. The nut must run up tight and its insulated skirt must overlap the insulation on the wires so that no bare wire is visible.

Running Cable. The code does not limit the

Table 7-4. Standard Gem/Junction Box Dimensions.

Box Dimension, Inches Trade Size or Type	Min. Cu. In. Cap.	Maximum Number of Conductors				
		#14	#12	#10	#8	#6
4 × 1¼ Round or Octagonal	12.5	6	5	5	4	0
4 × 1½ Round or Octagonal	15.5	7	6	6	5	0
4 × 2⅛ Round or Octagonal	21.5	10	9	8	7	0
4 × 1¼ Square	18.0	9	8	7	6	0
4 × 1½ Square	21.0	10	9	8	7	0
4 × 2⅛ Square	30.3	15	13	12	10	6*
4 11/16 × 1¼ Square	25.5	12	11	10	8	0
4 11/16 × 1½ Square	29.5	14	13	11	9	0
4 11/16 × 2⅛ Square	42.0	21	18	16	14	6
3 × 2 × 1½ Device	7.5	3	3	3	2	0
3 × 2 × 2 Device	10.0	5	4	4	3	0
3 × 2 × 2¼ Device	10.5	5	4	4	3	0
3 × 2 × 2½ Device	12.5	6	5	5	4	0
3 × 2 × 2¾ Device	14.0	7	6	5	4	0
3 × 2 × 3½ Device	18.0	9	8	7	6	0
4 × 2⅛ × 1½ Device	10.3	5	4	4	3	0
4 × 2⅛ × 1⅞ Device	13.0	6	5	5	4	0
4 × 2⅛ × 2⅛ Device	14.5	7	6	5	4	0
3¾ × 2 × 2½ Masonry Box/gang	14.0	7	6	5	4	0
3¾ × 2 × 3½ Masonry Box/gang	21.0	10	9	8	7	0
FS—Minimum Internal Depth 1¾ Single Cover/Gang	13.5	6	6	5	4	0
FD—Minimum Internal Depth 2⅜ Single Cover/Gang	18.0	9	8	7	6	3

number of junction boxes that may be used. However, the code is strict about the position of each box. Each box must be readily accessible. It cannot be covered by Sheetrock or wall panels. Thus a well-planned electrical job has very few junction boxes. Almost all the cables "run home" (all the way down to the fuse box or switching panel without a break).

Number of Outlets. The minimum number of outlets required is such that no plug-in electrical device need have a cord more than 6 feet in length. There is no limit to the maximum number of outlets other than their cost. See Fig. 7-16 for an example of how this 6-foot rule applies.

Wall Switches. Wall switches are mounted in gem boxes. Usually the wall switch is centered 48 inches above the finished floor.

Dimmers. Dimmers fit neatly into gem boxes, but they cannot be used with fluorescent lamps. They can only be used with incandescent lamps.

CHOICE OF CABLE

Two types of electrical wire or cable are used today. The trade name for one is Romex, and another type is generally called BX. Both types consist of two or more solid copper wires covered with plastic insulation, good for 400 volts. The Romex cable is covered with braided cloth dipped in wax or a similar preservative. The BX cable is covered with a continuous band of metal wound in a spiral. Both also contain a bare wire that is used for grounding.

Under ordinary circumstances, the Romex will last the life of the building. Nevertheless, a stray nail can be inadvertently driven through the Romex. Nails cannot be driven through the metalclad BX. See Fig. 7-17. Hungry mice will eat the Romex; they do not fare as well on the metal BX. The BX costs much more than the Romex, but this is one building item that should not be stinted.

Wire Size. The code stipulates that no wire less than No. 14 AWG gauge can be used for power

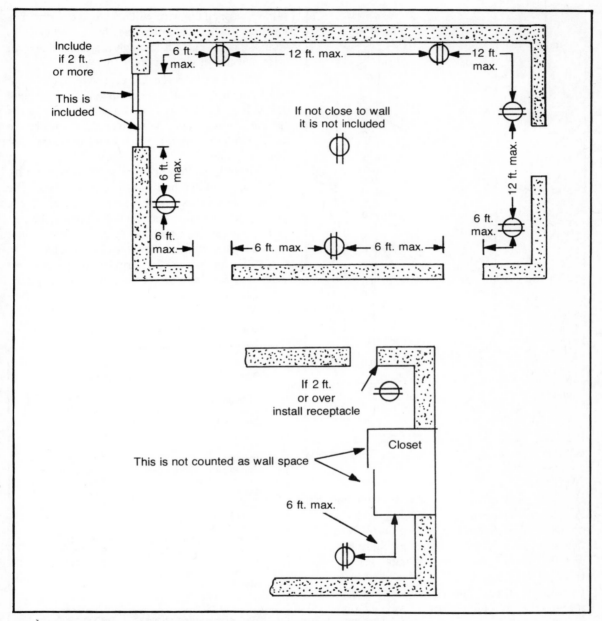

Include if 2 ft. or more

This is included

6 ft. max.

12 ft. max.

12 ft. max.

If not close to wall it is not included

12 ft. max.

6 ft. max.

6 ft. max.

6 ft. max. — 6 ft. max.

12 ft. max.

6 ft. max.

If 2 ft. or over install receptacle

Closet

This is not counted as wall space

6 ft. max.

Fig. 7-16. Basic code regulation concerning the number and placement of outlets.

circuit (lights, etc., smaller wire can be used for bells, thermostats, and the like). The choice of wire size depends upon the electrical current that will be drawn through that wire and the distance between the particular appliance and the main fuse box or switch box. See Table 7-5. No. 14 wire is rated at 15 amperes, continuous. Larger-diameter wires, which are classified by lower numbers, can carry more.

To find the current drawn by any appliance,

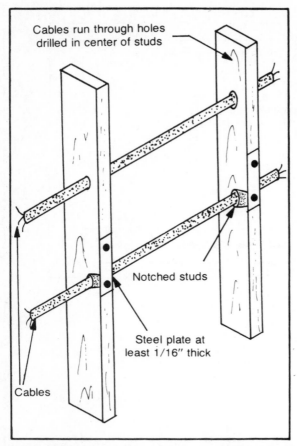

Cables run through holes
drilled in center of studs

Notched studs

Steel plate at
least 1/16″ thick

Cables

Fig. 7-17. Two methods that can be used to protect Romex
from stray nails.

temperature of the wire will not exceed warm. You
can use smaller diameter wire, but it will get hot.
Run sufficient current through the small-diameter
wire and it will get red hot.

120/240 Service Line. Today, most modern public utilities offer their customers a choice of
120-volt or 240-volt service lines. The utility runs
the cable from their pole to the side of your house
and their electric meter. You take it from there. See
Tables 7-6 and 7-7.

There is a difference in cost between the 120-
volt fuse or switch box and the 240-volt box. The
240-volt box costs a little more. You can, if you
prefer, draw nothing but 120 volts from a 240-volt
box or you can draw both as you prefer. You cannot
draw 240 volts from a box that is either connected to
a 120 line or has no 240 provisions. In the first
instances, you have to get the utility to change the
power line. In the second, you may have to change
the box.

Table 7-5. Electricity Drawn by Common Appliances.

Air conditioner	800-1500 watts
Blanket	150-200
Blender	250
Coffeemaker	600-1000
Deep fryer	1200 1650
Dishwasher	600-1000
Dryer, clothes	4000 87000
Food mixer	120-250
Freezer	300-500
Frying pan	1000-1200
Furnace blower	800
Garbage grinder	200-400
Grill	1000-1200
Heat lamp	250
Heater, portable 120 volt	600-1650
Heater, portable, 240 volt	2800-5600
Hot plate, each plate	550-1200
Iron, hand	660-1200
Ironer, machine	1200-1650
Motor ¼ hp	300-400
½ hp	450-600
1 hp	950-1000
Range, oven and all fires	8000-1600
Refrigerator	150-300
Rotisserie	1200-1650
Toaster	200-400
Vacuum cleaner	550-1200
Waffle iron	600-1100
Washing machine	400-800
Water heater	2000-5000

divide the wattage of that appliance by the voltage.
For all practical purposes, the voltage in a residential building is considered to be either 120 or 240.
Actually, the voltage might be anywhere from 110
to 120 or even 125. For our computations, 120/240
is sufficiently accurate.

Assume that you plan to plug in a frying pan and
a deep fryer into the outlet. Together (adding the
minimum wattages) you have 1200 plus 1000, which
gives you a total of 2200 watts. Dividing by 120
gives the current figure of 18.33 amperes. This
would overload No. 14 wire. For this *single* outlet
(which can supply two plug-in appliances), you have
to go to the next larger wire size (No. 12, rated at 20
amperes). Note that safe operation means that the

Table 7-6. Ampacities for Insulated Copper Wire.

AWG	Maximum continuous current in amperes
14	15
12	20
10	30
8	40
6	55
4	70
3	80
3	95
1	110
1/10	125

In a small cottage—that will never draw much more than 15 or so amperes on a single line—there is no need for 240 volts. In a larger home or a home where there might be a hot-water heater, clothes dryer and the like a goodly distance from the fuse box, you need 240 volts. The reason is the cost of copper. For a given wattage, you draw half the amperage and therefore require but half the copper (half the diameter wire). You can't go under No. 14. If you examine the table of recommended minimum wire sizes for various amperage, you can see how quickly wire size goes up (numbers become smaller) as wattage goes up.

Distance to Fuse Box. When electricity flows through a copper conductor, it heats that conductor and loses energy. The longer the wire the more energy that is lost. To compensate for the energy loss, wire size is increased. Ideally, a wire size is selected that will hold energy loss to under 3 percent. In practical terms, if you use undersize wire for the run you will warm the wire and not the dryer (even though the wire size is adequate for the amperage carried). To overcome this loss without spending a fortune on wire, you can go to the higher voltage or you can position your dryer, etc., closer to the fuse box.

Fuses or Switches. There is a tendency among home builders to replace the fuse box with a switch box (actually relay switches). These are automatic switches that open when the current exceeds a preset figure. They are safe, dependable, and comparatively costly. The old fuse box works just as well and just as dependably. A fuse will almost always blow under overload; a switch might stick. In any case, do not use the standard fuse. Use the slow-blow fuse. This fuse will carry the momentary overload produced by two appliances, particularly motors cutting into the line at the same time. They only cost a few pennies more.

Table 7-7. Minimum Wire Size for Various Currents and Distances.

Amperes	Distance in ft.								
	50	75	100	125	150	175	200	250	
15	14	12	10	8	8	6	6	6	
20	12	10	8	8	6	6	6	4	Wire
25	10	8	8	6	6	4	4	4	size
30	10	8	6	6	4	4	4	2	
35	8	6	6	4	4	4	2	2	
40	8	6	6	4	4	2	2	2	
45	8	6	4	4	2	2	2	1	
50	8	6	4	4	2	2	2	1	
55	6	4	4	2	2	2	1	0	
60	6	4	4	2	2	1	1	0	
65	6	4	4	2	1	1	0	2/0	
70	6	4	2	2	1	1	0	2/0	
80	6	4	2	2	1	0	0	2/0	
90	4	2	2	1	0	0	2/0	3/0	
100	4	2	2	1	0	2/0	2/0	3/0	

These are the values most often used for residential BX and Romex wiring. Under special conditions, values may be changed.

Service Line Costs. It is common for the utility not to charge for connecting your home to their power line, but only if they can make the connection directly from their line. If they have to install one or more poles because you are so far away from their power line, they will charge you for it. They will also charge extra if they have to run their power lines underground in ditches you dig for them. The reason is that the cable must be water resistant, and it is therefore more costly.

DEALING WITH ELECTRICIANS

Electricians very often price a job by the number of outlets they will have to install. From the contractor's point of view this is convenient. He can count the number of outlets, multiply by the cost per and come up with his electrical costs. But you have to make certain that the number of outlets are correct—figure each gem box and outlet—and that the figure includes everything else—wire, cable, fuse box, etc.

You also have to make certain that the print has the required outlets and switches and that the heavy-duty appliances, which require more than No. 14 wire, are indicated and will be taken into consideration. You should at this time pencil in red any additional switches, outlets, and the line you may want.

If you wait until the contractor has started the job, you will find the price of the additional outlets, etc., has gone up. Also make certain that the contractor understands that the electrical work also includes connecting the bells, the thermostat, the oil burner, and the like. Get it all in writing.

ELECTRICAL FIXTURES

Like bathroom fixtures and kitchen cabinets, electrical fixtures can be had in a wide variety of styles and prices. You can select them from showroom catalogs, visit the showrooms, or even leave the selection to the electrician. The latter is the more expensive route. In any case, connecting and installing the fixtures is part and parcel of the electrical contract.

Chapter 8

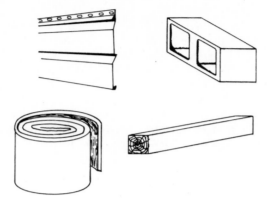

Working With Subcontractors

AS THE BUILDER YOU ARE THE PRIME CONTRAC-
tor. Those who work for you become subcontractors. In the course of erecting your home, you will
work with a dozen different subs representing as
many different building trades. The following is the
most important part of this book.

Subcontractors are subcontractors because
they relish their independence. They are self-
employed businessmen. Some have trucks and
crews and others have little more than a wheelbar-
row. They will try to sell their services for as much
as possible. Because their work is seasonal, they
will try to sign up as much work as possible, and
then hop from one job to another. This is how they
try to stretch their season and not be idle when it
rains. They will treat you with reasonable fairness
and expect to be treated the same way. You can
argue with them and cajole them, but you shouldn't
insult them. They are not under your thumb and
they are not your employees. Get them angry and
they will walk off the job and tell you to go stick it.
Losing money doesn't bother them. They won't put
up with abuse for the sake of a few hundred dollars.

CONTRACT VERSUS DAY RATE

In the process of gathering the information you
require to build your home, you might realize that
when you hire a subcontractor, and he hires a crew,
you are paying for his time and profit as well as for
that of the men he puts on the job.

It is penny-wise and dollar-foolish to hire a
craftsman to do a job when you have no experience
with the work. This is not to imply, for example,
that the carpenter who works directly for you will
do less than he will when he is working for a carpenter boss. He will do the same, but the results
will be less because you do not know (at this point)
how to keep him busy and how to program his work.
At the same time, without experience in the trade
you have no way of knowing his efficiency. Dili-
gence and effort do not automatically produce results. In most instances, you are well advised to
contract your labor on a per-job basis rather than on
time.

WRITE IT DOWN

You might encounter some contractors who are

accustomed to working with no more than a handshake. They might be insulted if you ask for a written agreement (a contract). They might be honest and they might be dependable, but people do forget. Don't do business on a verbal agreement. Get it in writing.

You can write the contract and you both can sign or he can write it up and you both can sign. Photocopies are fine, and you don't need a lawyer. Straight, plain English is all you need.

The following are some examples of contract wording you can use as a guide. Copy the guidelines or alter them as you see fit.

Excavation. The Ace excavating company herewith agrees to do the following work on the property known as 12 Tinker Street, lots 50 and 51, Elton Township, said property now owned by Mr. Joe Doe.

To clear the land leaving only those trees marked with a white X.

To remove the topsoil to uncover a area approximately 50 feet by 60 feet.

To pile the topsoil to one side of the property.

To excavate a flat-bottomed hole approximately 45 × 50 feet in size to a depth of 8 feet below existing grade.

To hold the bottom of the hole level to plus or minus 4 inches without replacing any soil.

To pile the removed soil to one side, leaving room for construction.

To return to the job site within one week of being called upon to do so to backfill.

To rough grade, with a power machine, to provide a gentle pitch away from the structure.

To replace and machine level the topsoil.

To begin the job on July 5, and continue until the excavation is done.

For the total sum of $800 to be paid according to the following schedule: 10 percent on signing of this contract; 40 percent upon completion of excavation. The balance upon backfilling and replacing the topsoil.

In the event rock too large to be moved is encountered, the rock will be blasted at an additional charge of $30.00 per cubic yard.

The contractor carries all necessary insurance, as required by labor law and local ordinance. The policy numbers are . . . . and is issued by the Atlas Company through their broker Mr. . . . . . .
.

Masonry. The Dependable Masonry Company herewith agrees to construct a masonry footing and foundation on the property known as . . . . . .
. , and belonging to . . . . , as described and detailed in the accompanying blueprint, for a total sum of $3000 for labor alone. All materials are to be supplied by the builder.

The footing shall be constructed of concrete and positioned as indicated on the plot plan.

The foundation shall consist of 10-inch concrete block, laid up in a neat, workmanlike manner, and all joints cleaned and pointed.

The mason will install foundation-wall windows, vents and doors, and provide whatever holes are needed by the other trades.

The foundation shall be capped, as indicated, and foundation bolts installed as indicated.

The exterior of the foundation will be parged with two, ⅜-inch thick layers of mortar cement. Following, when the mortar has dried, the exterior wall will be waterproofed with a trowel-applied layer of asphalt.

The contractor carries all the necessary insurance.

The schedule of payments are as follows, ...

Work is to begin on . . . . and is to be completed within two weeks, barring rain.

Carpentry. The carpentry contract reads the same way, but the requirements are, of course, different.

The Accurate Carpentry Company agrees to erect a wood-frame structure on a foundation provided by Mr. Joe Doe at 12 Tinker Street, lots 50 and 51, Elton Township as per the accompanying blueprint.

The Accurate Carpentry Company will frame the house, lay the subflooring, cover the roof (but will not apply the roofing), sheath the house, install all the windows, hang all the doors, install all the cabinets, install all the locks, install (or build) the stairs, and cut and patch for the plumber.

All work is to be done in a workmanlike manner and meet all local building code requirements.

The siding and the roofing might or might not be let out to the carpenter. In some instances, you can get a better price from people who specialize in siding or roofing.

Finishing. Sometimes called interior carpentry, this work involves putting up and taping the Sheetrock and putting the trim around the windows and doors. Again, this could be let out to one carpenter contractor or individual specialists.

Details. Obviously, we haven't listed every single bit of work that has to be done. It is up to you to review and list everything that has to be done.

Materials. We mention materials specifically at this point rather than farther along because it is common for the builder to purchase the carpentry materials—lumber, shingles, nails, roofing, gutters, leaders, etc.—and supply them to the crews. It is not necessary, but that is the way it is usually done when working with subcontractors.

If you don't have the time to supervise material deliveries, you can write the contracts to include material. In that case, you have to spell out every nail and every board.

Plumbing. The contract calls for good workmanship acceptable to the local plumbing inspector and applicable codes. You can take your plans to the local plumbing supply house and get a bid on all the pipes or you can have the plumber bid the entire job. In either case, you should spell out pipe material, pipe size, the necessary valves, the fixtures you want, and the hot-water system you want.

Heating. If you are going to use gas heat, see your local gas company and have them recommend the Btu size of your heating equipment you need. If you are planning on burning oil, see your local oil supplier. If possible, get them to specify what you need by the way of ducts and radiators, and then put those specs in your contract. Your heating man probably knows from experience what you will need, but it does not harm to double check.

Wells and Water Systems. You cannot get a fixed price on a well because the well digger doesn't know in advance the nature of the ground and the depth to which he will have to drill. He should be able to make a calculated guess based on his experience. To help him come to his decision, you should tell him how much water you expect to need. This will alter the pipe size he puts down and the depth to which he drills.

Water systems—pump, pressure tank, and controls—are often sold as a package. Knowing the quantity of water you expect to need, you can judge the size of the pump you will require to handle it. For the average-size home, you want water to enter at a pressure of about 30 psi (pounds per square inch). Set at this figure, your equipment will swing from 25 to 35 as the pump turns on and off (which will probably be fine).

If your home is a distance above the water pump, you need an additional 1 psi of pressure for every foot the water has to rise to enter your home (0.43 psi for gravity and 0.57 estimated friction loss).

DO SOME CHECKING

Before you sign any contract or hand over any money, take the time to protect yourself by checking on the subcontractor. Make certain the subcontractor actually is established and is not some itinerate mechanic from a neighboring state who will take your advance and scoot.

Get references and check the references. A few phone calls will do it. Did he do the job promised? Did he work on schedule? Is he reliable?

When the deal calls for the subcontractor to supply material as well as labor, demand to know his supplier(s). Phone them and ask if his credit is good. He might be so far in hock that they will take the money (your money) and apply it to old, unpaid bills, and you would have to fight to get your money back.

Check his bank. They won't give you his balance, but they will tell you if he is a depositor and how long he has been with them.

Last, but most important, check with his insurance agent. Are his policies in force? It is very unlikely that something will happen on the job, but if it does and the subcontractor is not insured, you are next on the hit list. You are responsible for a workman getting hurt or a foolish bystander falling into the excavation, etc. Make certain the subcontractor and you are protected.

Beware the "crying" contractor. These are gentlemen who come in with bids way below everyone else—which gives you a nice feeling. But halfway through the job they begin to cry. Their pencil slipped. They made a terrible mistake. They are losing money. They can't finish the job at the agreed-on price.

If you have given them a big advance, you are in trouble. You can't make a contractor swing his hammer any more than you can make a horse drink water. You can holler, you can threaten, or you can even sue if you don't mind waiting your turn in the courts. Your only defense is to be very careful with advance money. Small contractors need and often demand advance money. There is nothing illegit about this, but keep the sum small. If he wants progress payments, pay as he goes along but never let yourself be talked into more than the actual amount of work done and money earned.

Don't split contracts. Hire one contractor to do one specific job. Do not hire two contractors to split the work between them. If contractor number one believes he needs help, let him hire the second man or crew, and let him assume responsibility for the progress of the work.

Don't share work with a contractor. There is a tendency, if you have free time to offer, to do part of the work for the contractor in return for a lower charge. This usually leads to arguments and dissatisfaction. You will believe you are doing more than you are actually doing and he will believe you are doing less. Only two angels can get along under these circumstances.

If you want to lend a hand to speed things up, do so without expecting to be reimbursed. If you want to get paid, state your desires clearly. "I will drive the truck for so much an hour." Don't attempt to do some of the carpentry, while he does the rest, or any similar confusing, indefinite division of work.

BEWARE DISHONEST SUBCONTRACTORS

We are all aware that dishonest persons not only exist in our society but thrive. Unfortunately, you cannot distinguish a dishonest person from an honest person by his or her looks. But you can sometimes recognize them by their ploys. Let me tell you a true contractor story.

I was building two small houses in Mount Kisco, New York. Each was to have 1000 square feet of living space and the projected sale price was, at the time, $12,000. As I worked, a number of people came down the street to ask about the lots, building size, and price. Then they smiled. They were soon to be the proud owners of homes one-third larger for a cost of less than $12,000. Curious, I walked up the street and inspected my competitor's projects. There were three foundations, side by side, each certainly much larger than mine. I was impressed by my competitor's accomplishment.

Approximately two weeks later, the same people came to visit me. They were no longer smiling. "Where was the prime contractor, Mr. White, I believe was his name?" Then some of the subcontractors came by with the same question. Then a representative of the bank. And then the police. Why they believed I would know his whereabouts, I don't know. Eventually, the story became public.

Sometime during the week, Mr. White received a construction mortgage payment on the three buildings. He deposited the money in the Mount Kisco bank. On Friday, he went to a branch of the bank and asked a teller how much he had in his account. I assume the sum was $20,000 or more. He then went to the main office of the bank and withdrew the money.

Returning to the branch, he cashed a check for the same sum. As the teller had just checked White's balance, she did not recheck it. She handed the cash over to Mr. White. Mr. White, by all accounts, placed his family in a trailer and disappeared for parts unknown. The theft was not uncovered until some time during the following week. Mr. White purchased the lots on a subordinate mortgage; he did not pay for them beyond a small down payment. He did not pay any of the subcontractors. He took advances from the three buyers of his three homes, and he bilked the bank out of $40,000.

If my houses were priced to sell for $12,000, his houses should have been priced at $18,000 or $20,000. No one gives away one-third of the total price of anything. Apparently the bargain was so great that no one bothered to check. Double-check all big bargains.

SIGNING THE CONTRACTS

While you are in the planning stages, do *not* sign any contracts. Do not promise the work to any of the contractors at this time. For one thing, you are not absolutely certain that you will go ahead with the work. You are still in the planning and pricing stage. More important, no small contractor can really guarantee his presence at any specific time. No contractor of the size you will deal with will commit himself to a particular starting date. He does not know whether or not he will be free, and he certainly cannot be sure you will need his services at the time you state.

The last thing a contractor wants is open time without employment. You can bet all your subcontractors will assure you of their certain availability. Don't believe them.

Proper Handling. When the four or five subcontractors from whom you requested bids on each of the various crafts check with you—and they will call if they need the work—tell them they are being considered. When you are within two weeks of needing their services, you can call the subcontractor you want to hire and tell him or her you will be ready. If your first choice can't make the schedule, you still have the others to call. This is not unreasonable nor unfair. If any of these people secure work before you call them, they are going to take it. So the game works both ways.

Chapter 9

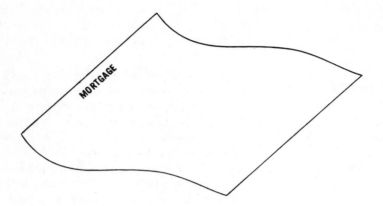

Getting a Mortgage

AT THIS POINT YOU HAVE CHOSEN A PIECE OF PROP-erty and you are fairly certain you can secure it or have made certain it can be held by purchasing an option on the land. You have selected house plans suited to your purse and your land. You have secured firm written bids from all the major subcontractors necessary to the construction of your building. You now believe you know exactly what the building will cost. Chances are that you are under by 10 percent to 15 percent, but you are close enough.

If you walk into a bank empty handed and tell a bank officer that you want to secure a mortgage to build a new home, he or she will say "That's nice," and dismiss you.

You need something tangible to show. You need proof of your ability to organize and direct the construction of a home. What is more important, you are not going to do it yourself with your own little hammer and saw. You have responsible, experienced building tradespeople who will do the actual work. If the bank has the money and you have the income necessary to carry the mortgage loan,

you have a good chance of getting the loan.

FINANCIAL PREPARATION

It is very important that you know exactly where you stand financially before you approach any mortgage lender. If there are any objections, you want to be prepared to counter them in advance.

Putting Your Best Financial Foot Forward. With pencil and paper go over all your assets. Put a dollar value on each and add the total. Include all property, stocks, bonds, jewels, insurance policies, etc.

Now compute your income from wages, interest, etc. If your spouse is working, include these figures too.

Job Record. Banks like borrowers with good, solid records of employment. If you voluntarily left one position for another, you need to state why. It had better be a good reason (more pay, greater opportunity, better company and so on). If you were laid off, you should (if possible) state how quickly you found stable employment elsewhere. The picture you want to present is one of a solid wage earner who doesn't job hop and who—when his employers flounder—doesn't go down with the ship, but soon finds other employment. In short, a hard worker the country needs.

Residence Record. A commitment to employment stability is residential immobility. Banks want borrowers who are rooted and remain rooted. They don't like people who move around very much no more than they care for people who change jobs very often. Explain why if you have had to move recently. There are families that have moved three or four times in one year because a house burned down, a company moved them, and so on. Without a detailed explanation, too many moves and you appear shiftless. At the same time, if you have been at one spot for five or ten years prior to all your moves, be certain to put it down on the application form.

Now make a list of your debts, (total sums, monthly payments). Add these figures. You now know your cash worth and your net income. If you are self-employed, bring along photocopies of your last two income tax returns. If you expect any changes—as for example, you expect to repay a loan shortly—that information should also be noted.

Creating a Credit Rating. If you are one of those rare birds who takes pride in never ever even being one penny in debt, you are in trouble unless you have considerable assets. When you have much more than you seek to borrow, banks never hesitate to lend. One way or another, default and they will get their money back. When you seek to borrow a sum that you plan to repay out of earnings, banks demand a good track record. In financial language, they will only lend to those with a good credit rating. If you have never borrowed, banks do not know how dependable you are when it comes to making payments. They have no way of checking your reliability.

The way out of this trap is simple and inexpensive. Go to your bank and borrow a sum small enough not to worry them. Deposit this sum in a CD or a savings account. Repay the loan promptly. Secure a few credit cards. Buy a few items on the cards. Pay the bills promptly. Your costs will be the

difference between what the loans cost you and what the saving account or CD pays you. In any case, it is a small sum. Now you have a good credit rating. You are a bank's type of customer. You pay your loans promptly. You can be trusted with money.

Clearing up Your Credit. If you buy on credit, if you use credit cards, sooner or later you will get into a hassle with either the credit card company or the seller of the merchandise or service. Errors in billing crop up, checks get lost, bookkeeping personnel goof, and so on. Most of us work too hard and long for our money to simply give it away when there is a discrepancy—so we argue.

If you have experienced any of this confusion, you know it can go on for months and even years. The shop, the company, whatever, argues that you owe them a sum that you deny owing. Meanwhile, this is reflected on your credit report. In the normal course of events, when you and your creditor come to an agreement, your failure to pay will be removed from your credit record. At least it should be.

Should there be any such confusion in your financial history, past or ongoing, it is most important that you know about it. You need to see a copy of your credit report. Before any bank commits itself to a mortgage, they will secure a credit report. If there is a black mark, legit or not, it will be held against you. Know your credit standing. If there is a mark against it, knowing the facts you can approach the bank with your explanation in hand, as it were, and put matters right. Whereas your explanation, "I'm not going to pay the repair shop for a muffler because they never installed a muffler on my car," is understandable and acceptable, a credit report stating that you have failed to pay $63.23 after being dunned for a year and a half doesn't make you appear to be financially reliable.

Securing a Credit Report. The Fair Credit Reporting Act of 1971 affects credit bureaus to the degree that they are supposed to release much of their information. If the credit company refuses to give you a copy of the report, your legal recourse is to the Federal Trade Commission (which you may as well forget because of the time delay). The more

117

practical recourse is to have a friend who is in business write the credit company asking (and paying for) a report. You could have your lawyer do the same. All it generally requires is a business letterhead. You can also ask the bank with which you are a depositor to do the same (assuming you are not yet approaching them for the mortgage).

Clearing up Your Credit. If you are in the process of informal litigation, it is wise to settle even if you believe yourself to be in the right. The way to do this is to approach the creditor and offer to compromise. This cleared up, you can ask the credit company for an updated report. If that is not forthcoming, you can bring along proof in the form of a quit claim from the creditor. This can simply be a note on the company stationary stating the bill is now paid in full, and the misunderstanding has been resolved.

PROCEDURES

Your first step is to decide what type of mortgage you want or what will be best for you: VA, FHA conventional. We cannot outline the factors you have to consider when making this choice, and we cannot provide you with the exact figure. They seem to change from month to month. What may be best for you at one time may not be best for you at another.

The VA Mortgage. First, a Veterans Administration Mortgage is not really a mortgage. It is a government guarantee for the first $27,500 of your mortgage loan. In effect, the government states, "If this person fails to pay, I will pay the bank, $27,500. The balance is your concern." In this way, the U.S. government increases your credit rating by that amount.

Second is that you have to be a veteran and meet the requirements spelled out in Fig. 9-1.

Third, you must contact your Regional VA office and secure an application (Form VA 26-1880).

Fourth is that the form is filled out and mailed or brought to your regional VA office along with a copy of military service. See VA Form 26-1880. The VA office then sends you a letter of eligibility. You bring this letter with you when you apply for a mortgage loan at a bank. Most banks will accept this

guarantee as part of your credit standing and will lend money if everything else meets their approval. They are not legally bound to accept it.

The VA sets a maximum limit on the interest rates that banks can charge VA borrowers. This discourages lenders. Nevertheless lenders (banks) can charge points (one-time fees) high enough to make up the difference in interest rates. Check this out before signing.

The VA loans are assumable. This means that when you sell the house the buyer can assume the existing mortgage at its going rate of interest. Banks do not care for this in times of rising mortgage interests. When a house changes hands, they want to hit the new buyer with a new mortgage at the higher interest rate.

The FHA Mortgage. The FHA mortgage is similar to a VA mortgage in that the government only insures a portion of the money you borrow. A bank does the actual lending. The FHA interest rate is fixed a distance below the current market rate, but the banks are allowed to charge points. This can add up to quite a sum. In one case, a bank charged 15 points when the FHA interest rate was 2½ percent lower than market. On a $100,000 mortgage, 15 points amounts to $15,000.

The procedure consists of finding a bank that is acceptable to the Federal Housing Administration. You then make an application for a loan in the conventional manner by providing the bank with your credit qualifications, plans, and specifications of the proposed building. If the bank accepts your application, they will take it from there and do the paperwork required.

It takes about six weeks to secure a FHA mortgage on an existing residential building. A building loan will take much longer. There will always be sufficient points charged by the bank to make up the difference between a lower rate and current market interest rates.

Conventional Mortgage. A conventional mortgage is simply a loan. It differs from an ordinary loan in several ways. First, the collateral is usually real estate, but it can be anything else. Second, the details of the loan are recorded at the local county clerk's office. Perhaps most important,

INSTRUCTIONS FOR VA FORM 26-1880

READ CAREFULLY BEFORE COMPLETING FORM.
USE TYPEWRITER OR PRINT CLEARLY.
COMPLETE ALL APPLICABLE ITEMS.

A. Privacy Act Information. No Certificate of Eligibility may be issued unless VA receives sufficient information to determine that you are eligible (38 USC 1802). You are not required to furnish the information, including the Social Security Number, but are urged to do so, since it is vital to proper action by VA in your case. Specifically, your Social Security Number is requested under authority of 38 USC 1802 and is requested only if the service department used your Social Security Number as a service number. Failure to provide a completed application will deprive VA of information needed in reaching decisions which could affect you. Any disclosure of the information collected, outside the VA, will only be made as permitted by law or the Privacy Act routine uses.

B. Use this form to request VA to determine your eligibility for Loan Guaranty benefits, and the amount of entitlement available.

C. To establish eligibility based on active military duty during World War II, the Korean conflict or the Vietnam Era, you must have been DISCHARGED OR RELEASED from active duty under conditions other than dishonorable (1) after active duty of 90 days or more any part of which was during the period September 16, 1940, to July 25, 1947, during the period June 27, 1950, to January 31, 1955, or during the period August 5, 1964, to May 8, 1975, or (2) by reason of a service-connected disability from a period of active duty, any part of which occurred during any of the above wartime periods.

D. To establish eligibility based upon active duty after July 25, 1947, and prior to June 27, 1950, after January 31, 1955, and prior to August 5, 1964, or after May 8, 1975, you must have been discharged or released from active duty under conditions other than dishonorable (1) from a period of continuous active duty of 181 days or more all of which occurred after July 25, 1947, and prior to June 27, 1950, or any part of which occurred after January 31, 1955, and prior to August 25, 1964, or after May 8, 1975, or (2) from active duty during such periods for a service-connected disability. In the absence of a discharge or release, you must have served on continuous active duty at least 181 days in active duty status.

E. Unmarried surviving spouses of eligible veterans seeking determination of basic eligibility for VA Loan Guaranty benefits are NOT required to complete this form, but are required to complete VA Form 26-1817 for that purpose.

F. This request should be sent to the VA office serving the area in which you reside.

G. Proof of Military Service. Attach to this request your most recent other than dishonorable discharge or separation papers from active military duty since September 16, 1940, which show active duty dates and type of discharge. If you were separated after January 1, 1950, DD Form 214 must be submitted. You may submit either your original papers or legible copies. In addition, if you are now on active duty submit a statement of service signed by the adjutant or personnel officer or commander of your unit or higher headquarters showing date of entry on your current active duty period and the duration of any time lost. A DD Form 13, Statement of Service, is acceptable for Loan Guaranty purposes. Any Veterans Benefits Counselor in the nearest Veterans Administration Office or Center will assist you in securing necessary proof of military service.

H. Instructions on specific numbered items:

1. Item 4. List all periods of active duty covered by discharges or separation papers from September 16, 1940 to the present. When listing periods of service, start with your latest, or current, period of service on line 4A, and then work back to your earliest service. If you are now on active duty show as the first entry in Item 4 the date you entered on your current active duty period, write the word "Present" in the column headed "Date To" and complete line 4A. Then list all prior periods of active duty covered by discharges or separation notices. If additional space is necessary, attach separate sheet. Enter your service number. (Enter Social Security Number if it serves or served as your service identification number.)

2. Item 5B. If you have ever filed a claim for any VA benefit, insert your VA file number.

3. Item 6. Attach to this request the Certificate(s) of Eligibility previously issued to you. Certificates of Eligibility relating to World War II entitlement are not valid if you are eligible for loan benefits by virtue of active military duty during the period June 27, 1950 to date. Certificates of Eligibility relating to Korean conflict entitlement (PL 550) are not valid if you are eligible for loan benefits by virtue of active military duty after January 31, 1955. All such certificates must be returned to the Veterans Administration.

4. Item 7C. Complete only if this is a request for a DUPLICATE Certificate of Eligibility.

5. Item 19. This request is not complete until it is signed in Item 19 and dated in Item 20.

6. Item 21. Print or type in Item 21 the name and address of the person or firm to whom you want the Certificate of Eligibility mailed.

☆ U.S. GOVERNMENT PRINTING OFFICE: 1980-624-229

Fig. 9-1. Veterans Administration eligibility information. (Continued on page 120.)

VA Veterans Administration

	TO	VETERANS ADMINISTRATION ATTN: LOAN GUARANTY DIVISION

REQUEST FOR DETERMINATION OF ELIGIBILITY AND AVAILABLE LOAN GUARANTY ENTITLEMENT

NOTE: Please read instructions on reverse before completing this form. If additional space is required attach separate sheet.

1. FIRST - MIDDLE - LAST NAME OF VETERAN	2A. ADDRESS OF VETERAN (No., Street or rural route, City or P.O., State and ZIP Code)

2B. VETERAN'S DAYTIME TELEPHONE NO. (Include Area Code)	3. DATE OF BIRTH	

4. MILITARY SERVICE DATA (SEE INSTRUCTIONS ON REVERSE - ITEM 4)

PERIOD OF ACTIVE SERVICE		NAME (Show your name exactly as it appears on your separation papers (DD214) or Statement of Service)	SERVICE NUMBER (Enter Social Security No. if appropriate)	BRANCH OF SERVICE
DATE FROM	DATE TO			
A.				
B.				
C.				
D.				

5A. WERE YOU DISCHARGED, RETIRED OR SEPARATED FROM SERVICE BECAUSE OF DISABILITY OR DO YOU NOW HAVE ANY SERVICE-CONNECTED DISABILITIES? ☐ YES ☐ NO (If "Yes," Complete Item 5B)	5B. VA FILE NUMBER C-	6. IS A CERTIFICATE OF ELIGIBILITY FOR LOAN GUARANTY PURPOSES ENCLOSED? ☐ YES ☐ NO (If "No," Complete Items 7A and 7B)

7A. HAVE YOU PREVIOUSLY APPLIED FOR A CERTIFICATE OF ELIGIBILITY FOR VA LOAN PURPOSES? ☐ YES ☐ NO (If "Yes," give location of VA office(s))	7B. HAVE YOU PREVIOUSLY RECEIVED SUCH A CERTIFICATE? ☐ YES ☐ NO (If "Yes," give location of VA office(s))	7C. THE CERTIFICATE OF ELIGIBILITY PREVIOUSLY ISSUED TO ME HAS BEEN LOST OR STOLEN. IF RECOVERED IT WILL BE RETURNED TO THE VA (Check if applicable) ☐

ALL APPLICANTS MUST COMPLETE ITEMS 19 THROUGH 21

8. HAVE YOU PREVIOUSLY ACQUIRED PROPERTY WITH THE ASSISTANCE OF A GI LOAN? ☐ YES ☐ NO (If "Yes," complete Items 9 through 18. Please attach a separate sheet if more than one loan is involved)	9. ADDRESS OF REGIONAL OFFICE WHERE LOAN WAS OBTAINED (City and State)

10. STATE TYPE OF LOAN (Home, Mobile home, Condominium, Direct, Farm, Business, etc.)	11. ADDRESS OF PROPERTY PREVIOUSLY PURCHASED WITH GUARANTY ENTITLEMENT	12. DATE YOU PURCHASED THE PROPERTY

13. DO YOU NOW OWN THE REAL PROPERTY DESCRIBED IN ITEM 11? ☐ YES ☐ NO (If "Yes," do not complete Items 14 through 18)	14. DATE THE DEED, IF ANY, WAS DELIVERED TO PURCHASER	15. IS THERE ANY UNDERSTANDING OR AGREEMENT WRITTEN OR ORAL, BETWEEN YOU AND THE PURCHASERS THAT THEY WILL RECONVEY THE PROPERTY TO YOU? ☐ YES ☐ NO

NOTE: It will speed processing if you can complete Items 16, 17, and 18.

16. NAME AND ADDRESS OF LENDER TO WHOM LOAN PAYMENTS WERE MADE	17. LENDER'S LOAN OR ACCOUNT NUMBER
	18. VA LOAN NO. (LH)

I certify that the statements herein are true to the best of my knowledge and belief.

19. SIGNATURE OF VETERAN	20. DATE SIGNED

FEDERAL STATUTES PROVIDE SEVERE PENALTIES FOR FRAUD, INTENTIONAL MISREPRESENTATION, CRIMINAL CONNIVANCE OR CONSPIRACY PURPOSED TO INFLUENCE THE ISSUANCE OF ANY GUARANTY OR INSURANCE BY THE ADMINISTRATOR.

THIS SECTION FOR VA USE ONLY

DATE CERTIFICATE ISSUED AND DISCHARGE OR SEPARATION PAPERS AND VA PAMPHLETS GIVEN TO VETERAN OR MAILED TO ADDRESS SHOWN BELOW	TYPE OF DISCHARGE OR SEPARATION PAPERS RETURNED	SIGNATURE AND TITLE OF APPROPRIATE OFFICIAL (If applicable)	STATION NUMBER

VA FORM 26-1880, APR 1980   DO NOT DETACH

IMPORTANT - You must complete Item 21 since the Certificate of Eligibility along with all discharge and separation papers will be mailed to the address shown in Item 21 below. If they are to be sent to you, your current mailing address should be indicated, or if they are to be sent elsewhere, the name and address of such person or firm should be shown in Item 21.

The amount of loan guaranty entitlement available for use is endorsed on the reverse of the enclosed Certificate of Eligibility. This certificate must be returned to the VA at the time a loan application or loan report is submitted.

NOTE - PLEASE DELIVER THE ENCLOSED PAMPHLETS AND DISCHARGE OR SEPARATION PAPERS TO THE VETERAN PROMPTLY

VA FORM APR 1980 **26-1880**   SUPERSEDES VA FORM 26-1880, JAN 1977, WHICH WILL NOT BE USED.

DO NOT DETACH

Fig. 9-1. Veterans Administration eligibility information. (Continued from page 119.)

the collateral—the property—cannot be confiscated by the lender the moment the borrower defaults.

To foreclose, to gain physical control and ownership of a piece of property, the lender must go to court and only with the permission of the judge can the lender take possession. Contrast this with the usual loan made on an automobile. Cars are sold with a chattel mortgage. Fail to pay and the sheriff can pick up your car as soon as he gets his hands on it.

A mortgage loan can be made by any individual or any organization (bank, credit union, club, insurance company, etc.). A building loan, such as you are seeking, is simply a loan made in "pieces." The money is handed over to the borrower as work progresses. When the building is complete, the borrower receives the balance of the money.

The Best Mortgage. The best mortgage is no mortgage. Following that ideal situation, the best is that which is best for you. You want to borrow sufficient funds to build the house and cover contingencies. You don't want to borrow much more because you will have to pay the money back and you will have to pay interest on the sum while it is in your hands.

You want the lowest possible interest and the lowest possible rate of amortization (repayment). On the other hand, the longer you stretch out the repayment period the more you pay in total to the bank. You have to find a balance between slightly higher payments and a shorter period of time.

You want a mortgage without a prepayment penalty. This gives you the privilege of paying off the balance at anytime (generally a minimum of a year has to pass). You want to be able to pay off the old mortgage and get a new one at a lower rate. In times of rising interest, you want a mortgage with as long a life as possible because money is going to get "cheaper" as interest and prices rise.

SECURING A MORTGAGE

Your first step is to learn the interest rates and the points the various banks in your area are charging. Savings banks generally do more mortgage business than commercial banks, but not always, and their rates are not always lower.

Start by phoning the banks in your area; begin with the one you do business with first. Ask for the mortgage officer and then state simply that you have a building lot and are seeking x number of mortgage dollars.

Banks prefer to lend to people in their area because there is a good chance that some of the money will find its way back to them. In addition, the physically convenient accounts are easier to service. When you have exhausted all the nearby banks, work your way outwards. In good times, banks will lend to distant accounts. In tight-money times they usually will not.

Mortgage Brokers. Mortgage brokers are people and companies engaged in securing mortgages for applicants and finding applicants for people and companies seeking to invest their money. Mortgage brokers are usually the last desperate measure to raise capital because they charge for their services. You end up paying the bank for the loan (in addition to interest) and then paying the broker. You can locate mortgage brokers by their ads in the papers, secure their names from real estate agents, and sometimes obtain information from banks.

In any case, the brokers arrange loans with banks, insurance companies, credit unions, and individuals. If you have a choice, avoid taking a loan from an individual. Should you miss a mortgage payment or be late, an individual is much more likely to be upset than a bank. Individuals are also much more likely to go for foreclosure and so obtain ownership of the property. Banks don't want property. Foreclosure is their last step.

Cosigners. If you have a rich uncle and he will sign the mortgage bond, a bank will be considerably more generous with their loan. It costs your uncle nothing unless you default. In that case, he becomes a creditor and is so protected.

TYPES OF MORTGAGES

There are many types of mortgages drawn up these days. Your problem is to determine which type of mortgage is best for you in terms of overall costs, monthly costs, and special provisions suited to your needs. At the same time, your choice is limited by what is offered. The banks are as interested in earning as much as possible as you are interested in keeping their earnings down.

Long Term, Fixed Rate. The fixed-rate mortgage is the old standard wherein you pay a fixed rate over a long period of time. Few banks grant this type of mortgage now because they are not at all sure of what will happen to interest rates in the months or years ahead. Generally, when such loans are made they are made at top interest rates.

Variable Rate. Your rate of interest is tied to the prime rate (the interest rate the big companies). This is fine when the prime remains stable or goes down. It becomes horrible when the prime goes up.

Negative Amortizer. You start out with a low interest rate when you have a negative amortizer. Nevertheless, the sum you borrow is increased every year so that after a given period you owe more than you did at the start. At this, agreed-upon time, you pay a higher rate and eventually pay the loan off. In numbers, you might borrow $40,000 for 30 years at 18¾ percent. The first-year payments are calculated at a rate of 13¾ percent—just interest—which comes to $466 a month. The 5 percent unpaid interest is added to the principal. After 15 years, you would owe $60,000 and pay the full 18¾ percent, plus amortization. By this time your income hopefully will have increased to where you can carry it.

Balloon. With a balloon mortgage, you borrow a sum and pay an agreed percentage for an agreed period of time. At this point the balance (the "balloon") becomes due. Monthly payments are comparatively low, but when the debt is due you have to pay it all at once.

MORTGAGE COSTS

Mortgage costs differ from interest paid on the loan. These are "tacked-on" costs you cannot avoid. Be prepared for them.

If your loan was secured through a middleman, you will pay in points. A point is 1 percent of the face value of the loan. Most banks charge points for their kindness. And most banks will stick you with

their lawyer. Thus you should expect the following mortgage costs—at a minimum:

- ☐ The mortgage broker's fee (if used).
- ☐ The bank's charge.
- ☐ The bank's lawyer.
- ☐ Title insurance.
- ☐ Your lawyer.
- ☐ County registration fee.
- ☐ Mortgage tax.

These are called closing costs. They are for the costs of closing the deal (in this case the mortgage) with the bank.

Title Insurance. Because few if any titles (ownership) to property in this country are ever perfectly free and clear of all legal encumbrances, a system of title insurance has been developed. Very simply, should time prove that someone is not dead, as believed, and returns to claim his land, the title company will settle his claim. If the title to the land has already been searched and insured—in the process of purchasing an option on the land—the search can be updated.

Closing. The closing is the meeting at which all of you gather for the changing of money for the promissory note—the mortgage. Make certain you have all the necessary documents before you go to the closing. Check and see if you need building department approval of your building plan in hand.

Bring your checkbook. You want a record of what you pay out and you cannot say, "Take it out of the mortgage money." Banks like to be neat. Taking from A to pay B and C makes for difficult record keeping.

SPECIFICATIONS

You specify in three ways the home you will construct. You have the plot plan showing the size and location of the land, plus the deed or the option on the property. You have the print with all its dimensions. In addition, you need a list of materials (the spec).

In the specs, you list all the major items and you do so emphatically. You fill the pages with a lot of "shalls." Construction shall be accomplished in a workmanlike manner and shall conform to all applicable building codes and good construction practices.

Footing. The footing shall be constructed of concrete, laid on perfectly firm, virgin soil.

Foundation. The foundation shall be of 10-inch concrete block, laid up properly in cement mortar.

Frame. The framing timbers shall be of building-grade fir, properly nailed and spaced as required by the building code.

Sheathing. The sheathing shall be of ⅜-inch, construction-grade plywood that is properly nailed to the studs.

Windows. The windows shall be double hung, double glazed, of the sizes indicated.

Roof. The roof shall be of ⅜-inch, construction-grade plywood, properly covered with 15-pound felt and 360-pound, asphalt shingles laid up 5 inches to the weather.

Insulation. Glass fiber batts, 4 inches thick in the walls and 6 inches thick in the ceiling, shall be installed.

Floors. Subflooring shall be of ⅜-inch plywood. Finish floor shall be of grade #2 oak, properly sanded and shellacked.

Interior Walls. The interior walls shall be of ½-inch Sheetrock, properly taped and sanded.

Interior Trim. Clam shell trim shall be used throughout, 2 inches at the base of the walls and 1¼ inches elsewhere.

Electrical. A 220-volt line and a suitable distribution box with fuses will be installed. Outlets and switches will be connected as shown.

Plumbing. The following fixtures shall be installed (list them). Piping of a size to provide adequate water flow and pressure shall be installed.

Hot Water. A gas-fired, hot-water tank with a total capacity of 85 gallons shall be installed.

Heating. A hot-water, oil-fired heating system capable of maintaining 70 degrees Fahrenheit within the building when the external temperature drops to 0 degrees Fahrenheit shall be installed.

Driveway. The driveway shall consist of a 10-foot-wide roadway made of crushed stone laid upon the earth.

There Is No Money in the Fancy Stuff. You can, if you prefer, drop $10,000 or more for fine hardwood paneling in the playroom or elsewhere. Don't expect the bank to finance the work. They view a room as a room. The quality of the walls, the trim, and the fancy fixtures mean very little to them. They are thinking of how your house will appear to a prospective purchaser should they have to foreclose. Buyers are primarily interested in location and then in size. Rooms, baths, and fancy add-ons don't justify their cost.

If You Write It, You Must Supply It. The less you specify, the freer you will be when it comes to actual construction. Of course, you might be asked to be more specific and to provide more details. To promise a particular make of window, when all you need do is specify a window, is to increase the difficulty of securing materials and increases your costs.

Chapter 10

Checklist

IN THE PRECEDING CHAPTERS, WE WENT THROUGH the various steps that you are advised to take on your way to the construction of your home. For the sake of clarity, the steps are repeated in this chapter.

Grouping the various steps and stages of construction might also help you secure a clearer picture of just what has to be accomplished and the sequence in which the various steps have to be completed. You can also use the following as a checklist to make certain nothing has been overlooked.

☐ Decide on the style of house you want.
☐ Secure the property.
☐ Prepare to apply for a mortgage.
☐ Secure a plot plan.
☐ Secure the house plans.
☐ Discuss the house plan with the local building department.
☐ Make enough copies of the plans to secure bids and to show the bank.
☐ Write up the subcontractors' specs.

☐ Total your material costs.
☐ Total secondary expenses.
☐ Total your expected costs.
☐ Determine the amount you must finance and add 10 percent for an error margin.
☐ Estimate living costs. See Table 10-1.
☐ Figure your yearly property taxes.
☐ Prepare a set of specifications for the bank.
☐ Secure a loan commitment.
☐ Obtain title to the land.
☐ Secure a building permit.

You might want to check with the building department first to make certain your plans are acceptable. You might also want to start your mortgage applications earlier to save time. And you might decide to purchase the property as soon as you see it rather than take an option or just hope no one else buys it first.

Minor variations in the procedures are not too important, but your basic approach is. It is planned to prevent you from getting into serious financial difficulty by buying a lot you cannot build on, com-

Table 10-1. Payments on a 19% $100,000, 30-year loan.

Mortgage Year	Interest Paid	Principal Paid	Total Payment	Total Principal Due (Balance)
1	$ 9,974	$ 562	$ 10,536	$99,438
2	9,916	620	10,536	98,818
3	9,851	685	10,536	98,133
4	9,780	756	10,536	97,377
5	9,699	837	10,536	96,540
6	9,612	924	10,536	95,616
7	9,516	1,020	10,536	94,596
8	9,410	1,126	10,536	93,470
9	9,290	1,246	10,536	92,224
10	9,162	1,374	10,536	90,850
11	9,018	1,518	10,536	89,332
12	8,857	1,679	10,536	87,653
13	8,681	1,855	10,536	85,798
14	8,487	2,049	10,536	83,749
15	8,273	2,263	10,536	81,486
16	8,036	2,500	10,536	78,986
17	7,774	2,762	10,536	76,224
18	7,485	3,051	10,536	73,173
19	7,166	3,370	10,536	69,803
20	6,813	3,723	10,536	66,080
21	6,422	4,114	10,536	61,966
22	5,991	4,545	10,536	57,421
23	5,517	5,019	10,536	52,402
24	4,989	5,547	10,536	46,855
25	4,409	6,127	10,536	40,728
26	3,768	6,768	10,536	33,960
27	3,060	7,476	10,536	26,484
28	2,278	8,258	10,536	18,226
29	1,412	9,124	10,536	9,102
30	458	9,102	9,560	0
Total	$215,104	$100,000	$315,104	

mitting yourself to a house you cannot afford or buying a lot on which the city will not let you build. Our suggestions might be the long way around, but it is the safe route.

Chapter 11

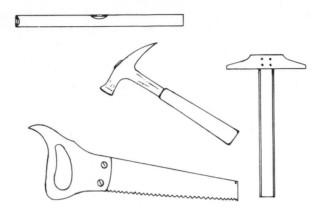

Construction Steps

CONSTRUCTION OF A HOUSE MUST FOLLOW the basic sequence outlined in this chapter; there can be little variation. You can stray a little, but if you go too far off course you will wind up repeating some of the steps and wasting time and material.

☐ Clear the land. You can start this work as soon as you take title to the property. Depending on the nature of the land and how much has to be cleared away, the work can take anything from one day to several weeks. Beware of hazards such as poison ivy. It is very common to second-growth timber lands, and it can take the form of a vine, weed, or bush. Consider the route the material delivery trucks will have to take and remove the trees from their path.

☐ Contact your shovel or dozer operator. Inform the man you are in the process of clearing the land and that you will need him on a specific day. If he can't make it, you have the option of waiting for him or contacting your second choice, and so on. You need to give these people a few days notice, but you might have trouble tying them down to a specific time and date.

☐ Check the position of the surveyor's stakes against the plot plan just to make certain there has been no confusion. Set up the batter boards. Stake the excavation (outlining the area that is to be excavated).

☐ Your dozer is committed or on its way. Contact the mason. Tell him when excavation will start and that you will be ready for the foundation the day following. Unless there are problems, such as rocks, or huge tree roots to remove, a cellar or a basement for a small home can be excavated in less than a day (two at most). Of course, bad weather might also intervene.

☐ Stake the foundation. If you are unsure of the technique, pay the mason to do this work. The mason will prepare the forms for the footings. The footing forms for a simple, rectangular structure will require two men less than half a day. For a complex structure in muck and mire, several days might be needed. With the foundation form completed, the mason will check it to make certain it is square and level.

☐ Contact the building department. Tell the

inspector the foundation forms are almost in and you would like his inspection as soon as possible. Try to learn when he can visit your site. If possible, you want to be there when he is there so that you can personally make note of any change needed. You don't want to lose the time it will take the inspector to make a report and write you a letter.

☐ If possible, have the mason present when the inspector arrives. When you get the okay, the mason can order the concrete. With luck you can have the footings poured the same day. The actual pouring and spreading of the concrete will not take more than an hour or two, but the concrete delivery truck might not be able to be there on time. Trucks get stuck and schedules go awry. It is not unusual for the mason and his crew to be held up half a day.

☐ Contact the plumber. Tell him you are getting the footings ready. Depending upon the elevation of the house in relation to the city sewer line or the septic tank, the plumber might need to run his sewer pipe beneath the footings. In such cases, it is much easier to do before the foundation is up.

☐ The concrete block and foundation hardware (bolts, windows, etc.) are ordered for immediate delivery.

☐ The concrete footings are given 48 hours to set up a little. Then the forms are stripped.

☐ The plumber can start installing his cellar pipes now.

☐ The mason constructs the foundation. One mason and a helper can erect a 14-course (block) foundation wall for a small, rectangular building in less than a week.

☐ Contact the excavator. Tell him where you are in the construction of the building. Tell him you will need him for backfilling in about one week.

☐ Provide footing drainage, if required.

☐ By this time, the plumber should have installed all the service lines—sewer, gas, and water—that have to enter the building through the foundation wall. The connections to the city service lines can be made at this point or some time later.

☐ Contact the carpenters. Tell them the foundation is going up. Tell them when you believe they can start work. This work can be started immediately after the foundation wall is done.

☐ Parge and waterproof the foundation wall. This consists of applying two successive coats of mortar cement to the exterior foundation wall and then covering the below-ground portion of the wall with a layer of roofing asphalt. It is one day's work.

☐ Do the backfill and grade work. The ditch around the building must now be filled with the earth that was previously removed. So long as the ditch remains, it is a danger and handicap to workers and visitors.

Grading is the process of giving the surface of the earth the desired pitch that should slope upward against the foundation. Place much more soil here and make the pitch much greater than what you first think is needed. The replaced soil is loose and will compact considerably with time and rain. You grade now even though some areas will be scuffed up and channeled by truck wheels because you have the dozer on the job now. To bring the machine back another time will cost a lot more money. On a small lot without obstacles and other problems, backfilling and grading should not take a full day.

☐ Excavate the driveway. The least expensive driveway, assuming the surface of the soil is not hard pan, is merely a layer of crushed stone placed on the earth. Because even the poorest soil has several inches of soft topsoil, you cannot lay the gravel directly on the earth. The gravel will soon sink out of sight. The topsoil must be removed. A couple of passes with a medium-size dozer to remove the dark topsoil is all that is required. Push the excess soil off to one side and spread it out to hide it. The driveway is done at this time because the machine is on the job.

☐ Order the frame lumber. Time the delivery to coincide with the arrival of the carpenters (whom you have already contacted and advised). You do not want the lumber lying about loose any longer than necessary. Don't accept much more lumber at any one time than your crew can handle in a day or two.

☐ The carpenters now frame the house. Two men and a helper can frame and sheath a small, five-room cottage in a week.

☐ Contact the building department, apprise the inspector of when you expect the framing to be completed. This will include rough floors and sheathing on the exterior walls and roof. Plan to be present when the inspector visits.

☐ Contact the roofers. They can start as soon as the roof is sheathed. Two men usually can do a roof on a small house in two working days.

☐ Contact the bank. The first building loan payment is generally made when the building roof is up. Call the bank for additional payments as per schedule or postpone their inspections and payments as long as you can to hold mortgage interests down.

☐ Contact the plumber, electrician, and heating craftsmen. They can start their work as soon as the roof is covered and there is little danger of water entering the building. The furnace will have to wait for the cellar floor to be poured (depending upon building design).

☐ Have the building department inspect and pass the electrical, plumbing, and heating work.

☐ Check to make certain all of the above is to your specifications (correct placement of outlets, bell wiring is in, etc.). You are now ready to close up.

☐ Have the insulation installed. Contact the Sheetrock specialists when you contact the insulation men. Two men should be able to apply insulation to a small home in one day. Order the Sheetrock for immediate delivery.

☐ Have the Sheetrock installed and taped. Two men should be able to install the Sheetrock in two days. Taping will take a week or so because three applications are needed, with a day for drying out between.

☐ Dig the well if required. A well can be driven in a day if there are no problems and the depth is under 50 feet. Capping and piping will probably take several more days.

☐ If required, construct and install the septic tank and drain field. Concrete tanks are generally constructed by a mason. The drain field and connecting piping is usually done by the plumber and a laborer. The tank and its connection to the house can take men a week. The drain field can take an equal amount of time. Note that these time estimates are very rough. Actual time can vary tremendously depending upon local conditions.

☐ Have doors, window frames, and other interior trim delivered. Inform carpenters that materials are on the site. Paint or have these items painted while they rest on the floor.

☐ Have masons pour the cellar floor.

☐ Have carpenters install exterior doors and window frames.

☐ Have the plumbing supplier deliver plumbing fixtures, the furnace, the boiler, etc.

☐ Inform the plumber and the heating man that materials are being delivered. They can do whatever has to be done in the cellar or basement the day after the floor has been poured.

☐ Carpenters or siding specialists can now go to work installing the siding and exterior trim. Depending upon the type of siding used and the size and complexity of the building, figure roughly two men need one day per house side (or eight working days).

☐ Meanwhile paint or have the interior of the building painted. On an average, one man can apply one coat of paint to one room in a day, assuming all the walls of each room are of the same color. Use a good water-base paint so there will be no time lost waiting for drying.

☐ Give the concrete cellar floor at least four days to dry and then have the wood-strip flooring delivered. You have to wait for the concrete to dry or the moisture will adversely affect the flooring. Contact the flooring craftsmen. Break the flooring bundles and give the flooring a few days to stabilize. The flooring can now be laid without shrinkage problems.

☐ If you are not going to lay the bath and kitchen tile yourself, contact the tradesmen. They can work while the wood flooring is being laid or a little sooner or a little later.

☐ As soon as one wood floor is laid and scraped (sanded), sweep and dust the floor perfectly clean and cover it with a wash coat of shellac. Mix wood alcohol with shellac (50/50). Let it dry; it takes about an hour. Then cover the floor with *red* building paper. In this way, you will keep following foot traffic from marring the finished floor.

☐ Have the carpenters complete the installation of the interior trim and the doors. If you have kitchen cabinets, now is the time to have them installed.

☐ Contact the gas company, the phone company, and the electric company to make their connections. If you will be using oil, have it delivered.

☐ Have the electrician, plumber, and heating man finish their work (install fixtures, etc.).

☐ Contact the building inspector. He might want to make a final inspection. He also might want to make or supervise a gas-line and sewer-line test before he gives his approval.

☐ Secure a certificate of occupancy from the building department.

☐ Contact the bank for their final inspection if you want to receive the last building loan payment.

☐ Paint the exterior of the building, if required.

☐ Complete the driveway with crushed stone.

☐ Landscape.

Chapter 12

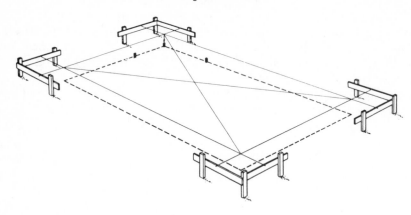

Excavating

AT THIS POINT, YOU OWN A BUILDING LOT, YOU HAVE A building-department approved plan in hand, and you have mortgage money. You are ready to start work.

CLEARING THE LAND

Clearing the land is something you can do yourself or with the aid of a few friends. Just be careful of the poison ivy and the poison oak, and don't let your early enthusiasm run away with you. Bear in mind that you will want some shade trees, but also that too many trees makes for difficulties in construction. Think of how the equipment will have to get in and out of the property and where the building materials will be dumped.

CHECK THE STAKES

If the brush is very dense, you will have to clear it before the surveyor (Fig. 12-1) will come in and place his stakes. If he can work with the lot the way it is, be careful not to disturb the stakes. If you do move the stakes and the surveyor has to come back to the lot, there will be another charge. In any case,

clear the area immediately surrounding the stakes so that no one trips over them and knocks them out of position.

STAKING THE EXCAVATION

Sometimes called setting up the batter boards, laying out the jobs or positioning the footing, staking the excavation is a process of determining the exact position of the building to be erected on the plot of land. This is easily accomplished by using the surveyor's stakes as accurate reference points. If you prefer, you can hire the mason to do this work for you. Of course that means an extra charge.

For simplicity's sake—and because this is a common situation—we will assume that the house is to be rectangular, and that the lot is roughly rectangular with parallel, long sides. Figure 12-2 shows the outline of the building on the lot. Note that the house is set back 25 feet from the property line at the road side (front), and that there is a side-yard space of 15 feet between one side of the building and the side edge of the property.

Fig. 12-1. Once the transit support has been adjusted to a horizontal position, as indicated by the spirit level, everything seen through the "scope" is at exactly the same elevation as the cross hairs in the scope.

Stretch the Side Lines. When we speak of a line, in the following paragraphs, we mean a stretched length of string. When we speak of the front of the building, we mean the side facing the public road. When we speak of the left side of the building, we mean the side to our left hand when we stand with our back to the road and face the building.

Two stakes demark the left side of the building lot. Take a long string and two sticks. Drive the sticks into the earth a distance beyond the stakes. Then stretch the line (string) from stick to stick. If

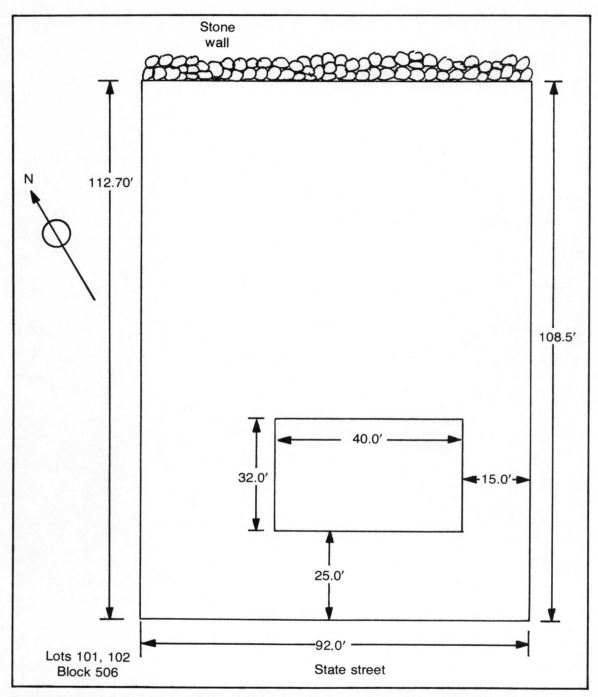

Stone wall

N

112.70'

108.5'

40.0'

32.0'

15.0'

25.0'

92.0'

Lots 101, 102
Block 506

State street

Fig. 12-2. This is more or less what the usual plot plan looks like. What makes it official is that it is drawn by a licensed surveyor who indicates the corners and other points with his stakes.

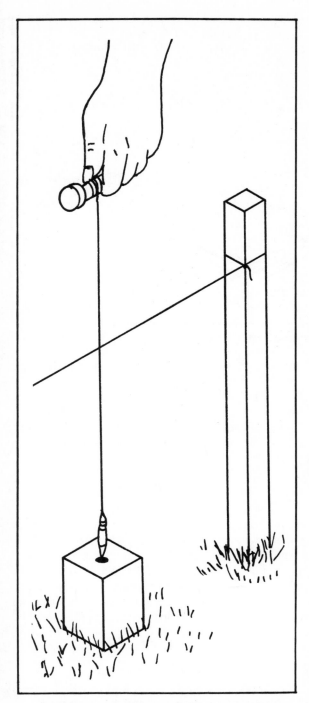

Fig. 12-3. To make certain a line is directly over a stake, drop a plumb bob.

necessary, move the sticks from side to side to position the line directly over the surveyor's stakes. To make certain the line is truly above the stake (actually the nail head in the stake) drop a plumb bob from the string. See Fig. 12-3.

Stretch a second line over the two stakes, marking the right side of the property. Stretch a line across the front of the property. Again use two sticks as supports and again position the line over the surveyor's stakes. This time work with the front two stakes. When this is accomplished, you have three sides of the property outlined with string.

Positioning the Corner Pegs. You know the setback of the house. In our example (and it states so on our plot plan), the setback is 25 feet. Using a steel tape, measure back from the front line a distance of 25 feet in two places. Drive two stakes into the earth to mark these two distances, and drive nails into the tops of the stakes for a more accurate definition. Next do the stick trick and stretch a line across these two stakes. Carry this line, which represents the front line or edge of the house, all the way out to the sides of the property.

Go to the left side of the property and measure 15 feet in along the front line. Begin the measurement at the left side line and mark the 15-foot point with another stake. You now have pegged the front left corner of the building. Because the building is to be 40 feet across its front, measure this distance along the same front line and mark this point with another stake.

Now you have the two front corners pegged. Go to the left, front corner peg and measure rearwards for the full depth of the house (in our example it is 32 feet). Peg this rear left corner. To make certain the left side of the building will be parallel with the left side of the lot, measure from the left rear peg to the side line. It should be 15 feet. See Fig. 12-4.

Locate and peg the rear right corner. Do this by following the same procedure and stretching a line across the rear two pegs.

Installing the Batter Boards. Batter boards can be made from anything that is convenient. Generally, there is nothing convenient on

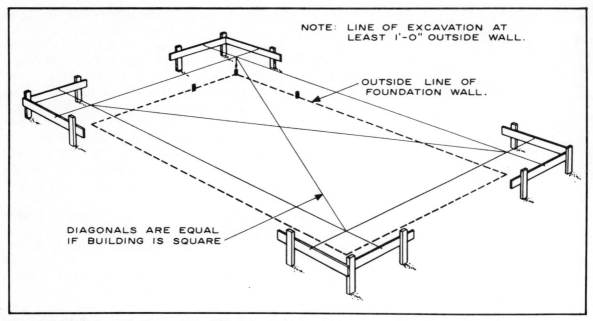

NOTE: LINE OF EXCAVATION AT LEAST 1'-0" OUTSIDE WALL.

OUTSIDE LINE OF FOUNDATION WALL.

DIAGONALS ARE EQUAL IF BUILDING IS SQUARE

Fig. 12-4. Batter boards and lines are used to define and locate a building's foundation.

hand so you end up using 1-×-6 roofers (cheap lumber) and 2 × 4s. In any case make them sturdy. They don't hold anything but string, but if they get knocked down you have to repeat the entire operation.

Each batter board is about 4 to 5 feet long and end supported by the aforementioned 2 × 4s that should be driven deeply into the ground. The boards should be fairly level and positioned some 8 to 10 feet clear of the corner pegs.

Transfer the Lines. Remove the front line and the side lines and the associate sticks. Remove the lines that demark the building (the lines that pass over the corner pegs). Replace the lines, wrapping their ends over the batter boards. Move the lines from side to side.

With the aid of a plumb bob, make certain the lines are directly over the corner pegs. Mark the position of each line on the associate batter board. Remove the line. With a saw, make a small slot at each mark. Now you can remove all the lines and the corner pegs.

Whenever you want to relocate the corners, stretch the string from slot to slot. Where the

strings cross is where the corner of your building will be. See Fig. 12-5.

The reason for all this will become obvious when you begin excavating. If you merely depend upon pegs, you would have to remeasure every time the dozer scooped some earth out of the ground.

REMOVE THE TOPSOIL

Almost everywhere the top few inches of soil are soft. You can't build on topsoil. Even if you are just going to pour a slab, you have to get down to firm subsoil.

Plan this move carefully. You don't want to lose any of the topsoil by having it mix with subsoil, and you don't want it in the way of work. Have the dozer pile it in some distant corner of the lot. See Fig. 12-6.

EXCAVATING DEPTH

The depth to which you are going to have your crew excavate will depend upon the design of the house (full cellar, partial cellar, slab, or what have you).

134

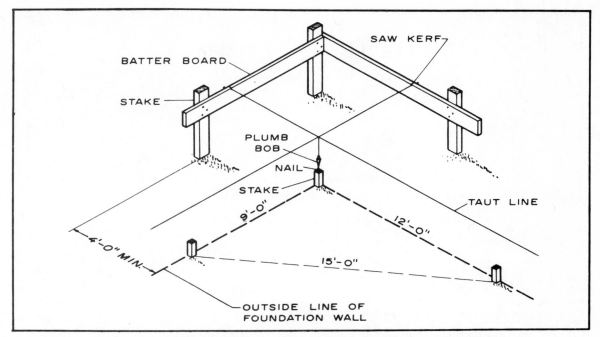

Fig. 12-5. A plumb bob can be used to transfer the batter board line's cross points to the earth below.

There are some other considerations you should have in mind as you supervise the work.

Sewer Depth. In order to avoid the use of a soil pump, your toilet must be higher than the sewer main by a difference that will give you a pitch of ¼ inch to the foot or more. If you are planning on a two-story building with a toilet on the ground floor, you might not be able to excavate at all. You might find you need to elevate the building to get gravity flow to the sewer. In some cases, you might find that, by confining yourself to a half-depth cellar, the problem is solved. It all depends upon the depth of the city's sewer main. This is information you can secure from your local city engineer.

Rock. If there is a chance of encountering bedrock, it is advisable to excavate in layers rather than go to the full depth at one end of the excavation and then work to the other. The latter method is more efficient. If you encounter rock with half a cellar at full depth and rock blocking the other, you will have to either blast the rock or have a new set of plans drawn up. If you encounter rock going down the full area a short distance at a time, you can always quit at rock level and build directly on the rock.

Never Replace the Soil. Once you or the machine has scooped up some dirt, you cannot replace it. It is not compacted. You must always keep sharp tabs on your progress to make certain you do not overdig. If you dig too deep, fill the low spots with crushed stone. If you must use soil, wet it down and pound it compact with a power driven compactor.

Excavation Area. For a perimeter foundation, you need about 2 to 3 feet of clearance between the edges of the hole and the footing. If you are going down 5 or more feet, you want a good 5 feet of clearance all around the footing to provide working room for the masons. If the soil is firm, you can have the hole sides cut straight up and down. If the soil is loose, you simply have to remove more of it.

Have the dozer move the soil off to one side. The machine operator will tell you it is not important and argue for making neat piles alongside the excavation. It might not seem important, but it does

Fig. 12-6. The batter board lines have been removed. The edge of the excavation has been outlined with lime to guide the dozer operator.

add to the work and the time the masons and carpenters will spend on the job. Remember, it is your time as well as their time that will be wasted.

HOLDING DEPTH AND KEEPING THINGS LEVEL

Except for piers, which don't especially need level support, all the other types of footings and slabs must be supported by reasonably level soil. To make the bottom of the excavation flat and level is the job of the dozer operator. You should keep tabs on his progress. If he digs too deeply, you are going to have to fill the area in with crushed stone or make your foundation walls higher.

Transit and Helper. The best and easiest way to keep tabs on the dozer's progress is by means of a transit and helper. A transit is a sighting telescope with cross hairs at each end. The transit is supported by an adjustable platform mounted on a tripod. The transit will have a spirit level along its length or two levels on its supporting platform. In the latter case, you adjust the support screws until both bubbles are centered, indicating the platform is perfectly level. When the level is attached to the telescope, you adjust one pair of screws to center the bubble and then swing the scope half way around and adjust the second pair of screws. In this way you make its platform level. See Fig. 12-7.

Now that the transit support is level, anything you see through the scope is on a level with the cross hairs. Have your helper stand a target stick vertically on the floor of the excavation. You can use a yardstick fastened to a pole. Read the number that appears on the cross hairs. Note the number. Have your helper position the target at another point.

Fig. 12-7. Sighting a target pole with a transit. As the helper carries the pole to various points in the excavation, sighting through the transit measures the depth of the excavation at that point.

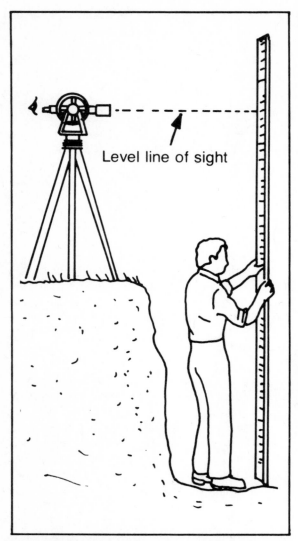

Fig. 12-8. A visual explanation of how the transit and target pole can be used.

Read the number. If it is the same, both points are on the same level. If not, one is higher than the other by the difference indicated on the yardstick. See Fig. 12-8.

Don't worry about the accuracy of the transit. Even the least expensive transit is far more accurate than you need. The best, called theodolites, are accurate to within 1/10 of an inch in a mile.

Incidentally, the hand-held sighting levels, and the spirit levels to which you attach sights, are not sufficiently accurate. Don't buy one. You are better off renting a scope.

Using a Line Level. The line-level method is accurate but cumbersome and requires that you stop the dozer. Very simply you stretch a line across the excavation, using a centered line level to make certain the line is level. Then you measure down from the line (string) at various points to ascertain depth. See Figs. 12-9 and 12-10.

Depth of Excavation. At a minimum you must get down below the topsoil. You have got to reach firm subsoil even if you are putting down a slab foundation. When and where you are going to lay down a footing, you have got to go below the frost line. If you don't, frost heave will move your

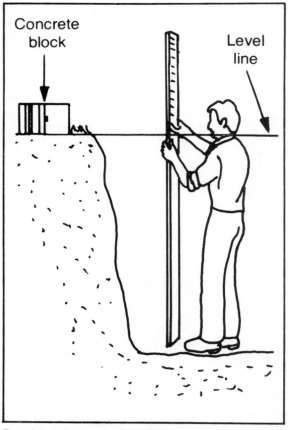

Fig. 12-9. A line level and string can be used in place of a transit to determine excavation depth.

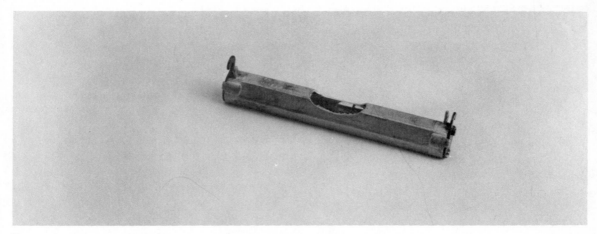

Fig. 12-10. Used correctly, the lowly line level is capable of accuracy of 1 inch in 45 feet or more.

foundation. Your building department will be able to tell you the frost depth in your area.

On the other hand, you don't want to go down too far. You want your finished grade to angle up to the side of the building, and you want at least 6 inches and preferably 12 inches of masonry between the grade and the house frame. You need this clearance to prevent rot and termite attack.

Accuracy. Don't worry too much about holding the bottom of the excavation perfectly level. Anything within a couple of inches will be fine. Actually, you can't do any better unless you shovel the job by hand.

SERVICE LINES

If your sewer line will enter the building below the footing, it is generally advisable to excavate for it now. This is not easily accomplished with a dozer, but is relatively simple with a small backhoe. Whether it pays to hire a backhoe just for this trench or to do the job with pick and shovel is something you will have to decide. In either case, if you trench for the sewer pipe before you pour the footing you have to provide some kind of temporary fill for the trench so that you won't fill it with concrete when you pour the footing.

DRAINAGE

Most house plans show a perforated pipe lying in a bed of gravel alongside the foundation. The same drawings also show 3 or 4 inches of crushed stone beneath the poured concrete slab or cellar floor. Both items are there for drainage and are very nice. The crushed stone under the floor helps if the water level is no higher than the stone. The drainage pipe helps but only if the pipe leads somewhere. The somewhere can be out the side of a hill or into a public storm sewer (if permitted). Drainage is mentioned here briefly because you will need to excavate narrow trenches for the drain pipes.

Chapter 13

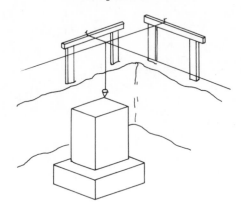

Footings and Foundations

THE FOOTING OF A BUILDING IS THAT PORTION WHICH rests directly on the earth. The foundation is that portion of the building that rests upon the footing. In some designs, the two are separate; in others they are one. So much for the nomenclature.

PIERS

A pier is both a footing and a foundation. It can be of wood, metal, or stone. Dimensions and materials are specified in the plan. Most important, the bottom of each pier must be below the frost line. The tops of the piers must be at the exact same height, and their position must be correct in relation to the building they are to support. See Fig. 13-1.

Positioning. Replace the lines on the batter board. Drop a plumb bob from where the lines cross one another. That will give you the *outside* corner of the pier. Check the height of one pier against another with the aid of a transit or a length of line and a line level. If you are working with brick or stone, you can raise a pier with the addition of a little cement. When working with wooden piers,

saw the high pier down. See Figs. 13-2, 13-3, and 13-4.

SLABS

The slab footing/foundation is constructed by pouring concrete into a wooden form. Locate the corners of the form by means of the batter-board lines. Bear in mind that you want the point of the bob to strike the inside corner of the form. Check to make certain the form is braced and perfectly level. Check to make certain that all the service lines that have to come up through the slab are in place.

Preparation. Unless the soil is rock hard and bone dry, it is advisable to lay down several inches of crushed stone as a support for the slab. If there is any possibility that there will be moisture coming up through the ground, you should seal the bottom of the slab with a sheet of plastic. Use a 5-mill film sheet and overlap the edges by 1 foot. Before you lay the sheet on the crushed stone, tamp the stones down to remove the sharp edges that could cut holes through the sheet.

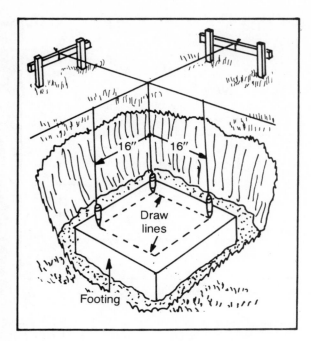

Fig. 13-1. A pier can be located exactly on its intended footing.

Fig. 13-2. The position of the erected pier can be checked in relation to the proposed building line. Note that the building line(s) are flush with the outside edges of the pier.

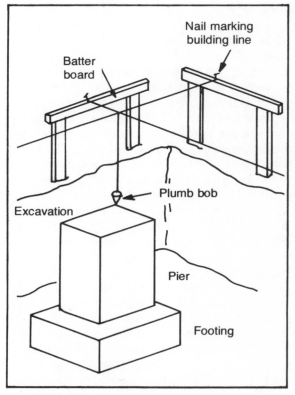

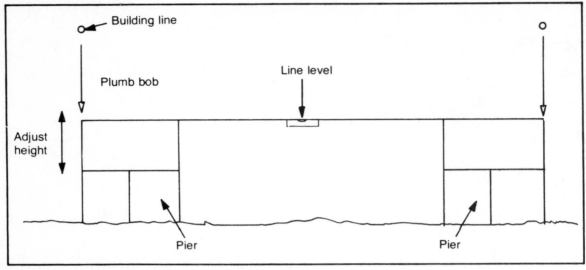

Fig. 13-3. A line level can be used to match the elevation of one pier against another.

Inspection. Check with the building department. They might want to inspect the site before you pour.

Insulation. The slab can be insulated as shown in Fig. 13-5. Insulation adds to the cost and complexity of the work, but it will more than pay for itself in increased comfort. Insulation is a must if you expect to use the slab for solar heating.

If you are going to erect a concrete block structure on the slab, the blocks are simply positioned in mortar atop the slab. If you are planning a frame building, you have to insert foundation bolts (heads down) in the edges of the concrete. Bolts have to be carefully positioned so that they do not come up in the middle of doorways or studs.

Pouring, screeding, and finishing. Pouring, screeding and finishing is physically a very difficult job. You need at least three men to handle the job properly. Bear in mind that on a hot day concrete can set up in 30 minutes. After that you would have to break it apart to change its shape.

The mason will probably pour the job in sections. Make certain he has a screed (a long, straightedged board or strip of metal) large enough to reach completely across the poured section. Insist that he machine trowel the screeded area. The machine will make the concrete harder and more

compact than is possible with a hand trowel. When the concrete has reached a preliminary set (it is stiff) have it lightly wetted down with water and covered with wet newspaper, burlap, sand or plas-

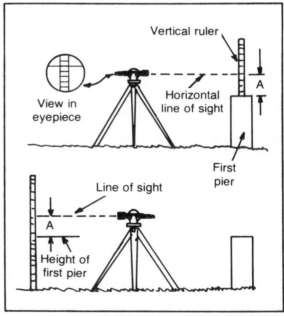

Fig. 13-4. A transit can be used to determine the relative heights of two or more piers.

142

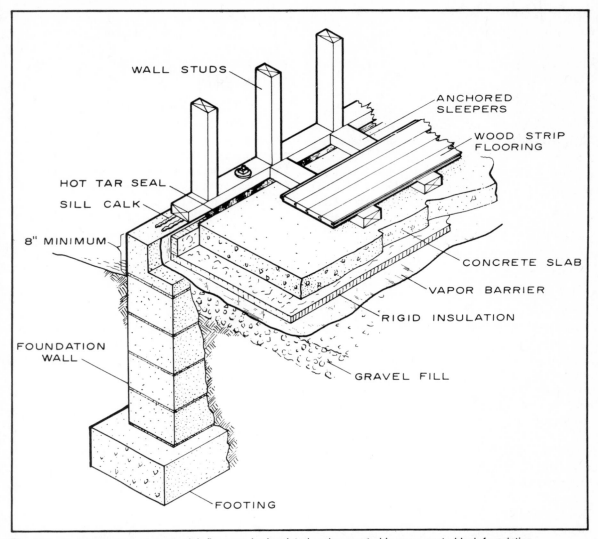

Fig. 13-5. An independent concrete slab floor can be insulated and supported by a concrete block foundation.

tic sheeting. This will speed curing and reduce the possibility of cracking. See Figs. 13-6 and 13-7.

PERIMETER FOOTINGS

Forms are constructed of 2-inch lumber set on edge and positioned with stakes. The method discussed previously is again used to locate the corners. This time the footing extends beyond the corner indicated by the plumb bob (Fig. 13-8). The width of the on-edge boards determines the height of the footing

and the space between the boards determines the width of the footing.

The footing must be level. You can't check this with a spirit level as you will pick up a fraction of an inch each time you move the level. Levelness can only be checked by means of a transit or a line level. In any case, you will find the footing up in some spots. Dig away to lower the footing at that point. Where the footing form is low, place stones underneath to raise it. You don't need absolute perfection, but you do want it to be level within an inch or so across its greatest dimension (Fig. 13-9).

In order to check for squareness measure the diagonals. When they are equal all the corners are square.

Inspection. Have the building department inspect your footing forms as soon as possible. Some soils become soft with exposure so you want to excavate and pour the footings as quickly as practical. See Table 13-1.

Pouring the Footings. Generally, a sloppy mix is used. This is done to help the concrete find its own level and reach all the corners. The form is filled to its top and screeded—a straight edge run over its surface. That is it. Two days later the form can be removed. If you let the boards stay in place too long, they become very difficult to remove. Move them too soon and you damage the concrete. See Fig. 13-10A through 13-10F.

FOUNDATION

The foundation can be laid up as soon as the concrete has set. Once again the corners are located by means of a plumb bob dropped from the cross lines. The corner blocks are the first blocks positioned. Then the corners are built up and then the middle sections are filled in.

Check to make certain the work is neat, that all

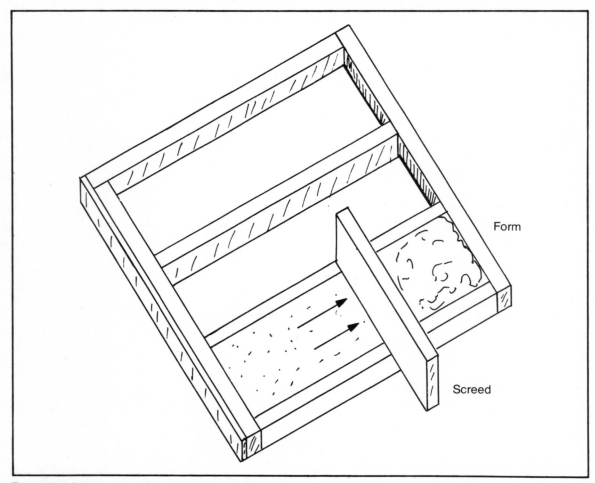

Fig. 13-6. A form and screed can be used to secure a level concrete surface in a cellar or elsewhere.

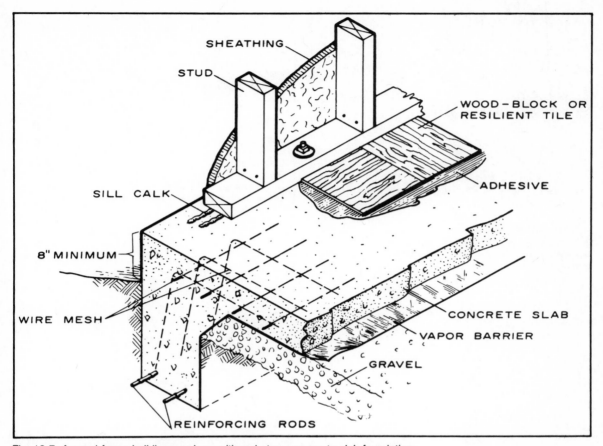

Fig. 13-7. A wood frame building can be positioned atop a concrete slab foundation.

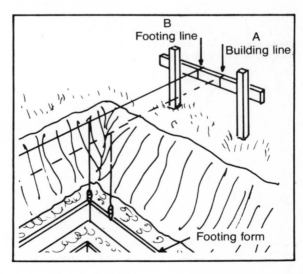

Fig. 13-8. Locating footings with the aid of batter board lines. Note how footing line B sets off the width of the footing.

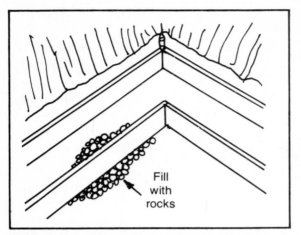

Fig. 13-9. If you dig too deeply for the footings, do not simply replace the soil, it is too soft. Fill the space with clean stones of any size.

Table 13-1. Load-Bearing Capacities of Various Soils.

Material	Approximate depth below grade	
	3 feet	8 feet
Soft silt and mud	0.1-0.2	0.2-0.5
Silt	1-2	1.5-2
Soft clay	1-1.5	1-1.5
Firm clay	2-2.5	2.5-3
Clay and sand	2-3	2.5-3.5
Fine sand	2	2-3
Coarse sand	3	3-4
Gravel and course sand	4-5	5-6
Soft rock	7-10	7-10
Bedrock	20-40	20-40
	(average 25)	

Fig. 13-10A. When footings other than perimeter footings must be positioned, the same batter-board line technique can be used. Measurements are made external to the job.

146

Fig. 13-10B. The width of the footings to be poured are determined by the spacing of the form board. Here the mason nails a spacer in place.

Fig. 13-10C. The form is ready to be poured. The mason is shoveling dirt up against the sides of the form to seal small holes.

Fig. 13-10D. The cement truck is backed into the middle of the job so that the concrete can be directed from the chute into the form.

the joints are pointed (a tool is run down the joint), and that the footing is kept clean. You can scrape it clean with a shovel or trowel.

Height. Your plan will tell you how many courses (how high) the foundation wall has to be. If there is any doubt, make it a course higher. That is always better than making it too low.

Details. Openings are now left for windows and doors and vents. The foundation is capped. According to some codes, the topmost blocks can be filled in. With other codes, you have to lay down 4-inch solids for the top course. The foundation bolts have to be installed at this time.

When the foundation wall is completed, its outside will be waterproofed. This is done by parging it; that simply means applying two ⅜-inch-thick

Fig. 13-10E. The mason and helper are "pulling" the concrete along to make it fill the form.

Fig. 13-10F. The concrete has been screeded flush with top of form. The mason's helper is puddling the concrete (vibrating it to make it settle evenly into all the spaces).

layers of mortar to the outside of the concrete block. Following that the mortar is permitted to dry hard. It is then given an asphalt coating.

Drainage. With the exterior of the foundation parged and sealed, you can install drain pipes. Unless you can lead the water somewhere, there is no point to having drain pipes. Use plastic or bituminous pipe with holes drilled into their sides. Place

Fig. 13-11. A plastic drain pipe (note the holes in its side) is positioned alongside the house footing and covered with gravel. Pipe must run downhill and lead water away if it is to have any value.

Fig. 13-12. A mason laying up the first course of block. The line is his guide.

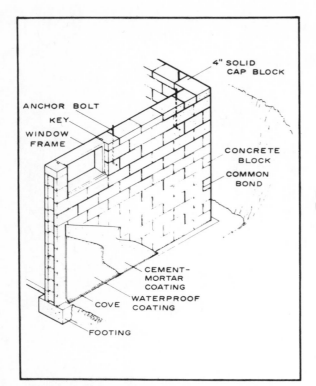

Fig. 13-13. A typical concrete block wall. Note the anchor bolts and window frame.

Labels in figure: 4" SOLID CAP BLOCK, ANCHOR BOLT, KEY, WINDOW FRAME, CONCRETE BLOCK, COMMON BOND, CEMENT-MORTAR COATING, WATERPROOF COATING, COVE, FOOTING

Fig. 13-14. This is what a good workman like job of laying block looks like. Courtesy Portland Cement Association.

Fig. 13-15. The corners of a concrete block foundation are usually erected first. The masons then fill in the open areas. Here the mason is using his transite to check corner elevation. If there is an error, he can pick up 2 or 3 inches by the time the topmost course has been laid.

Fig. 13-16. Parging the exterior of the foundation wall.

Fig. 13-17. A positioned basement window with the cement work completed.

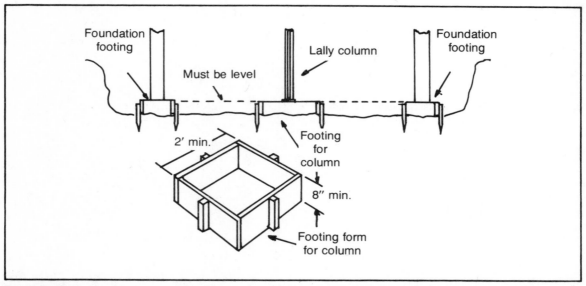

Fig. 13-18. A form that can be used to pour footing for the lally column(s). Note the height of form in relation to the footing.

the sides, and cover with more stone. Then cover the stones with tar paper and soil (Fig. 13-11).

Finishing. Cellar windows, doors, and vents are usually installed after the frame has been erected and the cellar floor—if there is one—is poured. See Figs. 13-12 through 13-18.

Chapter 14

Service Lines

WHILE THE MASON AND HIS HELPER ARE WORKING ON the foundation, you can supervise the excavating contractor in digging a trench for the sewer pipe and other lines. At the same time, you can have the plumber start his work. The plumber runs the sewer pipe and connects it to the city sewer main. The plumber runs the water service pipe, but the city engineers make the actual connections. You have to see to it that the trench is dug and the city is informed that you are ready for the water connection. See Figs. 14-1 and 14-2.

The Sewer Line. The sewer line should be as straight as possible. When and where you must have a turn, you must use a long-turn elbow. The line itself must be angled at ¼ inch to the foot. You can go to ½ inch to the foot, but no more. If you have to, run the line a short distance at 45 degrees rather than go beyond the ½-inch-to-the-foot pitch.

The Water Line. The only requirements with a waterline are that you run at least a ¾-inch copper line and that you position a shut-off valve in the line, as required by the city water department. See Figs. 14-3 and 14-4.

If you are running a cast-iron sewer pipe, do not place the copper pipe in the same trench. If they are physically close, galvanic corrosion will destroy the copper. If you have no choice but to run them alongside one another, wrap the copper in several layers of tar-impregnated cloth.

Septic Tank and Drain Field. At this point in your work, you have a backhoe on the site excavating your sewer trench. Because the cost of using the equipment is partially based on transporting the equipment, it is financially advisable to use the machine as much as possible at one session. If you are going to need a septic tank and drain field, excavate for them now even if you don't construct and install them until later.

Wells, septic tanks and drain fields are covered in Chapter 18.

Fig. 14-1. Installing a clay-pipe sewer line.

Fig. 14-2. When the water and sewer line are beneath the road, the cost of breaking a path through the concrete can be considerable. Here a workman is using an air hammer.

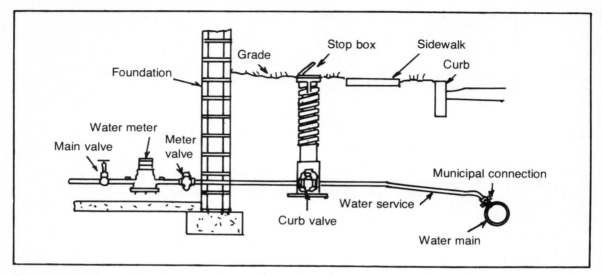

Fig. 14-3. The various parts comprising a water service line and its connection to the city main.

Fig. 14-4. A copy water-service line with a curb valve in position.

Chapter 15

Backfilling, Grading, and Driveway Excavation

BACKFILLING (FIG. 15-1) IS THE JOB OF REPLACING the soil around the building. Because a lot of soil generally has to be moved, it is usually accomplished by machine. Most often, backfilling is a portion of the excavation contract. The same subcontractor who dug the original hole comes back to the job site to complete the work. Because these people are selling their time, it is up to you to make certain they do what is required.

The first layer of soil placed over the service pipes must be positioned gently. If the soil contains a number of large rocks, it is advisable to hand fill the drain-pipe and sewer-pipe trench with a shovel. Use soft soil until the pipes are safely covered. Even then the subsoil cannot be tossed into the trench or the excavation where the rocks will go bounding down against the foundation.

The backfill must be free of debris such as cardboard boxes, lumber and the like. These materials decay with time. When they shrink they cause the surface of the earth to subside in spots.

The backfill, the soil that is actually repositioned within the excavation and the trenches,

will also subside and compact with time. Therefore, you must direct the dozer operator to pile the soil higher over these areas than elsewhere. See Fig. 15-2.

Rough Grading. The surface of the soil left behind after the passage of the dozer is called the rough grade. This surface should angle upward from all sides toward the foundation of the building. The angle need not be great; 1 inch per foot is plenty. You need it to direct the flow of rain water and melting snow away from the building. The piled soil must be higher than what you actually want because the replaced earth will settle with time.

Topsoil. If the land was originally covered with a decent layer of topsoil (perhaps a couple of inches), it paid you to have the excavator remove the topsoil and pile it up in one corner of the lot. Now that you have rough graded the lot, you want it back. This becomes another machine operation unless you don't mind a series of weekends with barrow, shovel, and rake. The topsoil is spread evenly over your grounds with the exception of the strip of earth that will become your driveway.

Fig. 15-1. Backfilling, replacing the soil around the foundation, being done beside a wood foundation. Courtesy American Plywood Association.

Fig. 15-2. The finished grade should slope gently upward toward the building foundation on all its four sides to provide rainwater runoff.

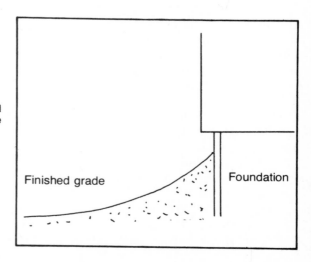

Finished grade

Foundation

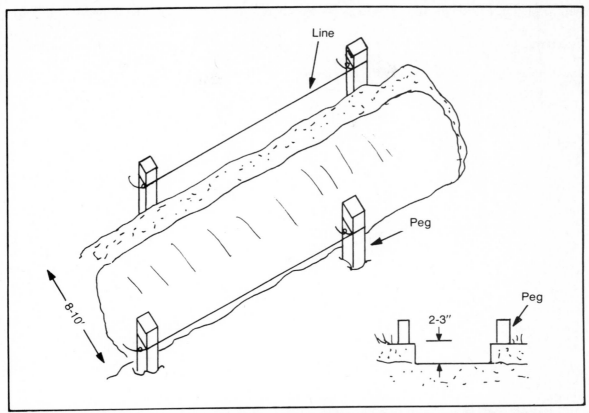

Fig. 15-3. Lay out the driveway with line and pegs. Then have the bulldozer remove the topsoil from the area.

If you have no topsoil, there are three things you can do. You can purchase topsoil by the cubic yard and have it dumped on your land and spread it yourself with a shovel and rake.

You can take the fast lane and purchase sod by the square foot and lay it down just as you would lay down a carpet. All you need do is water the sod and it will send its roots into the earth without further attention.

The last and least expensive method of adding grass to your land is to let the earth turn into topsoil. This takes time and effort, but if you have no topsoil it is the least expensive method. See Chapter 26.

Driveway. We call it a driveway, but all you really need is a hard stand alongside or terminating at the building or leading to the garage. If you are shooting for a minimum-cost home, there is no

point including a garage. Even a small garage incorporated into a building will occupy 25 percent of that structure. That is a lot of space to devote to a silent beast.

All you really need is sufficient space to get your car legally off the road. From the driveway, you can make do with a walk to the house. Use 2-inch-thick flagstones, 1 foot by 2 feet or so, simply laid down directly on the bare, exposed subsoil.

Using pegs and string (Fig. 15-3), outline the driveway you want. For a single automobile, you want a width of 8 to 10 feet. While the dozer is still on your property, have the man remove whatever topsoil is present between the staked lines. Then have him drag the dozer blade backwards down the length of the drive. This will smooth the surface of the driveway area.

Bear in mind that the drive must go all the way

to the road. If there is a curb the curb must be cut. In most cities, the building department issues permits for making this cut. It must be made to their specifications—so wide and so deep. Cutting can be done with a small sledge hammer and a cold chisel or it can be done by a subcontractor with an air hammer.

The least expensive driveway surface consists of crushed stone. You can lay the stone down now or later. See Chapter 25.

Chapter 16

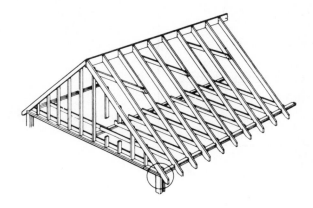

Framing, Sheathing, and Roofing

WITH THE FOUNDATION IN PLACE (ALONG WITH the foundation bolts—Fig. 16-1), framing can now be started. Foundation details can be completed at the same time. As the builder, there isn't very much for you to do at this time except keep the job clean and supervise. Make certain the materials are delivered on time and that the carpentry crew goes about its business.

Time Involved. While each job is different, you can estimate that it will take two masons and a helper about one week to erect a full basement for a small house. Another week will be required to finish the foundation (parge the walls, set the windows, etc.).

Two carpenters and a helper can frame a small house in a week and sheath it in another week. This is assuming that it is an ordinary, rectangular house without any special corners and shapes.

Care of Material. The lumberyard will dump the wood right on the ground. This is fine with everything except the plywood. You want to keep the plywood above the ground and covered with a sheet of plastic. All you need is a couple of blocks of concrete or wood. Letting the plywood remain in contact with the earth or get soaked will cause its layers to become unglued.

Your carpenter should check each 2 × 4 so as not to use any having very large knots. There are places where short pieces are needed and, with a little care, nothing is wasted.

Check to see that 8-penny nails are used and that each stud end has at least three nails. Check to see that none of the studs are badly bowed. If they are, have them replaced.

You might want to be on hand to check on material delivery if the deal calls for you to supply the lumber. We are not suggesting that the yard will shortchange you or that the carpenter will remove some lumber for use elsewhere. It is just wise to be on hand so there is no temptation.

Insurance. You can secure a construction policy that insures you against fire, but few insurance companies will protect you against theft. It is wise to make frequent appearances and keep an eye on things while the lumber lies in loose piles.

Accuracy. Right now you are dealing with

163

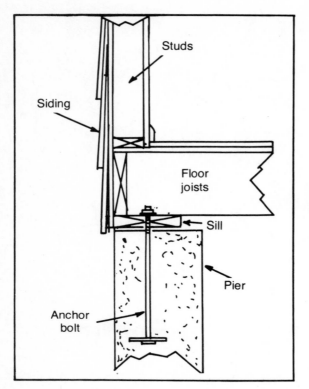

Fig. 16-1. The sill plate of a wood frame positioned atop a foundation. Note how the siding overlaps the sill plate and foundation.

Fig. 16-2. Another view of a sill plate atop a foundation. Note where the ends of the floor joists rest. Courtesy U.S. Department of Agriculture.

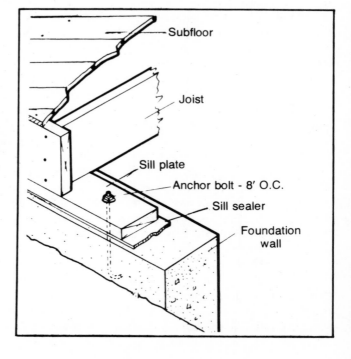

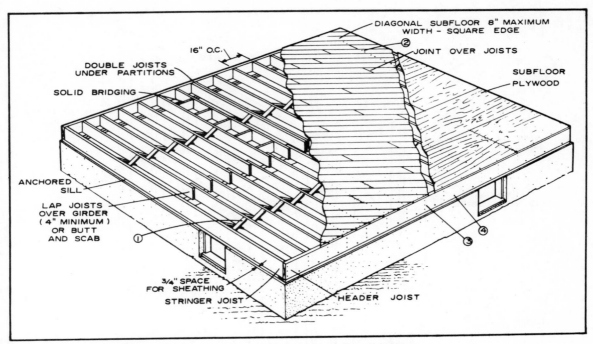

Fig. 16-3. Standard platform construction. Courtesy U.S. Department of Agriculture.

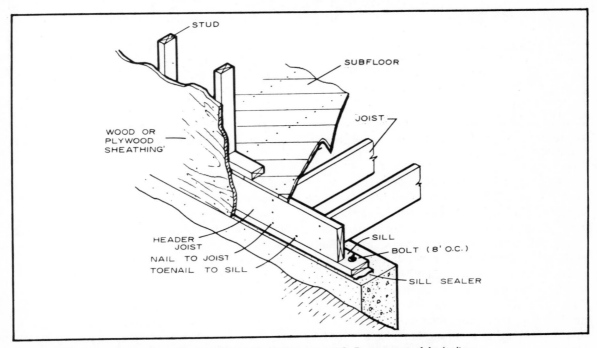

Fig. 16-4. The house frame (studs) rest on the platform. Courtesy U.S. Department of Agriculture.

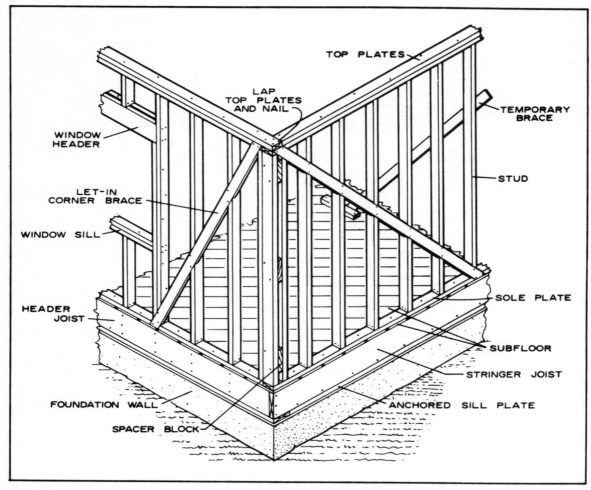

Fig. 16-5. The frame has been erected upon the platform. Braces are used to hold it temporarily vertical. Courtesy U.S. Department of Agriculture.

rough carpentry. Don't be surprised to see errors of up to ¼ inch. Nevertheless, the walls should be perfectly plumb. Check them with a spirit level. Bear in mind that some of the studs might be a fraction bowed. This means that you have to find a perfectly straight stud before you can make an accurate evaluation. The floor should be level to plus or minus 1 inch over its entire length. Because the floor will also have minor surface variation, you will need to take these variations into account. If the floor isn't level, shim up the low points by adding sheets of slate under the frame. A little mortar will

hold the slate permanently in place. See Fig. 16-2 through 16-4.

If you are using plywood or tongue and groove lumber, you do not need to install corner bracing. Most of the other sheathing requires corner bracing. This is best done before the sheathing is positioned. See Figs. 16-5 through 16-10.

Roof Deck. The roof deck is applied to the rafters. There is nothing special about its application except you must make certain there are no openings. Some carpenters are casual about the roof deck because it will be covered. The boards must be closely fitted and properly nailed in place. The deck is now trimmed to its preferred dimensions.

Roofing. Some carpenters will do the roofing, but some won't. In some cases, you will get a better price from a roofing specialist. You can also do the roof yourself. It is strenuous and repetitive work that requires careful attention to application instructions.

To find the quantity of roofing material you need, simply find the total square area of the roof in square feet. Divide by 100. This will give you the number of "squares" you need. Roofing is sold in squares, each square covers 100 square feet. Each shingle is 36 inches long. The light weight roofing comes three bundles to the square. The heavy weight roofing comes four and five bundles to a square. You can purchase less than a full square, but suppliers won't break a bundle. There is very little waste, but you have to figure a sufficient number of additional shingles to edge the eaves. You also need 15-pound felt as an undercover. Four rolls are usually enough for a small roof. See Figs. 16-11, 16-12, and 16-13.

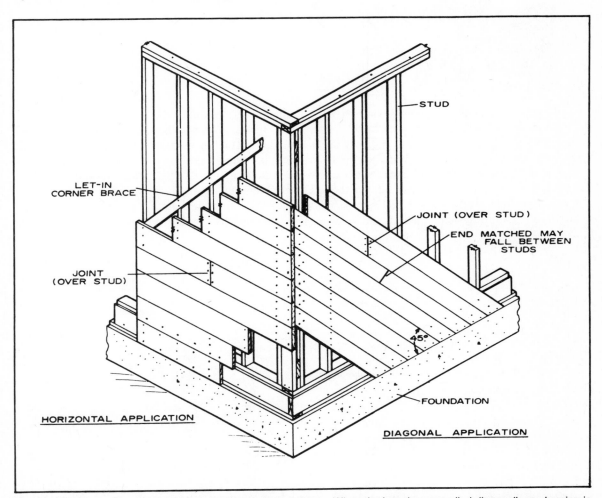

Fig. 16-6. Board sheathing can be fastened atop the house frame. When the boards are applied diagonally, no bracing is required. When the boards are applied horizontally, bracing is required. Courtesy, U.S. Department of Agriculture.

Fig. 16-7. A close up of "let-in" bracing on a house frame.

Roofing with asphalt shingles is easy when the roof is low and slightly pitched. The work is very difficult when the roof is steep and high, as in the case of a two-story building. With a one-story building, it is relatively easy to bring the material to the roof, easy to stay safely on the roof, and the low pitch tends to hid irregularities. A high, pitch roof is difficult to work on physically, and inaccuracies are immediately visible.

In any case, whether you do the work yourself or subcontract it the procedures are the same. The roof is covered with overlapping strips of 15-pound felt held in place with a few roofing nails and trimmed flush with all roof edges.

You start with a full, reversed shingle at a lower right-hand or left-hand corner. The shingle to

Fig. 16-8. Installing ceiling joists on a house frame.

Fig. 16-9. Called a header, this is a reinforcement that is positioned across window and door openings. Header dimensions are defined by the building code.

extend beyond the rake edge of the room by 1 inch and beyond the eaves edge by 1 to 1½ inches (more is not advisable). See Fig. 16-15. More shingles are positioned adjoining for the full width of the roof. Next, a right-side-up and "cut"-edge-down shingle is positioned atop the first shingle. More shingles are then nailed in place all the way across. The shingle package contains nailing instructions.

That does it for the first course. Now go back to the first corner or edge, using a shingle with one half tab cut off, position the first shingle of the second row 1 inch past the rake edge and 5 inches above the in-place, first course shingle. Nail down a row of shingles right across the width of the roof, take care to keep the line parallel with the first. The first shingle of the third course or row is cut back

Fig. 16-10. A partially constructed wood-frame house. In this design, the first-floor studs are short because they rest on a high foundation wall.

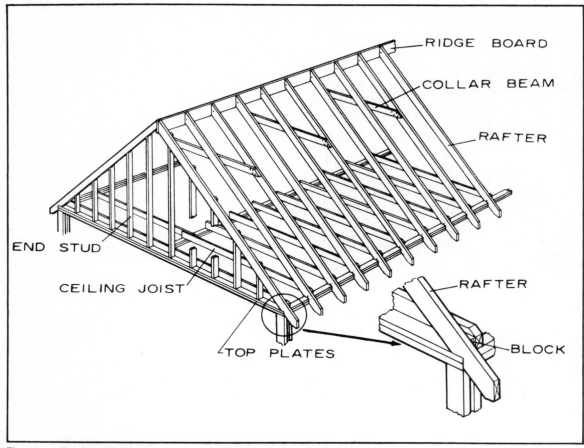

Fig. 16-11. Roof framing details. Courtesy U.S. Department of Agriculture.

one full tab. In this way, the tab of one shingle is always above the cut or indent on the next lower shingle.

Flashing. Flashing is the term used to denote metal that joins two differing building surfaces. Examples are a roof and a wall and a roof and a chimney. The best material to use is copper. The next best is aluminum. Do not use the copper-plated Kraft paper. The metal is too thin and is too easily damaged.

Flashing is never solid in the sense there are no openings. Instead, flashing provides a series of little roofs or guides that lead rain water away from the opening. If the joint is simple, as for example a roof to a vertical wall, you could do it yourself. If the joint is complicated, as for example a pitched roof

and a brick or stone chimney, it is best to hire an expert to do the flashing. It is easy to err with flashing, and you won't know you have not done the job properly until rain water leaks to the house interior.

The building inspector will want to see your work before you go any further. If there are any violations, he will "red tag" them, and technically you cannot proceed until you have made the required corrections.

Should your building be red tagged, don't feel the world has come to an end. Go see the inspector and find out what has to be done. Usually, it isn't very much, but make certain the inspector comes and removes the tag before you continue working. Some inspectors are very strict.

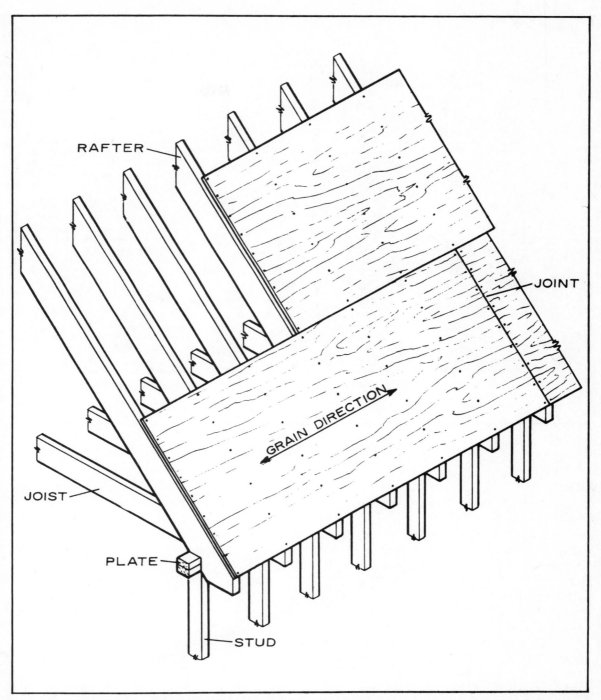

Fig. 16-12. The roof frame is covered with plywood sheathing. Note how the joints are broken up. Courtesy U.S. Department of Agriculture.

Fig. 16-13. This is a difficult roof on which to work. For one thing it is steep. For another, its very steepness makes all inaccuracies highly visible.

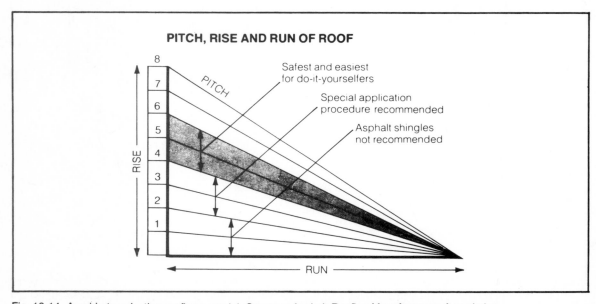

Fig. 16-14. A guide to selecting roofing material. Courtesy Asphalt Roofing Manufacturers Association.

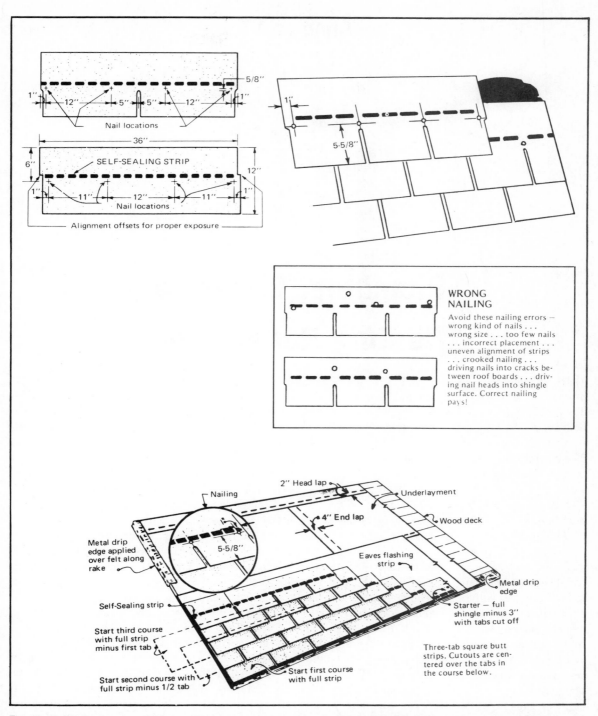

5/8"

1" **12"** **5"** **5"** **12"** **1"**

Nail locations

36"

6" SELF-SEALING STRIP **12"**

1" **11"** **12"** **11"** **1"**

Nail locations

Alignment offsets for proper exposure

1"

5-5/8"

WRONG
NAILING

Avoid these nailing errors —
wrong kind of nails . . .
wrong size . . . too few nails
. . . incorrect placement . . .
uneven alignment of strips
. . . crooked nailing . . .
driving nails into cracks between roof boards . . . driving nail heads into shingle
surface. Correct nailing
pays!

2" Head lap — Underlayment

Nailing

4" End lap — Wood deck

Metal drip
edge applied
over felt along
rake

5-5/8"

Eaves flashing
strip

Metal drip
edge

Self-Sealing strip

Starter — full
shingle minus 3"
with tabs cut off

Start third course
with full strip
minus first tab

Three-tab square butt
strips. Cutouts are cen-
tered over the tabs in
the course below.

Start second course with
full strip minus 1/2 tab

Start first course
with full strip

Fig. 16-15. Basic steps in applying asphalt shingle roofing. Courtesy Asphalt Roofing Manufacturers Association.

Chapter 17

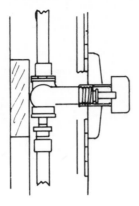

Plumbing, Electrical, Heating Rough Work

WITH THE ROOFING IN PLACE. YOU CALL IN THE plumber, the electrician, and the heating crews. They will either mark the holes they want cut in the building or they will tell the carpenter where they want the holes for their pipes and ducts to be cut. The cutting and the patching that follows is usually part of the carpenter's contract. See Figs. 17-1 and 17-2.

If you are building within a municipality, the plumber has to be licensed and his work has to be inspected. Therefore, you can be certain his work will be satisfactory from a technical plumbing point of view. You have to make certain the work is satisfactory from your point of view. This means that all pipes must be properly supported, nothing should just hang there. The pipes should run neatly and as close to the walls and ceiling as is practical. Make certain that the shut-off valves are installed as called for in the print and that there are a sufficient number of clean-outs in the sewer lines. This portion of the plumbing is called the rough plumbing. See Figs. 17-3 through 17-6. The fixtures are installed later.

The rough plumbing must be inspected by the city. If there is a gas line, the gas line must be subjected to a leak test as provided by the building code. The test will be checked by the city plumbing inspector.

The electrican can now do his work. He usually bores his own holes for the wires. The electrical contract usually includes all the wires, switches, and meter boxes. The local electric company installs the meter and runs the line to its pole.

Like the plumbing, the electrical work is not completed at this time. The gem boxes and switch boxes are installed, but the connections and covers are not put on until later. The electrical work has also to be inspected and approved.

Whether the heating crew opts to work now or later depends upon the type of heating equipment you are having installed and whether or not you are going to have a full cellar. If the heating system is above ground, they can usually go right ahead without problems. If it is to be in the cellar, they will wait for the cellar floor to be poured and place the unit on a slab of concrete atop the cellar floor.

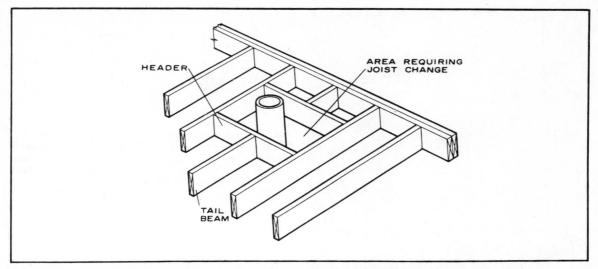

Fig. 17-1. It is the carpenter's responsibility to install headers in the joists to permit the installation of pipes.

In any case, it will be the carpenter's job to cut the holes needed for the heating pipes and ducts. If there are to be radiators partially set into the walls, now is the time to place reflective insulation in place so it will be behind the radiators. Note that the heating man does not make the electrical and control connections to the heating system. That is done by the electrician.

For some reason, the building department generally doesn't inspect heating systems. In any case, when the electrical, plumbing, and heating rough work is completed, have it inspected and passed by the building department. Until this is done you cannot close the walls.

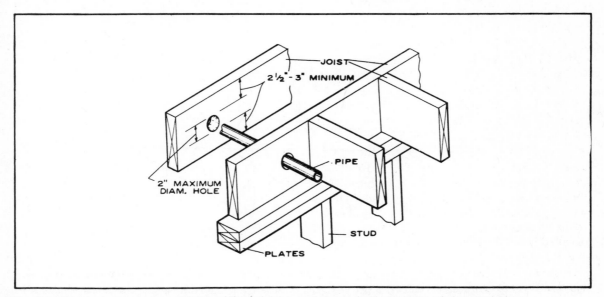

Fig. 17-2. Circular holes can be safely bored through joists and girders for the passage of pipes and wires.

Fig. 17-3. A plumber installing a floor flange for a toilet. The flange is made of PVC and so is the pipe section he is sanding preparatory to applying cement. Note the blocks of wood near the hole in the floor. Blocks will lift the flange to make it flush with the floor tile to be laid down later.

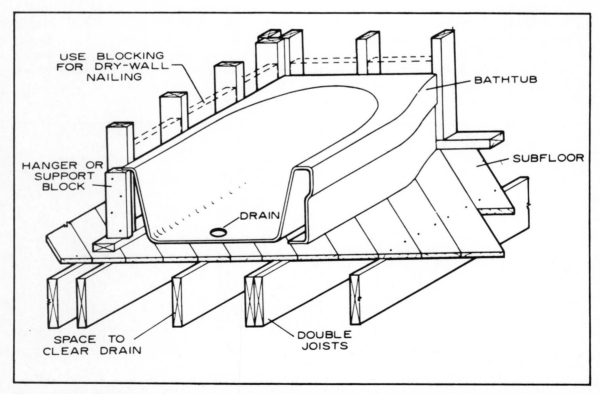

Fig. 17-4. The bathtub position and the supporting framing. Sufficient space must be left beneath the drain hole for positioning the trap and valve, if there is one. Courtesy U.S. Department of Agriculture.

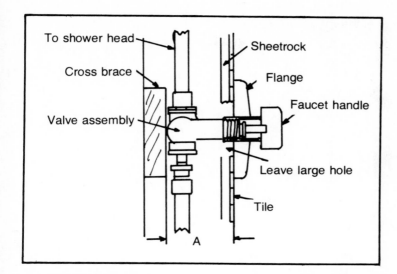

To shower head

Cross brace

Valve assembly

Sheetrock

Flange

Faucet handle

Leave large hole

Tile

A

Fig. 17-4. Shower valve assembly details. Use copper or brass screws and copper clamps to fasten the assembly to the brace. Do not use nails.

Fig. 17-6. Plastic drain and vent piping in place. Clean, round holes through studs do not weaken them materially.

Chapter 18

Well, Septic Tank, and Drain Field

WHATEVER EXCAVATING IS REQUIRED FOR THE well, septic tank, and drain field, the work should be done while the power equipment is on the job site. Not only will doing so save time, it will also reduce costs because the contractor and machine operator is spared the labor and expense of hauling his machines back and forth.

THE WELL

Unless you are in a frost-free part of the country, the well head and associate piping must be beneath the surface of the earth to prevent it from freezing. This can be done any number of ways. Whatever the final design, there must be provisions for access and repair to the well. Pumping equipment can be at the well head in a well house that is insulated or subterranean, or the pump and associate pressure tank and equipment can be placed within the building. It all depends upon the pumping system. In turn this depends upon the depth of the water in the well and the quantity that is to be drawn within a given time. If there is a need for an excavation around the

well head to be, now is the time to excavate.

Location. When there is a well, a septic tank and a drain field on the same land (or another source of pollution such as a barn or stable), the well should be positioned as far as possible away from the potential source of pollution. If possible, the well should be uphill from source of pollution. The reason for the choice of higher ground is that underground water generally travels from high-lying areas to low-lying areas. In other words, underground water generally flows in the same direction as surface rainwater flows. Placing the well uphill of the pollution reduces the possibility of trouble. The distance permissible between well and pollution source varies with the nature of the soil. See Fig. 18-1. This is a dimension you can and should secure from your local board of health. Generally, 75 feet is an acceptable minimum, but it can vary tremendously depending upon subsoil condition.

Depth. There are two depths to consider in the design of a well. One is the well itself. The other is the well head.

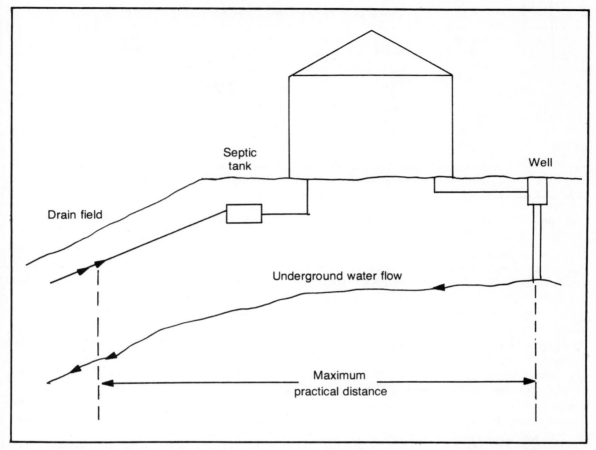

Fig. 18-1. The drain field should be positioned in an area of the property that is lower than the position of the well. The reason is that ground water usually flows in the same direction surface water does after a rain. The well should be placed as far away from the drain.

Depth costs money. The well digger charges per foot of depth, and you need to pay for the pipe that lines the well. The deeper you go the greater both these costs.

On the other hand, you cannot limit depth to a figure you would like. The well must reach down far enough to strike water-bearing rock or soil or it is worthless. It is wise to go down beyond this point as insurance against a lowering water table (underground water level). How much farther you should go to make certain the well never runs dry is difficult to ascertain with accuracy. Your well digger should know from experience in your region. Don't urge the well digger to go too far down after striking

water. He might go down past the water-bearing strata.

Well-head depth depends upon the frost line. You want the well head below the frost line and, of course, you want to run the water line from the well head to the building below the frost line. The alternative in cold-weather country is a heated or well-insulated well house and an insulated water line.

Placing the well beneath the house, when conditions permit, might appear to be a good decision, and I imagine that it has been done. But we advise against it. It is more than a little awkward getting the drilling equipment in place during construction. If well repairs require the removal of the well-pipe

179

Table 18-1. Minimum Recommended Septic-Tank Sizes.

Number of people	Approx. gallons	Inside width	Inside length	Liquid depth	Total depth
4	250	3'6"	3.0"	4'0"	5'0"
6	360	4'0"	4'9"	4'0"	5'0"
8	480	4'0"	5'0"	4'0"	5'0"
10	600	4'0"	6'0"	4'0"	5'0"
12	720	4'0"	7'3"	4'0"	5'0"
14	840	4'0"	7'4"	4'6"	5'6"
16	960	4'0"	8'9"	4'6"	5'6"

Based on 60 gallons of water per person per day usage. Note: If a garbage disposal unit is to be installed, increase the tank capacity by 50 percent.

liner, there is no practical way of doing the work.

Well Diggers. Your approach to hiring a well digger should be similar to that suggested for contracting any other subcontractor. You want an experienced person with a good reputation for dependability. You need to agree upon a fixed per-foot price for the drilling; who pays for the well pipe and fittings (the well screen); who takes care of the preliminary excavation (if needed); who completes the work around the well head (the concrete collar or similar protection); who furnishes the run of pipe to the house; who installs the run of pipe to the house; and who furnishes and installs the pump and tank and associate equipment.

The well digger cannot guarantee water at any depth, but he should be prepared to perform flow rate tests to your satisfaction before he packs his gear and takes off. Merely finding water is not enough. There must be water in sufficient quantity to make the well useful.

All these items require time, material, and labor. They should be spelled out. They are too easy to overlook and then the arguments ensue. Get it all down in writing and save yourself many headaches.

SEPTIC TANKS

A septic tank is a closed vessel into which the soil (toilet) and other waste material is discharged. The waste enters the tank and the contained solids are transformed to a liquid by bacterial action. The process takes about three days, depending upon the temperatures. The liquid is then directed out of the tank and into a drain field. Here the liquid seeps into the earth where more bacterial actions destroys its pathogens, thus eventually purifying the liquid.

Tank Size. Because the tank must hold the waste discharge from the house sewer pipe for three days, it must be fairly large. On the other hand, an overly large tank is a waste of money and labor. Tank size is computed on the basis of the expected number of people that will occupy the house or the number of bedrooms in the building. Table 18-1 provides the recommended minimum dimensions. If you want to rest assured your tank will not be overloaded, make or select a slightly larger tank. See Table 18-1.

Tank Position. A properly constructed and sealed tank produces no odor. Neither does a properly constructed drain field. Thus you can place either or both wherever it is convenient. If there is a well, you want the drain field as far away as possible. Although the tank can be placed alongside the building, it is usually placed a dozen or more feet away for the benefit of easy access to the clean-out door. Septic tanks are cleaned by truck-mounted pumps. When practical, the tank and its clean-out door are positioned within easy reach of the pump truck's suction pipe.

And also, since there may be some shifting of the tank relative to the building, a longer pipe between the tank and the building will have more joints and therefore permit more flexing without opening than a short, single length of pipe would. See Fig. 18-2.

So much for tank-to-house distance. Now we have to consider elevation; this is crucial. You should know exactly where the sewer pipe will exit the building. You know where the same pipe will enter the tank or you can adjust the pipe entrance elevation (height) if you are constructing the tank or having it built for you.

The ideal pitch for the sewer pipe going from the building to the tank is ¼ inch to the foot. If it is a long pipe and you feel there might be some slight sags developing with time, make the pitch ½ inch to the foot—but *no* more. If you are on hilly terrain and you need more pitch, run a portion of the pipe at 45 degrees (the balance at the aforementioned ¼ or ½ inch to the foot). At a lesser pitch, the solids will hang up in the line. At a greater pitch but less than 45 degrees, the liquid will run off and leave the solids in the line.

The rotation of the tank in relation to the side of the building from where the sewer pipe issues is also important. If the tank and building sides are parallel and the opening for the pipe in the building faces the opening in the tank directly, you can have the pipe run straight across. If this is not the case and the pipe has to be run at an angle, you want to angle the tank so that the connection can be made with standard fittings.

Tank Types. Tanks are made of steel, plastic, brick, concrete block, and poured concrete. Tanks can be purchased ready made in any number of sizes, shapes and materials. They can be made on the job. As the prime contractor, you will have to

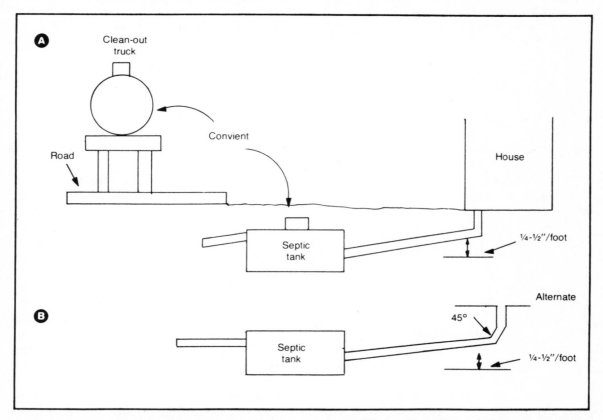

Fig. 18-2. Running the house sewer line to the septic tank: (A) tank-to-house distance permits a pitch of between ¼ and ½ inch to the foot, which is desirable. (B) the distance and tank depth is such that optimum pitch cannot be secured for the entire run. The solution is to run part of the pipe at 45 degrees or more and the balance at the lower angle. Note that the septic tank has been positioned within reach of the clean-out truck's suction pipe.

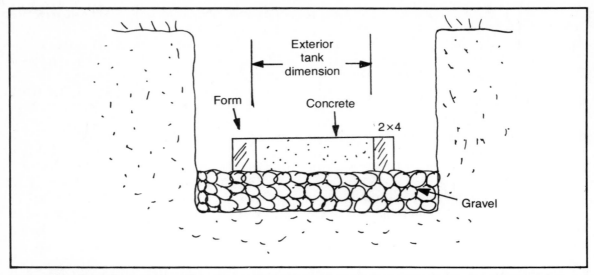

Fig. 18-3. The first steps in constructing a concrete-block septic tank. A hole is excavated to the proper depth. Its bottom is covered with 4 to 6 inches of gravel. A form is constructed and positioned. The form is then filled with concrete.

decide which is the least costly. Bear in mind when you price the ready-made tanks that you have to include the cost of delivery and positioning them within the excavation.

Because the tank is very heavy and position and elevation are crucial, the operation will require preparation, several men, and a power crane. The delivery truck will probably have a crane.

Making a Tank. Tanks can be made from brick, poured concrete and concrete block. Along with a poured floor and top, concrete probably provides the most economical method. The following design is probably the easiest to build in terms of material, skill, and labor.

Start by excavating a flat-bottomed hole in the earth 2 feet wider and 2 feet longer than the outside dimensions of the desired septic tank. You are going to cover the bottom of the excavation with 4 inches of crushed stone and 4 inches of concrete; make the hole's depth accordingly. Spread 4 inches of crushed stone across the entire bottom of the hole. Make the surface of the stone reasonably level. Construct a wood form of 2 × 4s on edge. Make the inside of the form just as big as the desired exterior dimensions of the tank you want to construct. See Fig. 18-3. Lay the form flat on the stone.

Adjust it to make it reasonably level.

Fill the form with concrete. use the high-sand mix (1:2¼:3) and lots of water so that the concrete finds its own level. Give the concrete 2 days to set and harden. If the air is very dry, spray a little water on the concrete after the initial set (about 1 hour) to speed curing and hardening.

Using 6-inch concrete block, build your septic tank. You can make it a single-compartment tank (Fig. 18-4) or a double-compartment tank (Fig. 18-5). The double tank is more effective than the single tank in keeping solid matter out of the drain field. In any case, make the second compartment roughly 50 percent as large as the first.

When you have layed up all the block, the inside surfaces of the tank are waterproofed with two sequential layers of mortar. Use mortar cement (which is 25 percent lime) in the ratio of 1 part cement to 2 or 3 parts sand. Give the mortar plaster a few days to dry hard and then further waterproof the interior of the tank, sides, and bottom with a thick coating of asphalt.

Next you need to construct or have constructed the roof of the tank, which needs one manhole if it is a single-section tank and two if it is a double-section tank. See Fig. 18-6.

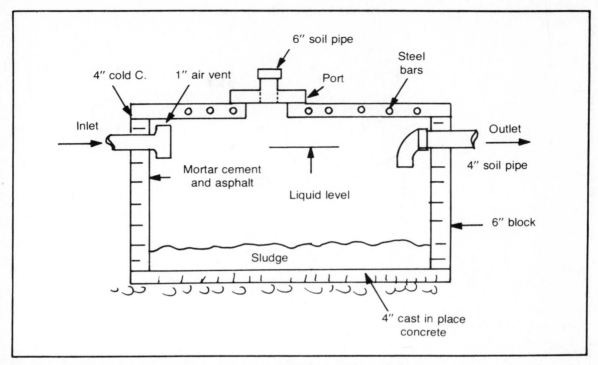

Fig. 18-4. A single-stage septic tank showing its crucial dimensions and part relationships.

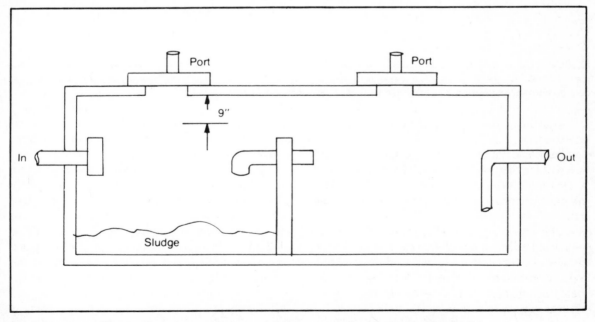

Fig. 18-5. A two-stage tank. Sludge must be removed when it reaches the pipe in the center wall.

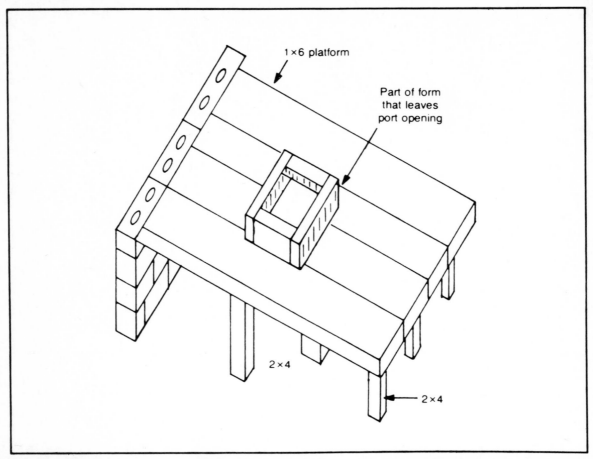

Fig. 18-6. The temporary concrete-support platform constructed within the septic tank walls. The port opening must be large enough for a man to enter and remove the form after the concrete has set.

Start by constructing a platform of 1-×-6 boards "tacked" to 2 × 4s to make a rectangle that is just large enough to fit inside the tank. Cut one or two rectangular holes in this platform. Each hole is to be approximately 1 foot by 2 feet; that is large enough for a man to slip through. Each hole is edged with 2 × 4s, on edge.

Next the platform is slipped over the tank and supported on a number of vertical 2 × 4s. The top surface of the platform is positioned flush with the top edge of the block. Use one 2 × 4 every 2 or 3 feet. Now the block tank must be edged with wood. The easy way is to backfill and then support a 6-inch board edging on pegs as shown in Fig. 18-7. The top

of the edge-board form is positioned 4 inches above the top surface of the concrete block. Now you have to pour and reinforce the top.

Use the same high sand mixture, but with just enough water to make the mix workable. Carefully spread a 2-inch layer of concrete over the entire platform surface. Now position the steel rods. Use the rod diameter and number suggested in Table 18-2. With this done, cover the rods and in-place concrete with more concrete. Screed flush with the top edges of the form. Wait for the concrete to set up and then float it.

Now you need to make one or two covers, as the case may be, for the manholes. Construct the

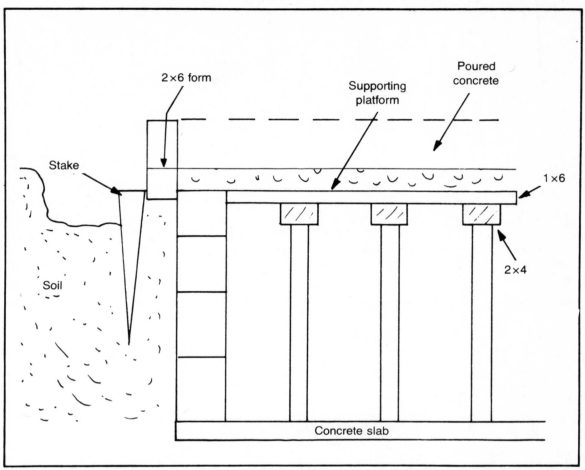

Fig. 18-7 A sectional view of the tank roof during construction. Note that the surface of the supporting platform is flush with the tops of the block.

form as shown in Fig. 18-8. Again use a high-sand mix. If you want to use one form for two covers, grease it first. Otherwise, you will probably have to destroy the form to remove it when the concrete has hardened. See Fig. 18-9.

Give the reinforced roof two full days to harden, and then gingerly enter the tank, remove the supporting posts, and remove the platform. If you have followed instructions and used just a few nails, you should have no difficulty.

With the preceding accomplished, the entire surface of the tank top is given a coating of asphalt. The manhole cover(s) is positioned and it too is

Table 18-2. Minimum Steel Reinforcing Bars and Spacing for Tank Covers.

Long bar	Spacing	Diameter
5 feet	19 inches	⅜ inch
6	14	⅜
8	10	⅜
10	10	½

Short bar (at right angles to long bars)

5 feet	15 inches	⅜ inch
6	14	⅜
8	10	⅜

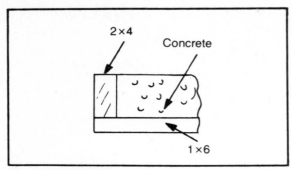

Fig. 18-8. The form showing concrete.

DRAIN FIELDS

In the septic tank, the sewage was attacked and digested by anaerobic bacteria that changed the solids into liquids. The liquid now must be treated by aerobic bacteria—air breathing bacteria—that safely converts the liquid into pure water. Obviously, you cannot simply direct the liquid out of the septic tank and onto the ground. There would be a constant puddle that would be a nuisance. There would be an odor because the bacteria do not work very rapidly, and in the winter the liquid would freeze; bacterial activity would almost cease.

The triple problem of water, smell, and frost is solved by discharging the septic tank's effluent underground. This cannot be accomplished at a single point because the earth will not absorb water that rapidly. The effluent is therefore spread out over an area by means of perforated pipe or short sections

given a coat of asphalt. As there is now a layer of asphalt between the cover and the tank top, the joint is sealed. Wait a week before you replace the soil atop the tank because the concrete is still weak. It takes a month for concrete to get close to full strength.

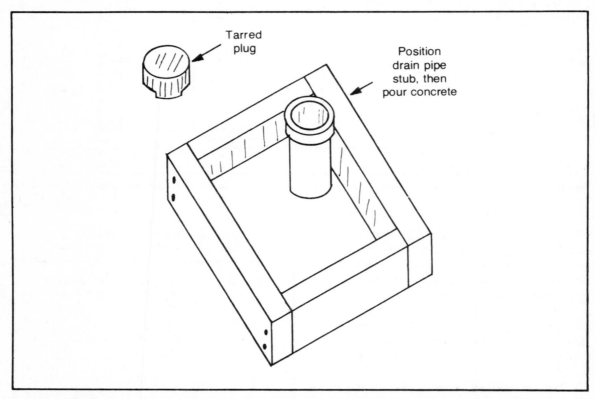

Fig. 18-9. The port covers can be constructed. The drainpipe stub is positioned before the concrete is poured. You may have to weigh it down to hold it in place during pouring.

of loosely joined pipe. The area in which the pipe is positioned is called the drain field.

While the effluent from the septic tank will not freeze as readily as pure water, it will freeze. Therefore the drain pipe must be below grade. At the same time, the bacteria you seek to encourage, the aerobic bacteria, must have air in order to live and do their important work. Thus there must be a compromise. The perforated drain pipe must be sufficiently deep to preclude freezing, yet not so deep the bacteria are starved for air. Drain pipe depth is therefore crucial. For best results, it is advisable to contact your building department or local health department. Where there is little frost, you need just enough cover soil to protect the pipes from damage. In deep frost country, you will need extra pipe length because the pipe has to be placed so deeply the bacteria cannot function very well.

Basic Considerations. The rate at which the soil in your backyard will absorb water depends upon the nature of the soil. If it is sandy, it will soak up water at a high rate. If it lies at the other extreme and is mostly clay, the rate of absorption will be very low.

Drain pipe length—meaning the pipe area that will be placed in the soil and will "present" the water to the soil—depends upon the quantity of water that will flow into and out of the septic tank over a 24 hour period and the nature of the soil.

To some extent local weather and local groundwater conditions are factors. In a high-rain area, the ground is going to be water soaked a good deal of the time. This makes it more difficult for the earth to absorb the effluent.

Estimating Absorption Rate. You need to know approximately how rapidly the soil into which you plan to place the drain pipe will absorb water. With soil capable of absorbing water at a high rate, you can get by with a comparatively short pipe. If the absorption is low, you will need a much longer pipe so as to spread the water over a greater area. If the pipe is too short for the rate of flow out of the septic tank, the drain field trench will be flooded. The bacteria will die for lack of air, and there will be an odor.

On the other hand, drain field piping and

Table 18-3. Ground Water Indicators

Grey (ferrous oxide):	Considerable ground water
Brown (ferric oxide, hematite):	Insignificant ground water
Red brown and grey streaks:	Fluctuating ground water

trenching cost time, labor and money. While it is true that an over-size drain field lasts longer, your goal should be a minimum initial cost. Properly sized and maintained, a drain field should last 20 years or so.

Very possibly local groundwater levels will rise and fall without any surface indications. In any case, absorption rates change for better and for worse now and again. But don't guess. You need a ballpark figure to work with if you are to avoid trouble.

There are two ways to estimate the absorption rate. One way is to examine the soil by checking its color and composition. See Table 18-3. The other way is called a percolation test. It consists of digging a hole in the earth, pouring in water, and measuring the rate at which the water level falls.

To examine your soil, dig a straight-sided hole 1 foot deeper than the depth at which you plan to lay the drain pipe. Check the color and the feel of the soil against Table 18-4.

For the percolation test, dig a straight-sided hole some 13 or 14 inches in diameter. Scrape all "smeared" soil from the sides of the hole. Cover the bottom of the hole with an inch or two of gravel or sand. Gently fill the hole with water. Wait until all

Table 18-4. Soil Texture.

	Recommended minimum drainpipe trench wall area*	
Coarse sand, small gravel	1.2 to 2	sq ft/gal/day
Sand	2.5	sq ft/gal/day
Clay/silt	4	sq ft/gal/day

*The figure is for one side of the trench only. Thus a trench 1 foot deep and 1 foot long would have 2 square feet of absorption area. The bottom of the trench is not included. The figures given are a compromise.

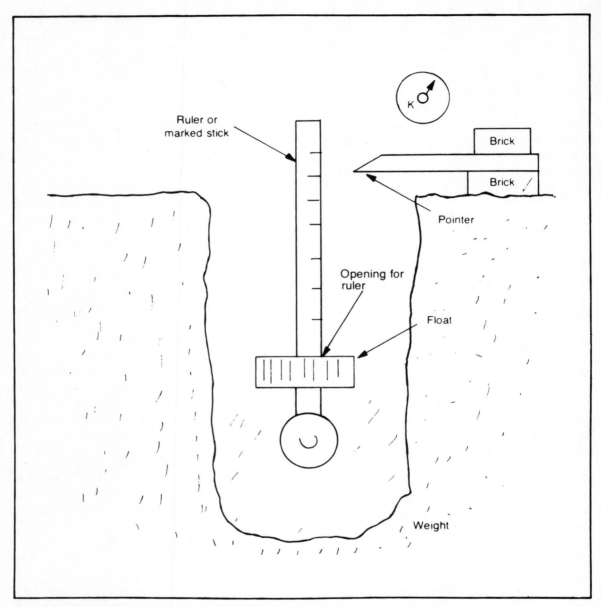

Fig. 18-10. A homemade scale for measuring the water drop in a test hole.

the water disappears. Fill the hole with 6 inches of water.

With the aid of a time piece and an arrangement such as shown in Fig. 18-10, time the rate at which the water drops exactly 1 inch. Refill the hole with clean water and repeat the test until the time re-

quired for the float to descend 1 inch is almost unchanged. This will indicate the rate has stabilized and duplicates (approximately) actual operating conditions. Use the time figure to find the drain field pipe length you need with the help of Table 18-5.

Table 18-5. Perculation Rates.

Rate minutes/inch	Recommended minimum drainpipe trench wall area* sq ft /gal/day
1 min or less	1.0
2	1.5
3	2.0
4	2.5
5	3.0
10	4.0
20	4.6
30	5.2
40	7.0
60	9.0
Unsuited	

*The figure is for one side of the trench only. Thus a trench 1 foot deep and 1 foot long would have 2 square feet of absorbtion area. The bottom of the trench is not included. The figures given are a compromise.

Computing Your Drain-Field Requirements. The average American family uses between 50 and 60 gallons of water per person per day. Assume that you have a family of four and guests once in a while. Using the 60 g/day figure, your drain field will be called upon to dispose of 4 × 60 or 240 gallons of water per day.

Upon examining your soil you find that it is red in color; it is not water saturated. You make a percolation test and come up with the figure of 1 minute. Table 18-5 tells you that the soil can handle 1 gallon of water per square foot of trench-wall area.

Assume further that you are in a mildly cold-weather area and plan to place the drain pipe 2 feet below grade (the earth's surface). The wall area above the pipe is not considered; you hope that there is never so much water that the pipe is flooded. Only the side wall area from the top of the pipe to the bottom of the trench is considered.

Assume you make the trench a total of 3 feet deep. See Fig. 18-11. That would give you 4 square feet of absorption area for every lineal foot of pipe. The bottom of the trench is not included in the calculation either because it has been found that the trench bottom is the first area to become clogged and is therefore useless.

Returning to our calculations, you need to handle 240 gallons per day. The earth can handle 4 gallons per day per lineal foot of pipe: $240 \div 4 = 60$ feet of pipe needed.

Variations. If the pipe is positioned closer to the surface of the earth (assuming there is no risk of frost), the effective wall area of the trench is increased and less pipe and trench are required proportionally. If the trench depth is increased, effective trench wall area is also increased proportionally. You require more gravel and the possibility of coming too close to underground hardpan or rock must be considered. The danger is that the effluent might move too rapidly between the soil and the rock and travel a great distance without aerobic treatment.

If the soil shows streaks of red and grey, you have to increase the length of the drain pipe or deepen the trench or both. Partically water-soaked soil naturally will not absorb as much liquid or absorb it as quickly as dry soil.

If the soil shows grey, meaning it is water soaked much of the time, you had best secure local engineering advice.

Installing the Drain Pipe. You can use any kind of pipe 3 to 4 inches in diameter except metal pipe and Orangeburg, which is mineralized paper pipe. When installing perforated drain pipe, the holes go at the pipe sides. When using drain tile, the short pieces of ceramic pipe are positioned about ⅛ inch apart and the joint is covered with a strip of tar paper.

The drain-field area has to be selected with care. It should be on the south side of the house and away from trees and other sources of shade. You want the field as warm as possible. It should be as far away from the well as practical and not where a car or truck is likely to back up and pass over it.

The drain pipe can make a straight line coming from the septic tank. It can spiral, twist, and turn or separate into several branches. This can be accomplished with a plumbing T or a distribution box. The latter is a concrete box with a heavy, removable cover. You can make it from block or you can make a form and pour it. In any case, the box is preferred to the pipe fitting because you can remove the box cover and clean out the drain pipe, or a portion of it, with a snake.

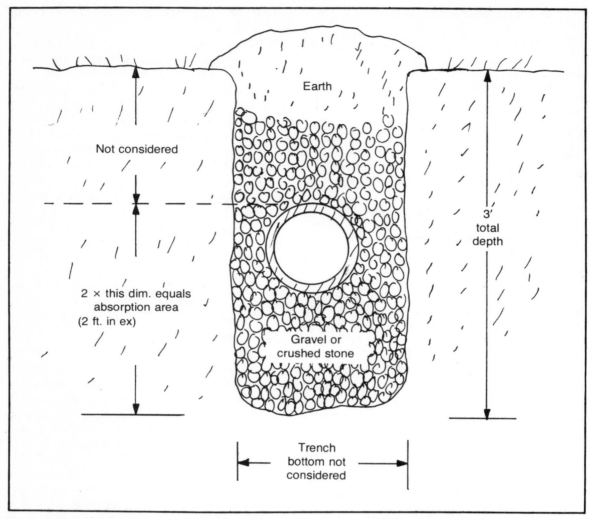

Fig. 18-11. A drainpipe should be positioned within the earth. Note that the pipe is not on the bottom of the trench, but about two-thirds from the bottom. Note too that only the side wall areas from the bottom of the trench to the top of the pipe are considered as being the effective absorption area.

The first few feet of drain pipe can be solid and pitched ½ inch to the foot or more. The drain portion of the pipe must be held to a very shallow pitch: 2 to 4 inches per 100 feet. Use a greater pitch and all the liquid will run down to the end of the pipe and the end will become clogged and useless long before its time.

The trick to establishing and holding this pitch is to position a guide board down the center of the length of the trench. See Fig. 18-12. Use a 4-inch furring strip that is positioned on edge and supported by short stakes driven into the earth. With the aid of spirit level and the gadget shown in Fig. 18-13, adjust the guide board to the desired pitch. Then gently fill the space to the sides and beneath the guide board with gravel. Now you can rest the pipe on the guide board and rest assured the pitch is correct. The pipe is covered with more gravel and

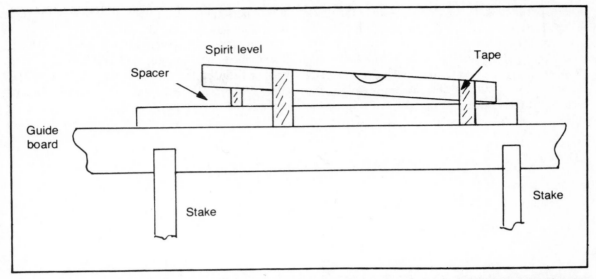

Fig. 18-12. The correct pitch on the guide board is secured. A spirit level is taped to a long, straight length of wood, with a very small spacer between one end of the level and the attached length of wood. This provides the pitch. When the bubble is in the center, the guide board is pitched at the same angle.

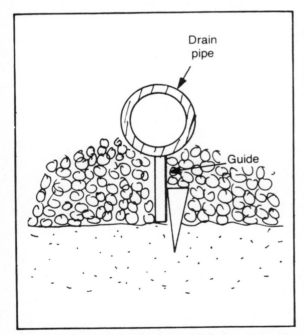

Fig. 18-13. Gravel is spread to the sides of the in-place guide board. The draintile or drainpipe is then position atop the guide board. When more gravel is added, the drain is permanently positioned at the preferred pitch. The guide board remains in place.

then topped with soil. The guide board remains in place.

Maintenance. Once a year you remove all inspection plug and insert a cloth wrapped pole all the way into the tank. Withdraw the pole and determine by inspection the depth of the solids on the

Table 18-6. Maximum Allowable Sludge.

Liquid capacity of tank	Liquid depth (feet)		
	3	4	5
(Gallons)	Distance from bottom of outlet to top of sludge (inches)		
500	11	16	21
600	8	13	18
750	6	10	13
900	4	7	10
1,000	4	6	8

When the sludge at the bottom of your septic tank exceeds the above figures, it is advisable to have the tank pumped clean.

191

bottom of the tank. Compare the depth of the muck as indicated by the soil on the cloth with the figures given in Table 18-6.

If the sludge exceeds the allowable accumulation level, have a septic-tank cleaning company come and pump out the tank. Avoid breathing the gas that might emanate from the tank. It can be deadly poisonous. Don't light a match near the test hole. The gas is flammable.

Do not pour fresh water into the tank, and don't worry about it being pumped perfectly dry. You want a little of the muck to stay. You need the anaerobic bacteria remaining to inoculate the soil and get the operation going again.

Chapter 19

Windows, Doors, and Trim

NOW IS THE TIME TO HAVE THE WINDOWS, DOORS and trim delivered. Have the material brought inside the building. Check the delivery and then paint. It is a lot easier and faster to paint the windows and trim while you are standing on the floor and the work is in front of you than when they are in place on the walls of the building.

Take your time. Give the windows two good coats of the paint. The trim can be painted the same color as the windows or different colors. If you believe you might want to change the color later, just paint it white. You can easily paint over white.

Painting the windows and trim before they are used will not eliminate all painting. You are going to have to follow up with putty in the nail holes and a touch of paint, nevertheless, you will cut your painting time way down.

The price of trim—moldings, quarter rounds and the like—depends upon the thickness of the piece of wood, its complexity, and the grade of the wood. The thinner the wood the simpler its outline and the less it costs. First-grade trim is knot free. But knot-free wood is getting more and more dif-

ficult to find so it costs more. Second- or third-grade trim has knots. When the knots are very large, the board must be cut and used in shorter pieces. When the knot is small and tight, you simply shellac the knot and paint over it. If you do not seal the knot with shellac, the rosin will "bleed" through the paint (dissolve it). Once the shellacked and painted trim is in place, it looks just like any other trim.

Whether the windows are installed (Fig. 19-1) at this time or later depends upon the sheathing and sidewall material used. When single-sidewall material—meaning the sheathing and sidewall are a single layer—is used the sidewall is applied first. Then the windows are installed. The window frame trim overlaps the sidewall. This would be the case when plywood siding or board and batten siding is used.

When the frame is sheathed and the sheathing is to be covered with clapboard, shingles, or a second layer of any material, the usual procedure is to install the windows atop the sheathing. Then you butt the sidewall against the window frame.

Fig. 19-1. Installing a double-hung window. Courtesy Andersen Corporation.

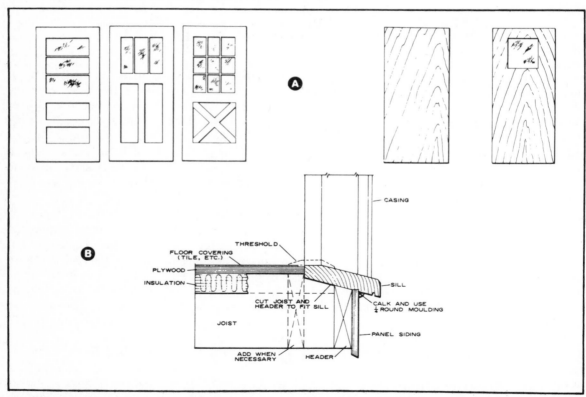

Fig. 19-2. Some common types of doors. The flush door (A) bottom left is the least expensive type. How an exterior door frame is positioned (B). Joist and header often have to be cut. Courtesy U.S. Department of Agriculture.

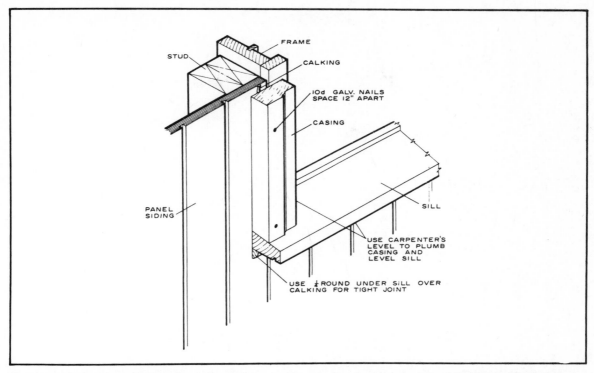

Fig. 19-3. How a double-hung window frame is installed. In this case, there is only a single layer of siding on the house frame. Courtesy U.S. Department of Agriculture.

There is nothing special about installing windows except to make certain they are fastened perfectly vertical. Some builders line the rough openings with building paper when the windows are installed prior to sidewall application. Some builders caulk the rough window openings when single-sidewall construction is used. Both practices are intended to reduce air leakage.

Generally, the frames are face nailed; the nails go directly through the front of the window frames and into the frame of the building. It sure looks crude and the nails have to be set and the nails have to be set and the holes puttied, but that is the way it is done. See Figs. 19-2 and 19-3.

If you have already given the windows two or three coats of paint, then filling the nail holes and touching up with a little paint won't require much ladder work and time.

Chapter 20

Finishing the Interior

WITH EVERYTHING INSPECTED AND THE WINDOWS and doors in place you are ready for the next steps.

INSULATION

Insulation is something you can do. Measure the square footage required. Price the insulation at the supplier and then price the complete job with a specialist. There might or might not be a considerable savings to doing it yourself. In any case, it is several days work for an inexperienced man. You cut the fiberglass batts with a razor knife and staple the batts in place with a staple gun. Just be certain to place the vapor barrier side of the insulation toward the center of the house. *Always* wear gloves. The glass fibers can easily enter your skin and cause misery.

PLASTERBOARD

With the insulation installed, it is time to cover the walls and ceiling with plasterboard. Sheetrock is a trademarked brand of plasterboard. Don't save pennies by using the ⅜-inch sheet; go to the ½-inch-thick sheets. Use sheets just as large as you can fit into the rooms. The larger the sheets the fewer the sheets. Use spiral or ringed (annular) Sheetrock nails. Do not use ordinary nails or the old, glue-covered nails. They don't hold.

There should be a nail every 6 to 8 inches. Hit the nails just hard enough to dimple the Sheetrock and bring the nail head below the surface of paper. Do not hit so hard that the paper is broken.

Every edge must be supported. If there is no stud or plate to which to nail the edge of a sheet of plasterboard, a nailer must be installed. A nailer is a board nailed to the house frame just for the purpose of supporting the Sheetrock edge. If you let an edge "float," it will eventually warp out of position.

Taping is the job of sealing the edges of the Sheetrock to make it appear as one smooth, continuous surface. It is done by applying taping compound, paper tape, and then two more layers of compound. Feather the edges with each pass of the trowel. It is not difficult to do, but is difficult to do well and quickly. If you do try doing it yourself, use

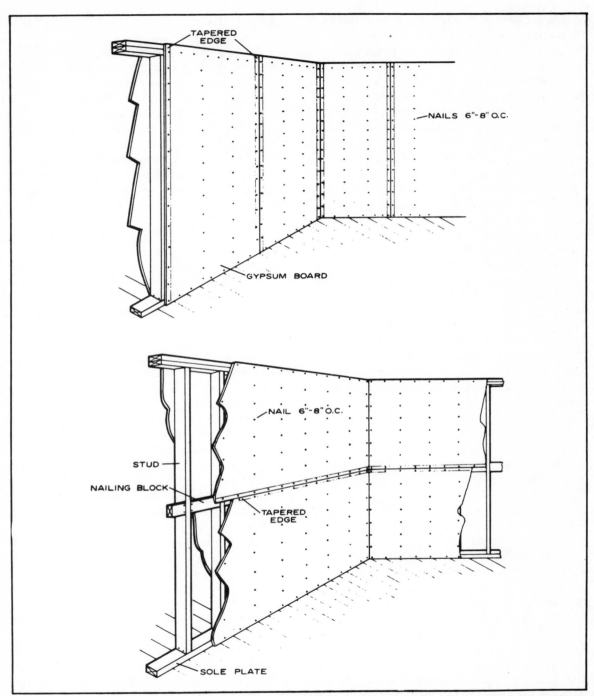

TAPERED EDGE

NAILS 6"-8" O.C.

GYPSUM BOARD

NAIL 6"-8" O.C.

STUD

NAILING BLOCK

TAPERED EDGE

SOLE PLATE

Fig. 20-1. Two ways to install Sheetrock. A horizontal application is usually preferred. Courtesy U.S. Department of Agriculture.

premixed compound. Keep your tools perfectly clean at all times by scraping one against the other. Never pick up and reuse any compound that has dropped to the floor.

You need to make three passes. Go over each joint and nail head three times. You must wait until one layer of compound is bone dry before applying the next. If you apply too much cement in any one place or if the results look too rough, you can go over the joint with a power sander. It is a lot of dusty work, but you can correct taping errors this way.

Taping should be done before the finished flooring is installed. The compound is highly alkaline and will stain wood flooring if permitted to remain more than a few minutes. In addition, the compound introduces a lot of moisture into the room. You want the room as dry as possible when you have the flooring installed or laid. If the flooring picks up moisture before it is laid, it will shrink afterwards and the fit will be poor.

Some carpenters will put up and tape Sheetrock. Others won't. There are Sheetrock specialists who do the work on a per-square-foot basis. If you measure out the Sheetrock area surface required, you can easily predetermine what the Sheetrock and taping will cost.

Sheetrock and taping contracts are let on a per-square-foot basis. All you need to do is multiply the subcontractor's rate against your required square footage.

On the other hand, if you are going to do the Sheetrock yourself, you have got to allow for waste. Sheetrock comes in 4-×-6, 8-, and 10-foot lengths. Some material is always wasted, but there is no rule of thumb for estimating loss.

Installation of Plasterboard. Plasterboard installation is not difficult, but two people are required. Use the longest sheets that you can. Always run the sheets across the studs and joists. Use annular nails. Indent the nail heads but not so deeply that the surface of the Sheetrock is smashed. Do not permit joints to line up. In other words, do not start all the sheet ends on the same stud or joist. Use 1 nail every 6 to 8 inches. Cut the white side with a razor knife; fold to break and cut the grey side. To keep your cuts straight, use a large, metal

T square. Use a small saw to cut holes for gem boxes and the like.

Taping. When you begin taping, start in the closets where your errors will not be visible. You will need taping compound (called mud), tape (a narrow strip of special paper), a scraper, a 4-inch wide putty knife, and a flat piece of metal with a centered handle at right angle to its surface (called a hawk). You work by removing some mud from its bucket, dumping it on the hawk, and then removing as much as you require from the hawk with your putty knife. To clean the putty knife or scraper, draw the tool against the metal edge of the hawk. See Fig. 20-2.

Start with an easy joint between the sides of two pieces of Sheetrock. These side edges are beveled so that a valley is formed between the sheets. Lay down a 1/16-inch layer of mud in this valley. Remove a length of tape from its roll. Lay the tape in the valley, and with your fingers gently press the tape onto the mud. Then gently run the putty knife down the length of the tape. The entire length of tape must be wetted by the mud and must be flat and in place. Take a 24-hour breather to let the mud harden or repeat the process in another valley while the first joint hardens.

Return and spread another 1/16 of an inch of mud down the valley atop the tape. With the scraper, spread this wet mud as evenly as you can down the length of the valley. Then once again give the mud time to dry bone hard.

Return to the same valley. Spread a third layer of mud down the length of the valley. This time you will need a layer about ⅛-inch thick. With your scraper, spread the mud to make a band 6 to 8 inches wide. You will have to make two passes to do this. When you are finished, the top of the valley should be flush or almost flush with the sides of the Sheetrock.

Now to the difficult joint. This is the joint between the ends of the pieces of Sheetrock. It is difficult because the ends are not beveled.

Again make the first pass with the 2-inch knife and lay down a very thin layer of mud. Next position the tape. Let it dry. Now make the second pass. This time you have to use the scraper and draw a

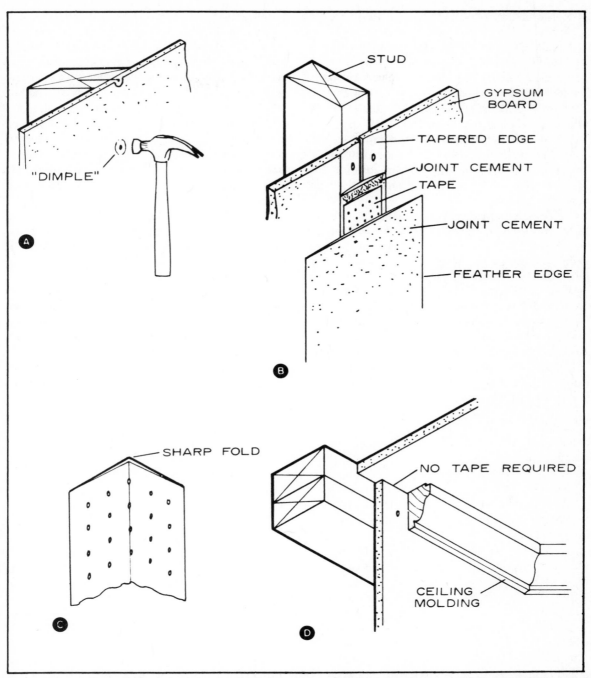

Fig. 20-2. Some basic steps in taping: (A) The nail heads are dimpled. (B) The joint, tap and more joint cement are applied in the sequence shown. (C) Tape is folded prior to insertion in a corner joint that has been coated with taping compound. (D) The use of ceiling molding eliminates the needs for taping the wall-to-ceiling joints. Courtesy U.S. Department of Agriculture.

4-inch-wide band. You do this with two passes (one along each side of the tape). Bear in mind that you are making a very gentle ridge. When the material is bone hard repeat the process. This time you make each pass 3 to 4 inches wide, centered on the center of the tape, that is now covered with a thin layer of mud. Bear in mind that the result is *not* a flat surface. It is a gentle ridge or hill.

To cover the nail holes, fill them with mud, and then run the knife across the surface of the Sheetrock. Let the spot dry, repeat, dry again, and repeat. It takes three passes to fill a nail hole because the mud shrinks.

To do an outside corner, you nail a metal outside corner over the Sheetrock joint. Then you cover the metal screening with mud; use the metal edge and the surface of the Sheetrock as a guide.

Inside corners are also easy but they require more care. Start by folding a length of tape down the middle. It has an indent for this very purpose. With the putty knife, spread a thin layer of mud down the length of the corner joint. Take care to keep the mud to one side and make the strip angular so that there is a little more down the center edge. Now repeat the process along the second side of the corner joint.

You now have two narrow bands of mud running down the parallel sides of an inside corner joint. Gently slip the folded paper tape into the corner and press it firmly into place with your fingers. Run the putty knife gently down each half of the tape to smooth it and remove excess mud. Let it dry. Spread a 2-inch band of mud along *one* side of the in-place tape. Run the scraper down the length of the tape so as to feather the edge of the mud and hide the tape. Let it dry. Repeat on the other side. Only two passes are required for an inside corner joint.

Some Do's and Don'ts. Keep your tools clean by scraping one against the other. Never pick up dropped mud; it will always contain dirt and will never be smooth. Keep your mud moist by keeping a layer of water on it when you finish for the day. Don't use semihard mud, it won't work right. Don't let drops remain on the walls or trim. You will have to sand them off. Don't let rough spots remain on the joints. Sanding them smooth is a hard, time-consuming task. If your taper says, "It doesn't matter," tell him you won't pay for the work until *he* sands the drips away.

Chapter 21

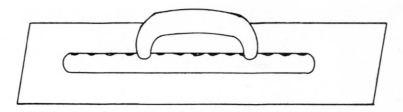

The Cellar Floor

A CELLAR FLOOR CAN BE A SIMPLE SEAL, AS IN THE case of a crawl space foundation, or it can be a smooth, concrete surface suitable for paint or covering with resilient flooring of one kind or another.

SIMPLE SEAL

All cellars, whether they are shallow crawl spaces beneath a building or full height areas, should be sealed. The earth must be covered with some sort of watertight layer that will prevent moisture from reaching the building. Failure to do so leads to early deterioration, cracking, and the like. See Fig. 21-1. It is also a constant source of moisture in the building.

Concrete. The simplest way to seal the surface of the earth consists of a wash of concrete. A watery mix is slushed over the surface of the crawl space after the perimeter foundation walls have been erected. It is then spread out with the aid of a rake. Order enough concrete to provide a 2-inch-thick layer. Push the concrete up against the masonry to seal the joint between the two.

Blacktop. Blacktop is crushed stone mixed with asphalt. It has to be spread while it is hot because it congeals into a hard solid. You can use a little less of the blacktop than concrete because blacktop is tenacious and forms a watertight surface. Order the blacktop with the smallest stones they have available because the tar with the smaller stones is easier to spread. While no special skill is involved in spreading blacktop, it does harden quickly in cool weather. Have several helpers on hand when the material is delivered.

Plastic. When bare earth is free of rocks and bumps and you can cover it with sheets of plastic. Use 5-mil sheets just as large as you can purchase. Overlap the sheet edges by 1 foot or more. Hold the sheets in place with 4-inch solids (concrete block). Use one block ever 4 feet. Bring the edges of the plastic flush with the inside surface of the foundation wall.

CONCRETE

Although pouring a concrete floor might appear to

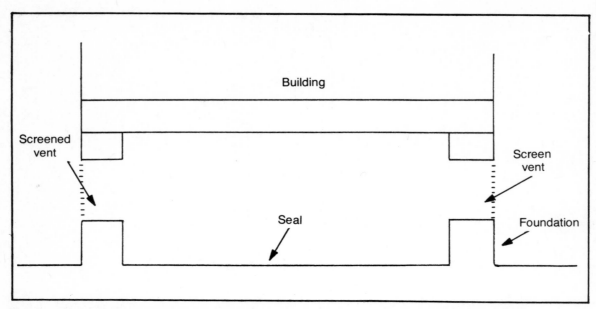

Fig. 21-1. Crawl spaces beneath buildings must be sealed and vented with at least two vents for circulation.

be a simple matter of pouring concrete and smoothing it out, it is neither simple nor easy. Physically it is the most difficult task in construction because there is the dead weight of the concrete that has to be moved into place. There also is the time element; you must finish before the initial set begins. And there is the confined space. Much of the time the mason is working ankle deep in the concrete. If you are planning to do any of the construction work yourself, don't do the concrete cellar floor unless you have several helpers and at least one person who has done the work before.

Time to Pour. You cannot pour the floor until everything has been prepared. You do have the choice of pouring before or after the frame is constructed. Before the frame is erected, you have an open area that is accessible from several sides. You can have the truck back up almost anywhere and drop its load. If the floor is large, you can have several pourings, each made from a different point around the foundation perimeter. In this way, you can reduce the distance the concrete has to be pushed. This makes the work a heck of a lot easier. See Fig. 21-2.

When you pour with the cellar open to the sky,

you have no protection against rain. A few drops of rain while the concrete is being floated (made smooth) is no problem. A downpour while the concrete is still soft will ruin the job. Once the concrete has reached initial set, rain can't harm it, but you could have a cellar full of water. The water will simply speed curing (hardening) of the concrete. A cellar full of water can be a nuisance. You must pump it dry and, generally, the water brings mud and that means a clean-up job.

Once the frame is on top of the foundation, access to the cellar becomes limited. You have to direct the concrete delivery chute through a window and then push and pull the concrete along to cover the floor. There is far less light. The moisture from the concrete tends to remain in the cellar, slowing set up a little. In cold weather, you cannot pour when the temperature goes much below freezing; you want the little protection offered by the enclosed space. Of course, the building's roof gives you protection. When the roof is up, however, the work is considerably greater.

Getting the Cellar Ready. Remove all trash, bits of wood, stone, and the like from the earth. A piece of wood in the concrete can swell and

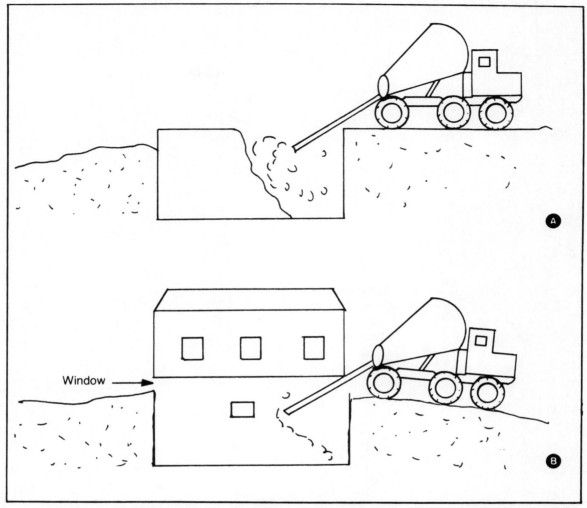

Fig. 21-2. Pouring a cellar: (A) If you pour before the frame is erected, the truck can be brought to several points around the building. This reduces the distance the concrete has to be moved by hand labor. (B) If you wait until the frame is erected, you are limited to the windows and doors present in the foundation walls. The concrete will have to be moved a considerable distance by hand labor.

crack the concrete. Tamp all the loose earth firm. Use a 2 × 4 with a couple of short pieces nailed to its end as a tamp. Clean the inside surface of the footing and the adjoining 6 inches of foundation wall. Knock all loose cement free. Wash all dirt off with water. See Fig. 21-3. You want these two surfaces to be damp and clean because you want the concrete floor to adhere to them.

You also want the concrete floor's edges to rest on the inside edge of the footing. Therefore, the cellar floor is covered with crushed stone to a level flush with the surface of the footing. See Fig. 21-4. If you believe that there might be water in the cellar excavation, the crushed stone is tamped smooth and covered with a layer of 5-mil plastic. The edges of the plastic are overlapped by 1 foot and brought onto the edge of the footing.

If there are any clean-outs or drainpipes that

Fig. 21-3. A homemade tamper.

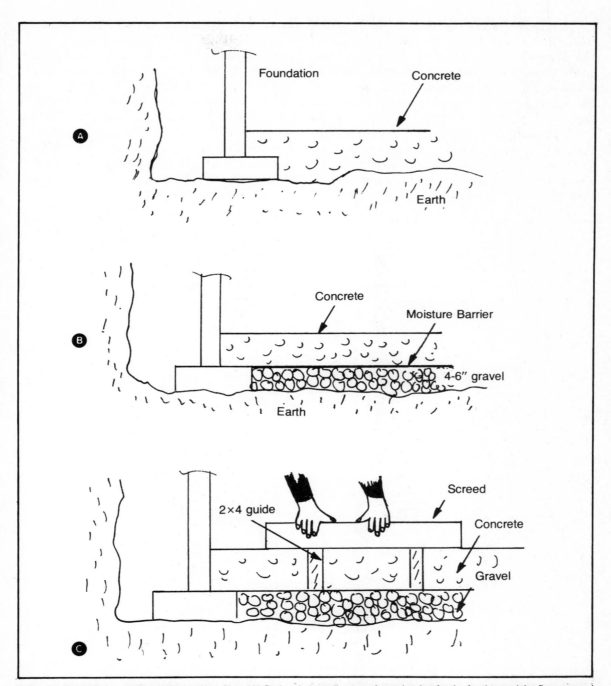

Fig. 21-4. Cellar floor and foundation wall profiles: (A) On hard, dry soil, a trench can be dug for the footing and the floor poured directly atop the earth. (B) Where there is a possibility of water, the cellar floor is poured atop gravel covered by a plastic sheet—a moisture barrier. (C) Guides can be used to secure a flat cellar floor. The guides are later removed and the spaces are filled with concrete.

are to project above the surface of the concrete cellar floor, now is the time to check their height. You do this by stretching a line from foundation edge to foundation edge. Because your concrete will be 4 inches thick, the surface of the projecting pipe, or whatever, must be this distance above the line.

Sumps. If you have reason to believe that water will be a problem, it is advisable to provide for the contingency by providing for a sump. This is a kind of well beneath your house into which you place an automatic pump. When the well fills with water, the sump pump empties it. This keeps the water level below that of the cellar floor.

To provide a sump, a hole is dug and a form is constructed. See Fig. 21-5. When the floor is poured, concrete is also poured into the form, making a tube or rectangle of concrete. The hole is usually dug 4 to 6 feet deep. The bottom is lined with crushed stone so the water can seep in. It is necessary to place a cover over the hole so that no one falls in. If and when water rises inside the well to a height that threatens to overflow into the cellar, you install the pump and put it to work.

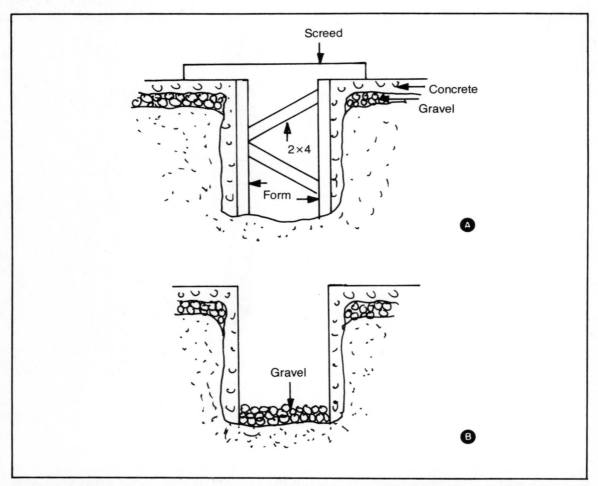

Fig. 21-5. A method for forming a concrete-lined sump pit. (A) A wood form is constructed within the pit. (B) When the concrete has been poured around the form and the concrete has set, the form is removed. Gravel placed on the bottom of the pit keeps the soil down.

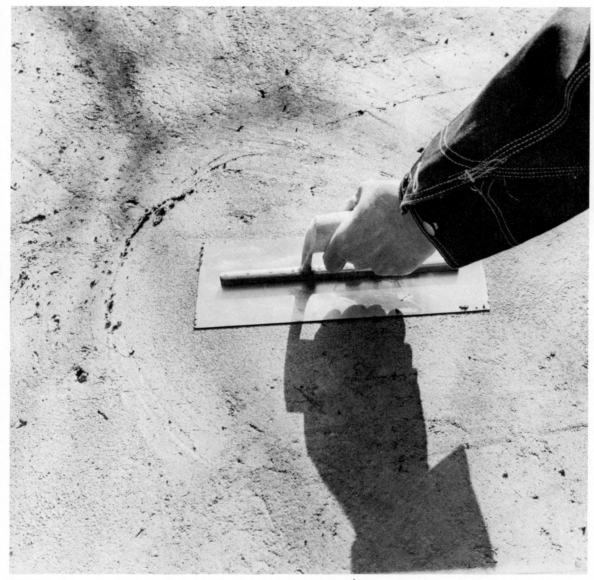

Fig. 21-6. For a hard, smooth surface that will take paint, the concrete is "finished" with a steel trowel.

Insist that the mason lay floor forms. These can be 2 × 4s on edge; the upper surface is used to locate the finished surface of the floor. Using the line, check to make certain the surfaces of the forms are level and at the right height. If you are going to have a cellar drain installed, check to see that the forms pitch properly. Do *not* let the mason judge the

floor level by eye. He can probably do it, but don't chance it.

The installation of guides or forms does not require very much work or materials. They can be constructed from 2 × 4s set on edge. Their top surfaces establish the top surface of the finished floor. Once the concrete has been poured and has set somewhat, the forms are removed and the spaces are filled in.

Pouring. Generally, small-size stones are used in the concrete mix and the mix is on the wet side to facilitate moving it along. Perhaps this is a good place to clear up a common misconception about concrete. When you purchase ready-mixed concrete (usually the least expensive way to purchase concrete), the mixture is set by the supply company: so much cement, so much sand, so much stone. The formula is more or less standard, and depends upon the use to which the concrete will be put. The quantity of water in the mix is determined on the job by the truck operator who works at the direction of the mason. The argument that the less water used in the mix the stronger the concrete is true. Nevertheless, for your purpose the concrete has several times the strength necessary. Forcing the mason to work with a "dry" mix just makes for a waste of energy and often for poor results because the concrete will not spread evenly. Don't be disturbed by the mason using a "sloppy" mix.

Finishing. When the concrete is first dumped onto the cellar earth or crushed-stone base, the surface of the concrete is not at one level. It is all hills and valleys. To make the surface one flat plane, a screed is dragged across the form. The screed pushes high areas ahead of itself. Low areas are filled in with a shovel by hand. Some 30 minutes to an hour is permitted to pass.

When the concrete is first dumped onto the cellar earth or crushed-stone base, the surface of the concrete is not at one level. It is all hills and valleys. To make the surface one flat plane, a screed is dragged across the form. The screed pushes high areas ahead of itself. Low areas are filled in with a shovel by hand. Some 30 minutes to an hour is permitted to pass.

Now a bull float is dragged across the surface of the concrete. The bull float is a flat strip of metal or wood about 1 foot wide and 4 or 5 feet long. This operation removes the stirations left by the screed.

Next the surface of the concrete is floated. This consists of rubbing the surface of the concrete with a wood or soft-metal trowel. Floating further smooths the surface of the concrete and leaves a smooth, sandy finish. This finish is fine if you are going to lay down tile or linoleum, but it will not take paint very well.

If there is a chance you will want to paint this floor, insist upon a steel trowel finish (Fig. 21-6). Very simply to the concrete is rubbeddown with a steel trowel. For best results and a very hard floor, a motor-driven steel trowel should be used. Ordinarily, the power trowel is unnecessary.

Chapter 22

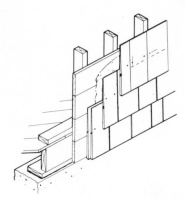

Sidewalls

IF YOUR HOUSE SHEATHING AND SIDEWALL ARE a single layer of material, then you had the windows installed following the application of the sheathing/sidewall panels or whatever. If your home is to have a two-layer exterior wall, the sheathing and the windows have been installed. Now the siding goes on atop the sheathing and is butted against the frames of the windows and doors.

Once again you have a choice of routes. You can hire a sidewall specialist on a limited contract, you can make the sidewalls part of the carpenter's contract, or you can do the sidewalls yourself. See Fig. 22-1.

Making the Choice. In choosing between specialist and carpenter there are two factors to consider. One is price and the other is time. The specialist will accomplish the work in less time than the carpenter, but the difference will not be more than a day or two. The work should be let on contract and not on a per-day or per-hour basis. The extra time it takes is the mechanic's problem not yours. Your problem is deciding who is more likely to show up and start the work at the promised time?

All things being equal, which they seldom are, the carpenter is more likely to be on hand when you need him than the specialist because the carpenter has other work at your job site. He is already there with his equipment and crew. He need lose no time installing the windows, or whatever, and then going on to the sidewalls. The specialist has to schedule your job along with others. All the subcontractors know that you are only building one house and you are not likely to build any more in the near future.

In comparing the two contracts, bear in mind the cost of your time. Every day that house is under construction is a day for which you pay mortgage interest plus rent (and other expenses) in your present abode. It is advisable to figure these costs accurately.

Assume your present rent and associate costs, not including food, heat and the like, that will not change no matter where you live amounts to $650 a month and you have already received half of the $60,000 mortgage at 18 percent. Thus "home" costs run to $650 plus 18 percent × 30,000 or $450 a month for a total of $1,100 per month. When you

Fig. 22-1. Hardboard strip siding designed to look like shingles. Courtesy Masonite Corporation.

receive the balance of your $60,000 mortgage, your monthly costs will jump another $450 for a total of $1,500 per month. This comes to $375 a week or $75 per working day (five days to the work week).

You must keep such figures in mind when making your decisions regarding one subcontractor or another or doing it yourself. If doing it yourself is going to hold up the job, you are well advised to take a weekend job and use the money to hire another subcontractor.

Doing the Sidewalls Yourself. If you cannot find a specialist who will start immediately and your carpenter has to go elsewhere for a spell, you might do the sidewalls yourself, assuming you have the free time.

Wood shingles and shakes are fairly easy to install (Fig. 22-2). First the surface is covered with building paper held in place with a few roofing nails.

The first course of shingles are usually doubled. The second course is held straight with the aid of a guide board temporarily nailed in place. With the second course in place, the guide board is removed and renailed higher up by the preferred shingle exposure distance. A very wide board is selected

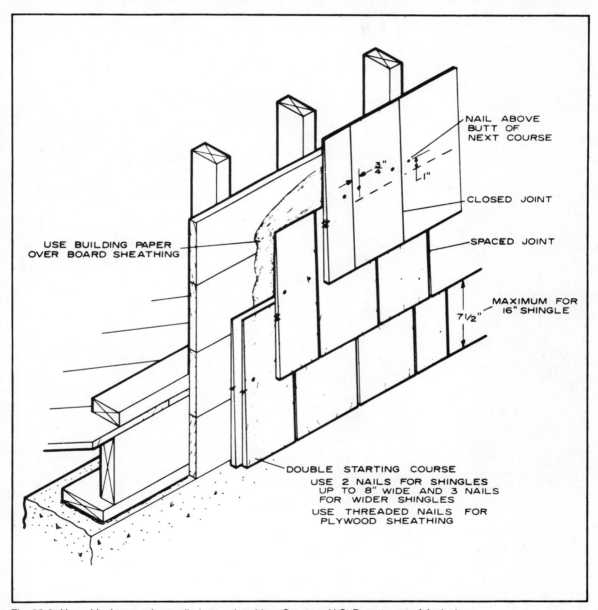

USE BUILDING PAPER OVER BOARD SHEATHING

NAIL ABOVE BUTT OF NEXT COURSE

3/4"

1"

CLOSED JOINT

SPACED JOINT

MAXIMUM FOR 16" SHINGLE

7 1/2"

DOUBLE STARTING COURSE
USE 2 NAILS FOR SHINGLES UP TO 8" WIDE AND 3 NAILS FOR WIDER SHINGLES
USE THREADED NAILS FOR PLYWOOD SHEATHING

Fig. 22-2. How shingles may be applied atop sheathing. Courtesy U.S. Department of Agriculture.

Fig. 22-3A. Redwood shingles (cedar). These are third-grade shingles. Notice the large, loose knots.

for the fascia so that there is no need for short shingles over the door and window frames. See Fig. 22-3A, 22-3B and 22-3C.

Asbestos shingles are somewhat more difficult to apply. You need a special cutter (which can be rented). You must place the strips of felt that comes with the shingle package behind each joint to keep it water tight. You cannot nail a guide board atop the in-place shingles because doing so may crack them. Therefore you have to snap a guideline across the shingle surfaces. This is done by stretching a chalk-coated string tightly across the shingles. The string is pulled away from the shingles. The string snaps back into place and in doing so makes a chalked line.

Asbestos shingles are larger than wood shingles and shakes, but snapping lines, placing the felt strips, and taking care not to drive the supporting nails too hard (which could crack the shingle) consumes time.

Boards and battens are relatively easy to apply. These are wide boards fastened side by side in a vertical position over the sheathing. The battens are narrow boards positioned vertically over

Fig. 22-3B. A shingle can be cut with a small plane.

Fig. 22-3C. A shingle can be cut with a backsaw.

the joints. Usually the boards are some 8 inches wide and the battens are usually 2 inches wide. The batten is centered over the board-to-board joint that is usually about ⅛ of an inch wide. Nails are then driven through the batten and through *one* board. A second board and batten is now positioned and the nailing is repeated. Note that only one edge of each board is nailed. The other edge is free to move under the batten. This allows for dimensional changes that always occur with changes in temperature and humidity.

Plywood sheet siding is more difficult to install because it requires very careful cutting to assure a tight fit around the doors and windows. If you don't mind the extra cost, you can always cover up the gaps poor carpentry leaves with moulding of one kind or another.

Hardboard strip siding is treated like giant shingles. The strips go up rapidly, but there is the problem of cutting them accurately to fit around the fenestrations (doors and windows).

Clapboard siding might appear to be easy to install, but it is not. Each piece must be cut accurately to length. Done correctly, there should be no gap between the ends of the siding boards and the sides of the window and door frames. Use aluminum finishing nails. Set them deeply and putty the holes.

Aluminum strip siding can be applied directly

Fig. 22-4. Aluminum strip siding. Courtesy The Aluminum Association.

atop sheathing although most people think of aluminum siding as a re-siding material. If you underlay the aluminum siding (Fig. 22-4) with up to ½ inch of insulation, you can increase the R factor of your walls without going to wider studs.

On the other hand, the cost is generally much higher for material and labor and it is not easy for a beginner to install. Covering the exterior trim with sheet metal can be tricky and time-consuming.

Still another siding with many advantages is stucco. This consists of a layer of building paper covered by wire lath covered by three successive ⅜-inch layers of mortar cement. The last layer usually made from white sand and white cement. Stucco provides a little insulation and a good stucco job can last better than 25 years without attention.

Chapter 23

Paint the Interior

AT THIS POINT, YOU HAVE COMPLETED APPLYING the sidewalls or someone else is working on the side walls. There are no doors except the exterior doors. There is no trim, flooring, kitchen or bathroom tile, and no toilet or electrical fixtures in place. The rooms are wide open. There is nothing or there should be nothing to interfere with your painting. This is when painting is a breeze.

Colors. The .colors are your choice but remember the colors that look so good and so bright in "chip" form in the paint store will overpower you if you apply them to the walls. Bright colors that look so good in magazine photos are often much too strong for everyday living. Pastels will make furnishings stand out (not the walls).

You could make the trim a different color than the walls, but we don't recommend it because in a small house two colors in a single room looks "busy." In addition, making the trim a different color than the walls almost doubles the work and increases the paint costs.

Buying paint. Don't purchase colored paint.

Purchase white paint and color it yourself. If you buy colors you will find yourself "stuck" with half a gallon now and again because it is impossible to know beforehand exactly how much paint you need. Purchasing paint by the quart is almost as bad because the smaller cans are much more expensive proportionally than the large cans.

Buy white in a 1- or 5-gallon can. Pour as much as you believe you will need for a day's work in one color (tint to be technically correct). Add a few drops of tint at a time until you secure the shade you want. Use only one tint.

If you find that you are going to need more paint of the same tint, stop and pour as much white paint as you estimate you will need in a second bucket. Now add a little tint to the white and mix thoroughly. When you believe you are approaching the shade you want, stop. With a stick, add a drop of the mixed paint to the second bucket. Now you have a drop of the "old" paint atop the new. You can easily and quickly see the difference. In this way you can secure a perfect match.

Assume that you have eight rooms to paint. The first room needs 1¼ gallons. The second needs ¾ of a gallon. The third needs 1½ gallons. The fourth needs 2¼ gallons. The fifth needs 1¾ gallons. The sixth needs just 1 gallon. The seventh needs ¾ of a gallon. The eighth needs 2½ gallons. Of the eight rooms, seven require something other than a full gallon. If you used eight different colors, you would end up wasting seven fractional gallons. If you used the system we suggested you could hold your waste to less than ½ gallon total.

Use a roller but not the standard amateur roller that is 8 or 12 inches long. A professional roller is 18 or 20 inches long and has a long handle. This will enable you to cover a lot more surface with one pass. You will, of course, need a large pan.

Do the ceilings first. To get the corners between the ceiling and the wall without climbing a ladder, fasten a 2-inch brush to the end of a long stick. With the stick-mounted brush, do the corners and then go over it with the roller. The roller will cover most of the brush marks.

Do not try to save money with inferior paint. The inferior paint will not cover as great an area as the better paint and so you will end up using more. Judge paint by its contents and not by weight or thickness or feel. If the paint's contents are not listed, don't buy the paint. Bear in mind that it is the metal and resin content tht makes one paint better than another. Buy the paint with the highest percentage of zinc or titanium oxide and the lowest quantity of water and neutral spirits. Note that calcium carbonate is a filler and adds little to the quality of the paint.

Chapter 24

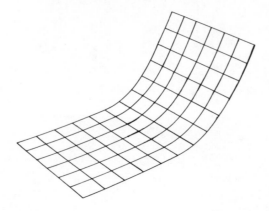

Floors

THE TILE ON THE BATHROOM FLOOR CAN BE INstalled any time after the tub is in and the walls have been taped and painted. The tile or linoleum in the kitchen should also be held until the same is done in that room. See Figs. 24-1, 24-2, and 24-3.

Wood flooring requires the same basic preparation for taping and painting. In addition there are two other precautions. The cellar or crawl space must be sealed. If it is a crawl space sealed with blacktop, there is no need to wait. If concrete is used, you must wait until the concrete is no longer green (in color) and is dry. When the concrete is thoroughly dry, the flooring is brought into the building and the bundles are broken open. Two or more days are permitted to pass to allow the wood to stabilize by reaching the same moisture content as the air in the building. If the flooring is dry when it is laid and it then absorbs moisture, the floor will buckle as each board expands a fraction of an inch.

CERAMIC TILE

Ceramic tiles are not difficult to lay. You can do a good job first time out if you take your time and follow our basic suggestions. Stay away from patterns and designs. We know that a mosaic on the bathroom floor will give the room a touch of Roman elegance, but patterns cost more and tend to exaggerate tile positioning errors. Go for muted colors and simple tile and not tiles with a riot of colors in each tile. As with the color chip, you cannot accurately assess the impact of a floor or a wall of tile by looking at a single tile. Cover a few square feet of flooring with the tile to see what they will look like in place.

Select nonglazed tiles for the floor. Glaze is fine, but it will wear off in spots in time and look bad. You can work easily with small tiles if they are preglued to a cloth backing. If not, stay away from tiles less than 4 inches across. It's too much fuss and bother. Avoid the foreign tiles. Not only are they prohibitively expensive, in most instances, many of them do not have nibs. Nibs are little bumps on the edges of the tile that space them automatically. Without the nibs you have to use toothpicks to space the tile.

Fig. 24-1. A ceramic tile floor in a kitchen. Courtesy American Olean Tile.

Fig. 24-2. An inlaid sheet vinyl floor with a brick pattern. Courtesy Armstrong World Industries.

Fig. 24-3. Laying cut-to-size sheet flooring of vinyl.

Rent a tile cutter and nibbling pliers to cut tile and make holes. Actually, you don't make holes in the tile. Instead you break the tile in half and then nibble a semicircle in each half. When reassembled, you have a hole and no crack is visible. See Figs. 24-4 and 24-5.

Check your walls with a steel square to make certain they are parallel and square. Check the tile against the space before gluing them in place. If you see that you have to end up with a sliver, which is bad, cut two tiles a little each to make them fit.

Use the properly notched trowel and a good quality mastic. Try not to apply too much and at the same time don't stint. You will know you have the correct amount when you feel the tile taking hold when you press it in place.

WOOD FLOORS

Wood floors are physically difficult to lay and very time consuming when accomplished without a power nailer. The problem is bending. The floor installer must work all day in a bent position. It is not easy, especially if you have never done this type of work before.

Select the type and grade of flooring (Figs. 24-6 through 24-9) you want while bearing in mind that the narrower boards, though costing less, require considerably more labor. Order enough material for the job, plus two or three bundles of odd-width pieces. These are narrower than usual and come in handy when all you need is half a width to finish up.

Give the flooring a couple of days to stabilize.

Fig. 24-4. Applying preglued (joined) ceramic wall tile. Courtesy American Olean Tile.

Fig. 24-5. Installing a sheet of ceramic floor tile. Courtesy American Olean Tile.

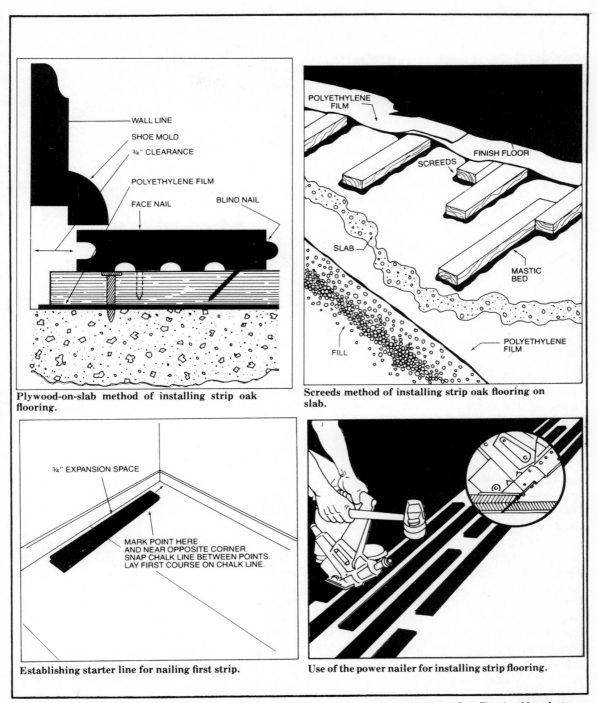

Plywood-on-slab method of installing strip oak flooring.

Screeds method of installing strip oak flooring on slab.

Establishing starter line for nailing first strip.

Use of the power nailer for installing strip flooring.

Fig. 24-6. The basic steps for installing wood flooring on different surfaces. Courtesy National Oak Flooring Manufacturers Association.

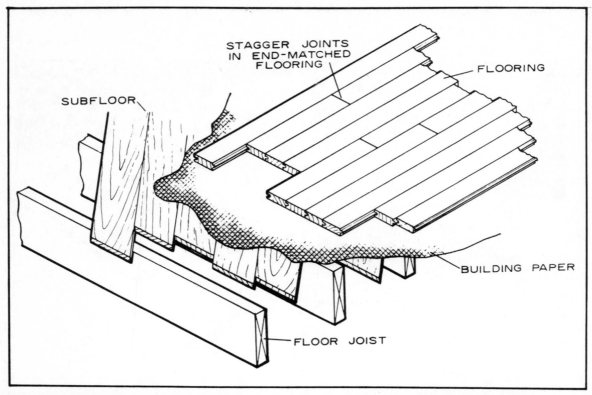

Fig. 24-7. The relationship of the various parts of a wood-strip floor on square-edged subflooring. Courtesy U.S. Department of Agriculture.

Cover the floor with red building paper. Use no nails. Start at the longest wall. You want to run your flooring lengthwise through the rooms (from one room to another) and through the halls without a break—if possible. Fasten your first strip ¾ of an inch away from the surface of the Sheetrock.

Using 7d or 8d screw or cut steel nails, face nail the first strip once every 2 feet or so along the side nearest the wall. The space and the nails will be covered by the moulding to be installed later. Now you have to nail the second strip of flooring in place. Select a piece that is shorter by 4 or more inches than the first. Position it. Now, place a scrap piece of flooring against the flooring you are planning to nail.

With a heavy, flooring hammer, drive the pieces of flooring together. You do this to make certain the tongue of the nailed flooring goes all the

way into the groove of the flooring that is to be nailed. Remove the scrap and nail the flooring in place. You need a nail every 8 or 10 inches. The nail point is positioned above the tongue of the flooring and driven through the flooring and into the subfloor at a 45-degree angle.

You cannot drive the nail home directly. To do so would mash the tongue. So you either lay the side of another nail against the nail head and hit it or you position the side of a nail set atop the in-place nail and use the set to help you drive the nail home without mashing the flooring. To speed things somewhat, you can rent a power nailer (which holds the nail for you).

Work your way across the floor. Take care to use pieces of varying lengths so that no joints are ever side by side. When you come close to the end of the floor, select a strip of flooring that will be short of the Sheetrock by the same ¾ of an inch or so. If you cannot secure flooring of the proper width, use a power saw to cut what you do have to size.

Finishing. If your subfloor is perfectly even and if you have a good grade of flooring lumber, chances are that the finished floor will be close to perfect. If it is not satisfactorily smooth, it has to be "finished." This consists of power sanding. There are specialists who do finishing or you can do it yourself.

Start by renting the largest drum sander available, the bigger the better. Put on shoes that will not leave marks. Use the coarse paper if there is a lot of wood to be removed or use fine sandpaper if only a little touch-up work is needed. Run the sander with the length of the boards. Do not work across the boards. Be careful not to remove too

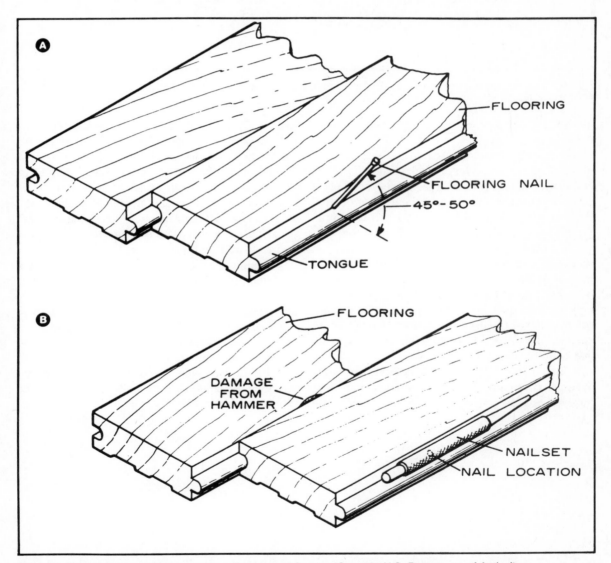

Fig. 24-8. The close-up of method used to nail strip-wood flooring. Courtesy U.S. Department of Agriculture.

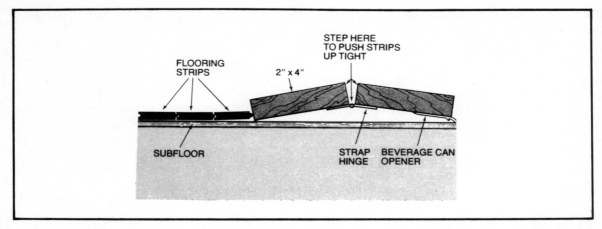

Fig. 24-9. A homemade lever that can be used to force strip flooring boards tight. Courtesy National Oak Flooring Manufacturers Association.

much. Follow the coarse paper, if you use it, with the fine sandpaper.

To reach areas inaccessible to the big drum, rent a small rotary sander or a belt sander. To reach corners too small for even these power tools, use a scraper. This is a sharp-edged, bent piece of steel that you repeatedly draw across the wood towards yourself—always with the grain of the wood.

Carefully sweep the floors clean of all dust and then seal the floors. All sorts of compounds and preparations are currently touted that promise beautiful floors that last almost forever. We still believe that good old shellac is the best compromise between cost and service. Use the white shellac. Make sure it is fresh. If it is orangy, it is old and will not harden properly.

Shellac is made from the shells of Lac bugs. When a container is marked 4-pound cut, that means there is 4 pounds of shellac in the can. The rest is alcohol. Thus 3-pound cut shellac contains only 75 percent as much "Lac" as the 4-pound cut, and is therefore that much less valuable.

Make the first coat a wash coat. Use a large bucket, a large, cheap brush (it will have to be discarded) and add an equal amount of alcohol to the shellac. Open all the windows or the fumes will get you. Apply an even coat of the thinned shellac to the entire floor. It will dry in less than a hour.

Sealing the wood floor prevents it from being permanently stained by accident. When the shellac is dry, you can give it two successive coats of full-strength shellac now, or you can let the final coats go until later. With full-strength shellac, it is best to allow several hours to pass between coats to make certain they are completely dry.

Either way, when the shellac is hard and dry, lay down red building paper walkways between the rooms to keep workers off the floor.

Chapter 25

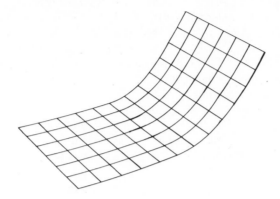

Finishing the Inside

THERE IS WORK STILL TO BE DONE TO THE INTERIOR of the building. The trim and doors have to be installed. The electrical and the plumbing fixtures have to be installed. There might also be a medicine cabinet in the bathroom and cabinets in the kitchen. Most but not all of this work can be done simultaneously.

TRIM

Trim is the term applied to the strips of wood used to complete the carpentry (shoe molding, floor molding, ceiling molding, and the like). If you prefer, you can purchase trim cut to fit specific window openings. This will eliminate 90 percent of the skill and experience required for the work. The other molding can be cut fairly accurately without too much difficulty. But there is a catch to it all: The doors.

DOORS

Hanging doors is technically the most difficult job a carpenter faces. The hinges must be installed per-

fectly or almost perfectly. If they are off a fraction of an inch, the door will not work properly. It is not a task for a beginner.

The answer to the problem would appear to be to hire a carpenter for the doors while you do the trim. This might work, but chances are the carpenter would relegate your doors to his back burner until it rains or he has nothing better to do. Many carpenters won't bother with small jobs. The unfortunate result might be that you will save money doing the trim by yourself, but lose money waiting for the carpenter to do the doors. Contracting both jobs is more likely to get immediate action. If the carpenter cuts the parts himself, the trim will cost you less. And, of course, you have to paint the trim.

PLUMBING AND ELECTRICAL WORK

The plumber and the electrician should be alerted well in advance of your flooring work so that they can come in as soon as it is done. If necessary, have them come in before the flooring is done. Just bear in mind that the toilet bowl and possibly the lavatory (bathroom wash bowl) are installed after the bathroom has been tiled. Both rest atop the tile.

If you have an ordinary kitchen sink, it is now hooked up. If you have kitchen cabinets or a built-in sink—meaning it is part and parcel of a cabinet of its own—now is the time to install the cabinet so that the plumber can make the connections while he is on the job.

The electrician will install the electrical fixtures, connect the heating equipment, and call for an electrical inspection. With this accomplished, he or you must contact the local power company so they can make their connection to your building.

Generally, the plumbing department makes no inspection at this time. Check to be certain.

KITCHEN CABINETS

You can secure kitchen cabinets from any number of different local sources, manufacturers or your carpenter. A carpenter can build cabinets for you right on the job. If you order them, give yourself plenty of lead time; delivery is usually erratic. Supply the manufacturer with a print of your kitchen, double check the actual dimensions with a steel tape and have whatever changes are required made by the manufacturer before he ships the units to you.

The cabinets simply slip into place and are usually nailed through their backs to the building itself. Usually, cabinet installation is a portion of the carpentry contract. If it is not, you can do it fairly easily yourself. Bear in mind that the spacer board is made to be sawn to fit. In this way, dimensional differences between your kitchen space and the more or less standard cabinets can be adjusted.

DETAILS

Now is the time to go over everything. Make certain nothing has been overlooked:

☐ The bell system is in.

☐ The heating equipment is connected and in operating order.

☐ All the lights and switches work.

☐ The phone company has been alerted to install a phone.

☐ Insurance on the house has been upped to cover the full value of the building.

☐ All the doors work properly.

☐ All the rooms and the cellar have been cleaned up and emptied of trash.

☐ The shellacking of the floors is complete.

Chapter 26

Finishing the Outside

AT THIS POINT, THERE IS STILL WORK TO BE DONE to the exterior of the building and the grounds, but it is ready to be lived in. Contact the building department now even though there is work to be done. They might issue a certificate of occupancy because the structure is habitable. If they won't issue a certificate, the department might tell you the minimum work required to secure the all important certificate.

EXTERIOR PAINT

If you have painted all the exterior trim, windows, and doors, all you need do is touch up here and there. If you have used bare wood shingles or shakes, you need not paint them at all. Painted wood shingles can also be safely ignored if they are made of cedar or cypress (neither will rot). If you are contemplating painting wood shingles, think twice. The bare shingles will soak up gallons of paint and will not present a smooth, solid appearance with less than two coats—probably three. A stain followed by a sealer is a better and more economical choice.

If you have used cedar or cypress for clapboard or board and batten, you can let them be if you have used aluminum nails. If you prefer, you can help preserve the color by using a sealer. Some home owners use a stain. The advantage of the stain is that it doesn't hide the grain, it is less expensive, and it is easier to apply because the passage of the brush leaves no marks.

If you are painting, use a good grade of paint that has been thinned somewhat for the first coat. Give the paint plenty of time to dry hard. Follow with a second coat of normally thinned paint. Permit more time to pass and finish up with a third coat.

Colors. The whites and the greys last the longest. The bright colors fade most rapidly and appear shoddy very quickly. The whites and the greys just get darker.

Use the same technique for purchasing and mixing the exterior paints (described in Chapter 23) as for use with the interior paint. Water-based (not water soluble) paints last as long or almost as long as the oil-based paints so why go to the bother of using the oil-based paints.

COMPLETE THE DRIVEWAY

When the bulldozer was on the job site, you had the operator clear an area for your driveway or hardstand. You had the topsoil removed to expose the lighter-colored subsoil. Now you have to pave this area unless the city will permit you to let it be. In the latter case, you must be concerned with dust in the summer and mud in the spring.

The least expensive and simplest pavement you can secure for your drive is a layer of crushed stone. Purchase the large stones that are 2½ to 3 inches in size. Crushed stone has sharp corners and edges; when it is spread over soil it tends to remain in place. The smaller crushed stone is easier to spread, but it is too easily kicked and poked out of place. Do not use gravel. Gravel consists of round stones. They will roll and otherwise move out of place.

Assuming that the dozer removed 4 inches of topsoil, you want to bring the top of the driveway at least flush with the adjoining topsoil, and preferable 2 inches higher. That will make the drive surface flush with the normal height of cut grass (which is 2 inches). Thus you want a layer of 4 to 6 inches of gravel. To compute your need, secure the total square footage of the driveway and multiply it by either 4 or 6 inches (as you prefer).

Assuming your driveway is 10 feet wide and 20 feet long, that works out to $10 \times 20 = 200$ square feet. Assuming you want a 4-inch layer, 4 inches is .333 of a foot ($200 \times .333 = 66$ cubic feet). Crushed stone is sold by the cubic yard. One yard = 27 cubic feet ($66 \div 27 = 2.44$ cubic yards). Because the supplier won't bother with a split yard, you have to order 3 yards.

Have the delivery truck *back* down the driveway to its end. Direct the driver to tilt the cargo hold, open the door, and move forward slowly. In this way, the load of stone will be distributed down the length of the drive. It will be your task to spread it out evenly.

Improvements. Should you any time in the future want to add blacktop or concrete to the driveway, you can do either directly atop the crushed stone. It makes a good base for a more permanent path. By itself, the crushed stones tend to pack together and eventually will present a fairly hard, smooth surface.

GRASS AND SHRUBS

You can add grass to your property by purchasing sod and laying it down like a carpet. Doing this costs money but it gives you immediate greenery. You return the topsoil to its original position (if you have topsoil) or you can purchase topsoil and spread it over the earth.

Growing grass in the soil that you have is the least expensive method. Although the grass will eventually become luxurious, a lot more time will pass than it would if you seeded topsoil.

If you grow grass in exposed subsoil, loosen the top inch or two of the soil with a rake or a shovel. Remove the loose stones (you'll have to remove more stones after each rain) and plant a mixture of winter rye and whatever grass is suited to your locality.

To plant you simply broadcast the seeds as evenly as you can, roll the earth with a garden roller, and spray lightly with a fine mist of water. The rye comes up very quickly and encourages the other grasses to grow. You must cut the rye (and other grass) before it goes to seed or it will become a nuisance, replacing itself season after season. If you have topsoil, you can do without the rye.

Little shrubs grow into big shrubs, but don't purchase shrubs so tiny that they die. You will see "bargains" advertised in the pages of newspapers and magazines. They read something like this: DOZEN YEWS FOR $2.00. When they finally arrive, you find that each "tree" is 2 inches high and three-fourths dead. You have to nurse them for five years to get anything.

Think about going into the woods and pulling some small, ordinary trees. They will look good when they grow. Visit a local horticulturist. Ask for his inexpensive trees and shrubs. They often have small, misshapen plants you can have for a few dollars, but which can be pruned and trained.

Glossary

Glossary

amortize—Pay off loan.

backer board—Insulation slipped behind siding.

backfill—Replace excavated soil.

broker—A middleman, an agent who buys and sells or who arranges sales and purchases.

building permit—Official permission to build granted by the local municipality.

BX—Metal-clad electrical cable.

cesspool—A hole in the earth into which sewage is deposited.

chattle mortgage—The lender owns the property or object until the loan is completely repaid.

clause—An add-on agreement or restriction added to a contract.

covenants—Special restrictions, privileges, and agreements between buyers and sellers of property.

creative financing—Mortgage arrangements other than conventional methods.

drain field—A leaching field; buried, perforated pipes that lead septic tank effluent into the earth.

earnest money—A deposit given by a buyer to the seller to indicate the buyer is in ernest.

easement—The legal right to traverse the property belonging to another.

elevation—Height above a reference point.

escrow—Monies held by a third party to insure all terms of a contract are met.

FHA—Federal Housing Administration.

float—Smoothing wet concrete with a wood or soft metal trowel.

footing—The lowest portion of a structure; that which actually rests on the soil or rock.

foreclose—Legal action in which a judge orders the property owner to turn over title to a creditor.

frame—The wooden portion of the building; the timber that give it its shape.

gem box—Metal box that holds receptacles, etc.

improved land—Property that has structures and/or city services.

joist—On edge timbers that support floor and/or roof.

judgment—A law court order giving the creditor legal right to a debt.

junction box—Metal box in which one electrical cable is connected to another.

lien—A debt charged against a property and registered with the local county clerk.

line—A tightly stretched length of string.

line level—A spirit level that is hung from a line to determine whether or not the line is level.

mortgage—The registered agreement indicating what property, etc., that is put up as collateral for the loan.

mortgagee—One who borrows with a mortgage.

mortgagor—One who lends money on a mortgage.

pier—A wood or steel or stone post positioned vertically to support a building.

plan view—A drawing that presents the details of a building lying directly below the viewer.

plumb bob—A pointed weight hung on a line to fix a point vertically beneath another point.

points—Fee charge by banks for providing mortgage money. One point equal 1 percent of the total sum borrowed.

quit claim—A written statement acknowledging the full payment or satisfaction of a debt.

receptacle—A female socket that accepts the male plug on an appliance cord.

right of access—The legal right to cross the property of another.

restriction—Limitations on a building design and/or use of property.

Romex—Trade name for electrical cable wrapped in cloth.

second mortgage—A mortgage that can be paid off only when all claims of the holder of the first mortgage are met.

seepage pit—A deep hole in the earth into which effluent from a septic tank may be led.

spirit level—A glass vial filled with liquid. When the vial is perfectly level, the bubble in liquid is centered in the vial.

steel trowel—A tool used for final smoothing of wet concrete.

stud—A vertical framing timber.

subordinate mortgage—A second mortgage.

survey—Legal measurement and staking of a property and a drawing of a map of the property.

tax claim—A claim by a municipality for past due real estate taxes.

title—Legal ownership.

title guarantee—An insurance policy supporting a legal title.

transit—A sighting device for determing vertical and horizontal angles and alignments.

VA—Veteran's Administration.

water table—Elevation of water's surface beneath the earth.

Index

Index

Other Bestsellers From TAB

☐ **MASTER HOUSEHOLD ELECTRICAL WIRING—2nd Edition—James L. Kittle**

Update dangerously old wiring in your house. Add an outdoor, dusk-to-dawn light. Repair a malfunctioning thermostat and add an automatic setback. You can do all this and more—easily and safely—for much less than the cost of having a professional do it for you! You can remodel, expand, and modernize existing wiring correctly and safely with this practical guide to household wiring. From testing to troubleshooting, you can do it all yourself. Add dimmer switches and new outlets . . . ground your TV or washer . . . make simple appliances repair . . . set up outside wiring . . . put in new fixtures and more! 304 pp., 273 illus.

Paper $15.95   **Hard $24.95**
Book No. 2987

☐ **THE COMPLETE FOUNDATION AND FLOOR FRAMING BOOK—Dan Ramsey**

Dozens of drawings and diagrams illustrate the fundamentals of planning, estimating, and installing foundations and floor frames! With the help of this confidence-building guide, you can construct or repair the foundation or flooring in a new or older structure without fear or hesitation. This comprehensive sourcebook provides you with plenty of hands-on instruction and meaningful advice for getting the job done as easily and professionally as possible. 220 pp., 275 illus.

Paper $14.95   **Hard $21.95**
Book No. 2878

☐ **DREAM HOMES: 66 PLANS TO MAKE YOUR DREAMS COME TRUE—Jerold L. Axelrod**

If you are planning on—or just dreaming of—building a new home, you will find this book completely fascinating. Compiled by a well-known architect whose home designs have been featured regularly in the syndicated "House of the Week" and *Home* magazine, this beautifully bound volume presents one of the finest collections of luxury home designs ever assembled in a single volume! 86 pp., 201 illus., 8 1/2" × 11", 20 pp. of full-color illus.

Paper $16.95   **Hard $29.95**
Book No. 2829

☐ **ADD A ROOM: A PRACTICAL GUIDE TO EXPANDING YOUR HOME—Paul Bianchina**

Overflowing with helpful diagrams, photographs, and illustrations, this indispensable guide focuses on the professional details that make the difference between a room addition that blends in and one that looks like an afterthought. It's far more than a volume of plans or architectural ideas . . . it's a complete how-to-do-it manual that leaves no question unanswered. The types of rooms you can build using this guide include a garage, a room on top of your garage, a sunspace or greenhouse, a family or rec room, a bathroom, and many others. 400 pp., 360 illus.

Paper $17.95   **Hard $27.95**
Book No. 2811

☐ **PRACTICAL STONEMASONRY MADE EASY—Stephen M. Kennedy**

The current popularity of country-style homes has renewed interest in the use of stone in home construction. Now, with the help of expert stonemason Stephen M. Kennedy, you can learn how to do stonework yourself and actually save money while adding to the value, charm, and enduring quality of your home. This book provides step-by-step guidance in the inexpensive use of stone for the relatively unskilled do-it-yourselfer. 272 pp., 229 illus.

Paper $16.95   **Hard $24.95**
Book No. 2915

☐ **BUILD YOUR OWN KIT HOUSE—Jonathan Erickson**

Building a house from a kit is an affordable choice. Erickson makes it possible for you to buy and build a kit home of your own from scratch. It answers real-life questions potential kit homeowners should pose to lending institutions, contractors, dealers, and others. The pros and cons of time, cost, and quality are examined so that you can make decisions from a solid knowledge base. 272 pp., 153 illus.

Paper $14.95   **Hard $22.95**
Book No. 2873

☐ **SUNSPACES—HOME ADDITIONS FOR YEAR-ROUND NATURAL LIVING—John Mauldin, Photography by John H. Mauldin and Juan L. Espinosa**

Have you been thinking of enclosing your porch to increase your living space? Want to add a family room, but want the best use of the space for the money? Do you want information on solar energy and ideas on how you can make it work in your home? If "yes" is your answer to any of these questions, you'll want to own this fascinating guide! 256 pp., 179 illus.

Paper $14.95   **Hard $21.95**
Book No. 2816

☐ **THE COMPLETE BOOK OF HOME WELDING—John Todd**

Highlights new arc welding equipment and single-phase wire feeders that greatly simplify the welding process and make it feasible for even novice do-it-yourselfers. The author provides actual step-by-step welding projects complete with detailed illustrations that make even complicated welding projects amazingly easy to perform. Just a few of the things you'll be able to construct and repair include garden carts, car racks, trailers, spiral staircases, wood-burning stoves, piping systems, auto engines, and others. You'll find endless applications for your new skill! 498 pp., 464 illus.

Paper $19.95   **Hard $29.95**
Book No. 2717

Other Bestsellers From TAB

☐ **THE ILLUSTRATED DICTIONARY OF BUILDING MATERIALS AND TECHNIQUES—Paul Bianchina**

Here's a one-stop reference for do-it-yourselfers and professionals that gives you clear, straightforward definitions for all of the tools, terms, materials, and techniques used by builders, contractors, architects, and other building professionals. It includes almost 4,000 terms and abbreviations from the simple to the complex, from slang to the latest technical information. 272 pp., 172 illus.

Paper $14.95 **Book No. 2681**

☐ **ROOFING THE RIGHT WAY—A Step-by-Step Guide for the Homeowner—Steven Bolt**

Install a new roof on your home at half the contractor-quoted cost. Here's all the information you need to install just about every type of roofing imaginable—fiberglass shingles, wood shingles or shakes, metal shingles or shakes, sheet-metal roofing, or roll roofing . . . Includes advice on everything from preparing for shingle delivery to nailing the last ridge cap. 192 pp., 217 illus.

Paper $11.95 **Hard $19.95**
Book No. 2667

☐ **TILE FLOORS—INSTALLING, MAINTAINING AND REPAIRING—Dan Ramsey**

Now you can easily install resilient or traditional hard tiles on both walls and floors. Find out how to buy quality resilient floor products at reasonable cost . . . and examine the types and sizes of hard tiles available. Get step-by-step instructions for laying out the floor, selecting needed tools, and adhesives, cutting tile, applying adhesives, and more. 192 pp., 200 illus. 4 pages in full color

Paper $12.95 **Hard $22.95**
Book No. 1998

☐ **HARDWOOD FLOORS—INSTALLING, MAINTAINING, AND REPAIRING—Dan Ramsey**

This comprehensive guide includes all the guidance you need to install, restore, maintain, or repair all types of hardwood flooring at costs far below those charged by professional builders and maintenance services. From details on how to select the type of wood floors best suited to your home, to time- and money-saving ways to keep floors in top condition. 160 pp., 230 illus., 4 pages in full color

Paper $10.95 **Hard $18.95**
Book No. 1928

☐ **BASIC ROOF FRAMING—Benjamin Barnow**

Would a new gambrel roof make your home more attractive . . . and increase its value? Want to enlarge your attic with dormers to add to your family's living space? Or are you thinking of building an addition to your home? Then this is a sourcebook that will save you hundreds, maybe thousands of dollars in contractor's costs by showing how even a novice carpenter can successfully master roof framing! 192 pp., 250 illus.

Paper $11.95 **Book No. 2677**

☐ **THE METALWORKER'S BENCHTOP REFERENCE MANUAL—Joseph W. Serafin**

This one-stop, ready reference contains all the information and instructions on metalworking that you need to complete any metalworking endeavor. By illustrating new approaches and unusual machining methods it will help you solve practically any metalworking problem you encounter. The ideal answer book for anyone interested in the craft of metalworking, as well as for those in the profession, this all-encompassing sourcebook covers techniques for working with all types of metals. Packed with illustrations to ensure absolute understanding! 320 pp., 360 illus.

Paper $16.95 **Hard $25.95**
Book No. 2605

☐ **BUILDING OUTDOOR PLAYTHINGS FOR KIDS, WITH PROJECT PLANS—Bill Barnes**

Imagine the delight of your youngsters—children or grandchildren—when you build them their own special backyard play area! Best of all, discover how you can make exciting, custom-designed play equipment at a fraction of the cost of ordinary, ready-made swing sets or sandbox units! It's all here in this step-by-step guide to planning and building safe, sturdy outdoor play equipment! 240 pp., 213 illus.

Paper $12.95 **Book No. 1971**

☐ **DO YOUR OWN DRYWALL—An Illustrated Guide—Arnold Kozloski**

Proper installation of interior plaster board or drywall is a must-have skill for successful home building or remodeling. Now, there's a new time- and money-saving alternative: this excellent step-by-step guide to achieving professional-quality drywalling results, the first time and every time! Even joint finishing, the drywalling step that is most dreaded by do-it-yourselfers, can be a snap when you know what you're doing. 160 pp., 161 illus.

Paper $9.95 **Hard $10.95**
Book No. 1838

Other Bestsellers From TAB